SCOTLAND: AN UNWON CAUSE

Other Books by Paul H. Scott

1707: The Union of Scotland and England (1979)
Walter Scott and Scotland (1981) (Paperback edition, 1994)
John Galt (1985)
In Bed with an Elephant (1985)
The Thinking Nation (1989)
Cultural Independence (1989)
Towards Independence: Essays on Scotland (1991)
Andrew Fletcher and the Treaty of Union (1992) (Paperback edition, 1994)
Scotland in Europe: A Dialogue with a Sceptical Friend (1992)
Defoe in Edinburgh and Other Papers (1995)

Edited:
(with A.C. Davis) *The Age of MacDiarmid* (1980) (Paperback edition, 1922)
Sir Walter Scott's *The Letters of Malachi Malagrowther* (1981)
Andrew Fletcher's *United and Separate Parliaments* (1982)
(With George Bruce) *A Scottish Postbag* (1986)
(With A.C. Davis) *Policy for the Arts: A Selection of AdCAS Papers* (1991)
Scotland: A Concise Cultural History (1993)
(With Daniel Szechi) *Scotland's Ruine: Lockhart of Carnwath's Memoirs of the Union* (1995)
(With Ian Gordon) John Galt's *The Member and The Radical* (1996)

Contributions to joint volumes in:
(Ed. by J.H. Alexander and David Hewitt) *Scott and His Influence* (1983)
(Ed. by M. Anderson and L. Dominguez) *Cultural Policy in Europe* (1984)
(Ed. by Douglas Gifford) *The History of Scottish Literature, vol. 3* (1988)
(Ed. by Angus Calder) *Byron and Scotland* (1989)
(Ed. by C.J.M. MacLachlan and D.S. Robb) *Edwin Muir: Centenary Assessments* (1990)
(Ed. by Noelle Watson) *Reference Guide to Short Fiction* (1994)
(Ed. by Horst Drescher and Susanne Hagemann) *Scotland to Slovenia* (1996)
(Ed. by Kenneth Simpson) *Love and Liberty, Robert Burns: A Bicentenary Celebration* (1996)
(Ed. by Alan Reid and Brian Osborne) *Discovering Scottish Writers* (1997)
(Ed. by Tom Crawford and Christopher McLachlan) *Boswell in Scotland and Beyond* (1997)
(Ed. by Colin Milton) *Elphinstone Institute Papers* (1997)

SCOTLAND
An Unwon Cause

AN ANTHOLOGY WITH A COMMENTARY

Paul H. Scott

CANONGATE

First published in Great Britain in 1997
by Canongate Books Ltd, 14 High Street
Edinburgh EH1 1TE

Copyright acknowledgments
Extract from *The Break-Up of Britain* by Tom Nairn reproduced
by kind permission of Verso;
extract from *The Democratic Intellect*
by George Elder Davie reproduced by kind permission of
Edinburgh University Press;
extract from *Scottish Journey* by Edwin Muir
reproduced by kind permission of Mainstream Publishing;
'A Backward Nation' by Gordon Donaldson reproduced by
kind permission of Scottish Academic Press.

ISBN 0 86241 700 7

British Library Cataloguing-in-Publication Data

A catalogue record for this book is available on request.

Typeset by Palimpsest Book Production Limited,
Polmont, Stirlingshire
Printed and bound in Great Britain by Biddles Ltd.

CONTENTS

'You talked of Scotland as a lost cause and that is not true. Scotland is an *unwon* cause.'

John Steinbeck in a letter to Mrs John F. Kennedy

INTRODUCTION

I was encouraged to compile this book by two events. The first was a remark by Professor Ted Cowan at the annual commemoration of Andrew Fletcher of Saltoun in September 1996. He said some kind things about my book, *Andrew Fletcher and the Treaty of Union*, but also made a very fair critical point. He said that although I had discussed the foreign intellectual influences on Fletcher, I had not paid sufficient attention to those in Scotland itself. There are elements in Fletcher's thought which can be traced back through George Buchanan and John Mair to the Declaration of Arbroath and forward through Hume and Walter Scott to the present. This suggested an interesting line of enquiry. An opportunity to explore it was provided by a proposal from Hugh Andrew of Canongate Books that I might edit a collection of texts from early times to the present to show the development of the Scottish national consciousness.

The existing source books of Scottish history by W.C. Dickinson and Gordon Donaldson and others are very useful but they are largely confined to state papers. There have been other excellent prose anthologies of a more literary kind, such as those edited by Moray McLaren, Maurice Lindsay and Douglas Dunn. What I propose here is something between the two, a mixture of official documents and literary comment. All are related to the theme of the national consciousness and therefore inevitably to constitutional and political matters.

Scottish national consciousness exists because Scotland was an independent country for centuries and has been partially autonomous since then. The two things depend on one another. We became a nation because we were a political entity and because we are a nation most of us feel the need to give it political expression again. In other words, this is not simply an exercise in history, but a contribution to the debate on the future of Scotland.

The book is not a comprehensive treatment of the subject; that would take several volumes. It contains the key passages from some of the major documents in Scottish history and from comments by writers either at the time or since. I have provided a commentary which attempts to set the extracts in their historical context. I hope that it will provide an introduction to some aspects of Scottish history and a stimulus to further enquiry.

Although Scotland is small, it is also, as MacDiarmid pointed out, a very diverse country. Like everywhere else, change is constant. Even so, it seems to me that there are some obvious lines of continuity in our collective consciousness, an instinct for egalitarianism and social justice, a respect for education and logical thought, an open response to ideas from abroad, a desire to accept responsibility for our own affairs. As John Steinbeck said, Scotland is an unwon cause. Many people have been trying to remedy that state of affairs for more than a century and we may now be close to a solution. It is more important than ever that we should try to discover how we arrived at this position.

I am grateful for the help of a number of people, especially Bernard Crich, Lauree Fiorentini, John Gibson and James Mitchell.

Paul H. Scott
Edinburgh, January 1997

PROLOGUE

The earliest recorded statement attributed to an inhabitant of the place which we now know as Scotland occurs in the work of a Roman historian. This was in the *Agricola* of Tacitus, written in about AD 97. Agricola, who was the father-in-law of Tacitus, was the governor of Roman Britain from 78 to 84. During that time, he made a determined attempt to extend Roman control to the north of the Tweed. In 84 he defeated the Caledonians at a place which Tacitus calls Mount Graupius, which was somewhere north of the Tay. He tells us that the leader of the Caledonians, Calgacus was 'a man of outstanding valour and nobility' and he gives us the 'substance of what he is reported to have said' in a speech to his troops before the battle. His words curiously anticipate both Bruce's speech before Bannockburn, as reported by Barbour and echoed by Burns (7.12), and the Declaration of Arbroath. (1.4)

(P.1) 'They Create a Desolation and Call it Peace'

When I consider the motives we have for fighting and the critical position we are in, I have a strong feeling that the united front you are showing today will mean the dawn of liberty for the whole of Britain. You have mustered to a man, and all of you are free. There are no lands behind us, and even on the sea we are menaced by the Roman fleet. The clash of battle – the hero's glory – has now actually become the safest refuge for a coward. Battles against Rome have been lost and won before; but hope was never abandoned, since we were always here in reserve. We, the choicest flower of Britain's manhood, were hidden away in her most secret places. Out of sight of subject shores, we kept even our eyes free from the defilement of tyranny. We, the most distant dwellers upon earth, the last of the free, have been shielded till today by our very remoteness and by the obscurity in which it has

shrouded our name. Now, the farthest bounds of Britain lie
open to our enemies; and what men know nothing about they
always assume to be a valuable prize. But there are no more
nations beyond us; nothing is there but waves and rocks, and
the Romans, more deadly still than these – for in them is an
arrogance which no submission or good behaviour can escape.
Pillagers of the world, they have exhausted the land by their
indiscriminate plunder, and now they ransack the sea. A rich
enemy excites their cupidity; a poor one, their lust for power.
East and West alike have failed to satisfy them. They are the
only people on earth to whose covetousness both riches and
poverty are equally tempting. To robbery, butchery, and
rapine, they give the lying name of 'government'; they create a
desolation and call it peace.

Nature has ordained that every man should love his
children and his other relatives above all else. These are now
being torn from us by conscription to slave in other lands.
Our wives and sisters, even if they are not raped by enemy
soldiers, are seduced by men who are supposed to be our
friends and guests. Our goods and money are consumed
by taxation; our land is stripped of its harvest to fill their
granaries; our hands and limbs are crippled by building
roads through forests and swamps under the lash of our
oppressors. Creatures born to be slaves are sold once for
all, and, what is more, get their keep from their owners. We
Britons are sold into slavery anew every day; we have to pay
the purchase-price ourselves and feed our masters into the
bargain. In a private household the latest arrival is made the
butt even of his fellow-slaves; so, in this establishment where
all mankind have long been slaves, it is we, the cheap new
acquisitions, who are marked out for destruction. For we have
no fertile lands, no mines, no ports, which we might be spared
to work in. Our courage, too, and our martial spirit are against
us: masters do not like such qualities in their subjects. Even
our remoteness and isolation, while they give us protection,
are bound to make the Romans wonder what mischief we
are up to. Since you cannot hope for mercy, therefore, take
courage before it is too late to strive for what you hold most
dear, whether it be life or honour. The Brigantes, with only
a woman to lead them, burned a Roman colony and stormed
a camp; and if success had not tempted them to relax their
efforts, they might have cast off the yoke. We, who have never

been forced to feel that yoke, shall be fighting to preserve our freedom, and not, like them, merely to avenge past injuries. Let us then show, at the very first clash of arms, what manner of men Caledonia has kept in reserve.

Do you imagine that the Romans' bravery in war matches their dissoluteness in time of peace? No! It is our quarrels and disunion that have given them fame. The reputation of the Roman army is built up on the faults of its enemies. Look at it, a motley conglomeration of nations, that will be shattered by defeat as surely as it is now held together by success. Or can you seriously think that those Gauls and Germans – and, to our bitter shame, many Britons too – are bound to Rome by genuine loyalty or affection? They may be lending their life-blood now to the foreign tyrant, but they were enemies of Rome for more years than they have been her slaves. Terror and intimidation are poor bonds of attachment: once break them, and where fear ends hatred will begin. All that can spur men on to victory is on our side. The enemy have no wives to fire their courage, no parents ready to taunt them if they run away. Most of them either have no fatherland they can remember, or belong to one other than Rome. See them, a scanty band, scared and bewildered, staring blankly at the unfamiliar sky, sea, and forests around them. The gods have given them, like so many prisoners bound hand and foot, into our hands. Be not afraid of the outward show that means nothing, the glitter of gold and silver that can neither avert nor inflict a wound. Even in the ranks of our enemies we shall find willing hands to help us. The Britons will recognize our cause as their own; the Gauls will remember their lost liberty; the rest of the Germans will desert them as surely as the Usipi did recently. And beyond this army that you see there is nothing to be frightened of – only forts without garrisons, colonies of greybeards, towns sick and distracted between rebel subjects and tyrant masters. Which will you choose – to follow your leader into battle, or to submit to taxation, labour in the mines, and all the other tribulations of slavery? Whether you are to endure these for ever or take quick vengeance, this field must decide. On, then, into action; and as you go, think of those that went before you and of those that shall come after.

There is another anticipation in the *Agricola*. The Romans failed to hold Caledonia for any length of time, but they systematically incorporated the territory to the south in their Empire. Tacitus comments on this process in a way which is not dissimilar to the theories, nearly 2,000 years later, of Michael Hechter and Tom Nairn about the control of subject peoples through voluntary assimilation. (10.16 and 10.17)

A Feature of their Enslavement

(P.2)

The following winter was spent on schemes of social betterment. Agricola had to deal with people living in isolation and ignorance, and therefore prone to fight; and his object was to accustom them to a life of peace and quiet by the provision of amenities. He therefore gave private encouragement and official assistance to the building of temples, public squares, and good houses. He praised the energetic and scolded the slack; and competition for honour proved as effective as compulsion. Furthermore, he educated the sons of the chiefs in the liberal arts, and expressed a preference for British ability as compared with the trained skills of the Gauls. The result was that instead of loathing the Latin language they became eager to speak it effectively. In the same way, our national dress came into favour and the toga was everywhere to be seen. And so the population was gradually led into the demoralizing temptations of arcades, baths, and sumptuous banquets. The unsuspecting Britons spoke of such novelties as 'civilization', when in fact they were only a feature of their enslavement.

TACITUS, *The Agricola and the Germania.*
Translated by H. Mattingly. Penguin Books,
1980. pp. 72–3 and 80–3

CHAPTER ONE

Wallace, Bruce and the Declaration of Arbroath

(1.1)   ## Sen Alexander Our King Wes Deid

Sen Alexander our king wes deid
  That Scotland left in luve and ^alee,   ^apeace
Away wes ^asonse of aill and breid,   ^a abundance
  Of wine and wax, of gamin and glee.
The gold wes changit all in leid,
  The frute failyeit on everilk tree.
Christ succour Scotland and remeid
  That stad is in perplexitie.

The Penguin Book of Scottish Verse. Ed. by Tom
Scott. Harmondsworth, 1970, p. 59

These lines were written in about 1300 and is probably the earliest poetry in Scots to have survived. The peaceful and prosperous Scotland of the reign of Alexander III was devastated by the events which followed his accidental death in 1296. There was no clear succession to the throne. Edward I was invited to arbitrate and took the opportunity to attempt to impose his will on Scotland. The repeated English invasions and occupations were carried out with such ruthlessness, slaughter and destruction that they provoked an outburst of popular resistance of a kind which was then new. In the feudal Europe of the time ordinary people were not expected to assert themselves or influence events. William Wallace, not a great feudal magnate but the son of a small landowner, emerged as its leader. G.M. Trevelyan describes the consequences:

(1.2)   ## Democratic Patriotism

All seemed finished. All in fact was about to begin. Deserted by her nobles, Scotland discovered herself. The governors whom

Edward I left behind him were incapable and cruel, and the foreign soldiery made the Scots feel their subjection. In the following May a guerrilla chief of genius, a tall man of iron strength, who suddenly appears on the page of history as if from nowhere, defeated at Stirling Bridge end an English army under its blundering feudal chief the Earl of Warenne, of *quo Warranto* fame. Thence William Wallace broke ravaging into Northumberland and Cumberland.

This unknown knight, with little but his great name to identify him in history, had lit a fire which nothing since has ever put out. Here, in Scotland, contemporaneously with the very similar doings in Switzerland, a new ideal and tradition of wonderful potency was brought into the world; it had no name then, but now we should call it democratic patriotism. It was not the outcome of theory. The unconscious qualities of a people had given it reality in a sudden fit of rage. Theories of nation-hood and theories of democracy would follow afterwards to justify or explain it. Meanwhile, it stood up, a fact.

G.M. TREVELYAN, *History of England*. Edition
of 1937. London, p. 218

Edward I had attempted to expunge all memory of Scotland as a sovereign, independent kingdom. He removed to England the Stone of Destiny, as the symbol of that sovereignty, along with the Great Seal and the historical records. He proposed to rule Scotland through a puppet king and barons all bound homage to himself. What he in fact achieved was the opposite; the consolidation in Scotland of a spirit which we now call nationalism, popular determination to resist foreign aggression. At that time this was unprecedented and astonishing. Europe, in Trevelyan's words, had been divided, not perpendicularly into nations, but horizontally into feudal strata. Events in Scotland changed that conception. In this sense, Scotland is the oldest nation in Europe.

Wallace was captured, taken to London and executed with the extreme barbarity of the English law on treason. His work was continued by Robert Bruce who was crowned King of Scots and won a great victory at Bannock-burn in 1314. The first major works of Scottish literature were the epic poems Blind Hary's *Wallace* and John Barbour's *Bruce*. Some of the best known lines in the whole of Scottish literature are these on freedom from Barbour's *Bruce*:

(1.3)   Freedom is a Noble Thing

Ah! freedom is a noble thing!
Freedom ᵃmays man to haiff liking;   ᵃmakes
Freedom all solace to man giffis:
He ᵃlevis at ease that freely levis.   ᵃlives
A noble hart may haiff name ᵃeis,   ᵃease
ᵃNa ellis nocht that may him pleis,   ᵃnor anything else
ᵃGiff freedom faill: for free liking   ᵃif
Is yarnit ᵃowre all other thing.   ᵃover, above
Na he that ay has levit free
May nocht knaw weill the property,
The anger, na the wretchit doom
That is couplit to foul ᵃthirldom.   ᵃthraldom

Bot giff he had ᵃassayit it,   ᵃexperienced it ('thirldom')
Than all ᵃperquer he suld it ᵇwit;   ᵃpar coeur ᵇknow
And suld think freedom ᵃmar to prize   ᵃmore
Than all the gold in warld that is . . .

Quoted in Moray McLaren, *The Wisdom of
the Scots*. London, 1961, p. 37

David Daiches has said that this is probably the first time in literature that
the word 'freedom' is used in the sense of self-determination, the freedom
from external domination.[1] That is only part of the truth. I think that it is
clear from the passion in Barbour's words that he was not thinking of an
abstract principle, but of the harsh reality of foreign occupation.

In his autobiographical letter to John Moore of 2nd August 1787, Robert
Burns said that the first two books he ever read in private and which gave him
more pleasure that any two books he ever read again were the life of Hannibal
and the history of Sir William Wallace. He goes on to say that 'the story of
Wallace poured a Scottish prejudice in my veins which will boil along there till
the flood-gates of life shut in eternal rest'. Generations of Scots might say the
same. We have seen it again recently in the reaction to the film *Braveheart*.

The Scottish attitude which emerged from the Wars of Independence
was expressed in the Declaration of Arbroath of 6th April 1320. It was a
document with a diplomatic purpose: to explain the Scottish case to Pope
John XXII. In its original Latin, the Declaration is a masterpiece of eloquence,
persuasiveness and controlled passion. One of its editors, and the author of
the translation which follows, Sir James Fergusson, speaks of the sonorous
music of its Latin and the sweep and cadence of its sentences. Its author

was almost certainly Bernard de Linton, Chancellor of Scotland and Abbot
of Arbroath, one instance among many of the vital role of the Catholic clergy
in the defence of independence.

The following translation is of the whole text with the exception of the
first paragraph. This gives the names and titles of those in whose names the
Declaration was issued and adds 'and the other barons and freeholders and
the whole community of the realm of Scotland'.

(1.4)   The Declaration of Arbroath

Most Holy Father and Lord, we know and from the chronicles
and books of the ancients we find that among other famous
nations our own, the Scots, has been graced with widespread
renown. They journeyed from Greater Scythia by way of the
Tyrrhenian Sea and the Pillars of Hercules, and dwelt for a
long course of time in Spain among the most savage tribes, but
nowhere could they be subdued by any race, however barbarous.
Thence they came, twelve hundred years after the people of
Israel crossed the Red Sea, to their home in the west where they
still live today. The Britons they first drove out, the Picts they
utterly destroyed, and, even though very often assailed by the
Norwegians, the Danes and the English, they took possession of
that home with many victories and untold efforts; and, as the
historians of old time bear witness, they have held it free of all
bondage ever since. In their kingdom there have reigned one
hundred and thirteen kings of their own royal stock, the line
unbroken by a single foreigner.

The high qualities and deserts of these people, were they not
otherwise manifest, gain glory enough from this: that the King
of kings and Lord of lords, our Lord Jesus Christ, after His
Passion and Resurrection, called them, even though settled
in the uttermost parts of the earth, almost the first to His
most holy faith. Nor would He have them confirmed in that
faith by merely anyone but by the first of His Apostles – by
calling, though second or third in rank – the most gentle Saint
Andrew, the Blessed Peter's brother, and desired him to keep
them under his protection as their patron for ever.

The Most Holy Fathers your predecessors gave careful heed
to these things and bestowed many favours and numerous
privileges on this same kingdom and people, as being the special
charge of the Blessed Peter's brother. Thus our nation under

their protection did indeed live in freedom and peace up to the time when that mighty prince the King of the English, Edward, the father of the one who reigns today, when our kingdom had no head and our people harboured no malice or treachery and were then unused to wars or invasions, came in the guise of a friend and ally to harass them as an enemy. The deeds of cruelty, massacre, violence, pillage, arson, imprisoning prelates, burning down monasteries, robbing and killing monks and nuns, and yet other outrages without number which he committed against our people, sparing neither age nor sex, religion nor rank, no one could describe nor fully imagine unless he had seen them with his own eyes.

But from these countless evils we have been set free, by the help of Him Who though He afflicts yet heals and restores, by our most tireless Prince, King and Lord, the Lord Robert. He, that his people and his heritage might be delivered out of the hands of our enemies, met toil and fatigue, hunger and peril, like another Maccabaeus or Joshua and bore them cheerfully. Him, too, divine providence, his right of succession according to our laws and customs which we shall maintain to the death, and the due consent and assent of us all have made our Prince and King. To him, as to the man by whom salvation has been wrought unto our people, we are bound both by law and by his merits that our freedom may be still maintained, and by him, come what way, we mean to stand.

Yet if he should give up what he has begun, and agree to make us or our kingdom subject to the King of England or the English, we should exert ourselves at once to drive him out as our enemy and a subverter of his own rights and ours, and make some other man who was well able to defend us our King; for, as long as but a hundred of us remain alive, never will we on any conditions be brought under English rule. It is in truth not for glory, nor riches, nor honours that we are fighting, but for freedom – for that alone, which no honest man gives up but with life itself.

Therefore it is, Reverend Father and Lord, that we beseech your Holiness with our most earnest prayers and suppliant hearts, inasmuch as you will in your sincerity and goodness consider all this, that, since with Him Whose vice-regent on earth you are there is neither weighing nor distinction of Jew and Greek, Scotsman or Englishman, you will look with the eyes of a father on the troubles and privations brought by the English upon us and upon the Church of God. May it please you to admonish and exhort the King of the English, who ought to be satisfied with what belongs to him since England used once to be enough for seven kings or more, to leave us Scots in peace, who live in this poor little Scotland, beyond which there is no dwelling-place at all, and covet nothing but our own. We are sincerely willing to do anything for him, having regard to our condition, that we can, to win peace for ourselves.

This truly concerns you, Holy Father, since you see the savagery of the heathen raging against the Christians, as the sins of Christians have indeed deserved, and the frontiers of Christendom being pressed inward every day; and how much it will tarnish your Holiness's memory if (which God forbid) the Church suffers eclipse or scandal in any branch of it during your time, you must perceive. Then rouse the Christian princes who for false reasons pretend that they cannot go to the help of the Holy Land because of wars they have on hand with their neighbours. The real reason that prevents them is that in making war on their smaller neighbours they find quicker profit and weaker resistance. But how cheerfully our Lord the King and we too would go there if the King of the English would leave us in peace, He from Whom nothing is hidden well knows; and we profess and declare it to you as the Vicar of Christ and to all Christendom.

But if your Holiness puts too much faith in the tales the English tell and will not give sincere belief to all this, nor refrain from favouring them to our prejudice, then the slaughter of bodies, the perdition of souls, and all the other misfortunes that will follow, inflicted by them on us and by us on them, will, we believe, be surely laid by the Most High to your charge.

To conclude, we are and shall ever be, as far as duty calls us, ready to do your will in all things, as obedient sons to you as His Vicar; and to Him as the Supreme King and Judge we commit the maintenance of our cause, casting our cares upon Him and firmly trusting that He will inspire us with courage and bring our enemies to nought.

May the Most High preserve you to His Holy Church in holiness and health and grant you length of days.

GIVEN at the monastery of Arbroath in Scotland on the sixth day of the month of April in the year of grace thirteen hundred and twenty and the fifteenth year of the reign of our King aforesaid.

The Declaration of Arbroath. Ed. by Sir James Fergusson. Edinburgh, 1970

The Declaration is remarkable, not only for its impressive pledge to resist English rule 'as long as but a hundred of us remain alive', but also for two other things. Robert Bruce was a popular and successful king who had won a great victory, but there is an undertaking to expel him 'if he should give up what he has begun'. At a time when kings were absolute rulers, it was a revolutionary idea that one could be dismissed if he failed to carry out the wishes of his people. The other point is the contention, which only began to be asserted universally in the 20th century, that powerful rulers should not make war on their smaller neighbours. We shall find frequent echoes of all of these ideas in the pages which follow. The Declaration of Arbroath is the foundation of Scottish political thought.

George Buchanan makes no mention of the Declaration in his history of Scotland nor in his essay about the limitations on the right of kings (2.5): but his ideas on this subject are in the same tradition. The Declaration was first printed in 1680 by Sir George Mackenzie of Rosehaugh, the founder of the Advocates' Library. Shortly afterwards, it was published again by Gilbert Burnett who was then a tutor in the household of Andrew Fletcher of Saltoun, whose views (5.2) are again in the tradition of the Declaration. The text was printed again in 1689 and the dismissal of James VII in that year by the Claim of Right also follows the tradition.

When James Boswell was in Leipzig in October 1764, in the course of his grand tour, he came across a copy of Anderson's *Diplomata Scotiae*, which contains a facsimile of the Declaration. He records in his Journal: 'My old spirit got up, and I read them some choice passages of the Barons' letter to the Pope. They were struck with the noble sentiments of liberty of the old Scots, and they expressed their regret at the shameful Union. I felt true patriot sorrow. O infamous rascals, who sold the honour of your country to a nation against which our ancestors supported themselves with so much glory. But I say no more, only Alas, poor Scotland.'[2]

Four years later Boswell wrote his *Account of Corsica*, of another small country struggling for its independence. On the title page, he quoted the most famous passage from the Declaration and in his Introduction he praised freedom in a passage reminiscent of Barbour's *Bruce*.

In the 19th century John Galt in his novel, *Ringan Gilhaize*, quotes from the Declaration and he gives the entire text of it as an appendix. In the present century the Stationery Office have published a facsimile and several translations of the text have been published. References to it are now very frequent and its significance is widely recognised.

CHAPTER TWO

David Lindsay and George Buchanan

James IV, who came to the throne in 1488, was a true Renaissance prince. He was a patron of the arts and sciences, responsive to new ideas and ready to play a constructive part in the affairs of Europe. His reign was marked by the first great efflorescence of Scottish poetry in the work of Robert Henryson, William Dunbar and Gavin Douglas. He built the most powerful warship of the time, the *Great Michael*. He encouraged science and promoted the founding of a third Scottish University in Aberdeen. All of this bright promise was brought to an abrupt end by the catastrophic defeat by England at Flodden in 1513, where the King and many of the leading men of the time were killed.

One of Henryson's major works was a series of fables in the manner of Aesop. Among them is 'The Wolf and the Lamb'. This tells how the wolf picked a quarrel with the lamb by accusing him of fouling the water by drinking in the same river. The lamb replies in a manner which is very Scottish by pointing out that this was untrue and contrary to reason because he was drinking downstream. Even so, the wolf makes a meal of him. In the moral Henryson says that the lamb signifies the poor and the wolf their extortioners and oppressors. He ends with these lines:

(2.1)   The Wolf and the Lamb

O thow grit lord, that riches hes and rent,
Be nocht ane wolf, thus to deuoir the pure!
Think that na thing cruell nor violent
May in this warld perpetuallie indure.
This sall thow trow and sikkerlie assure:
For till oppres, thow sall haif als grit pane
As thow the pure with thy awin hand had slane.

God keip the lamb, quhilk is the innocent,
From wolfis byit and men extortioneris;

God grant that wrangous men of fals intent
Be manifest, and punischit as ªeffeiris;   ªas is proper
And God, as thow all rychteous prayer heiris,
Mot saif our king, and gif him hart and hand
All sic wolfis to banes of the land.

> ROBERT HENRYSON, *The Poems*. Ed. by
> Denton Fox. Oxford, 1987, pp. 102–3

Thus the work of one of the earliest of our great poets identifies with the suffering of the poor and condemns the exploiters. This is a note which sounds constantly through Scottish literature.

During the reign of James IV the Scottish Parliament passed an Education Act which is said to be the first act of its kind in Europe. It applied only to the eldest sons of the barons and freeholders so that they would be qualified to discharge their judicial functions in due course; but it was followed by a long series of Scottish laws intended to spread education through the whole community.

(2.2)   ## The Education Act of 1496

It is statute and ordanit throw all the realme that all barronis
and frehaldaris that ar of substance put thair eldest sonnis and
airis to the sculis fra thai be aucht or nine yeiris of age and till
remane at the grammer sculis quhill thai be competentlie foundit
and have perfite latyne and thereftir to remane thre yeris at
the sculis of art and jure sua that thai may have knawlege and
understanding of the lawis. Throw the quhilkis justice may reigne
universalie throw all the realme sua that thai that ar schreffis
or jugeis ordinaris under the kingis hienes may have knawlege
to do justice that the pure pepill sulde have na neid to seik our
soverane lordis principale auditouris for ilk small iniure. And
quhat baroune or frehaldar of substance that haldis nocht his
sone at the sculis as said is haifand na lauchfull essonye[1] bot
failyeis heirin fra knawlege may be gottin thairof he sall pay to
the king the soum of xx pounds.

> *A Source Book of Scottish History*. Ed. by W.C.
> Dickinson, Gordon Donaldson &
> I.A. Milne. Edinburgh, 1958, vol. II, p. 122

At about the middle of the 16th Century the policy of the King of England,

Henry VIII, was to secure control over Scotland by persuading the Scots to agree to the marriage of the infant princess Mary to his son Edward. The 'Rough Wooing' was rough indeed. The Earl of Hertford in his invasion of 1545 destroyed the Border Abbeys, five market towns, sixteen fortified places and 243 villages. Not surprisingly, the Scots preferred to maintain their auld alliance with France and Mary went there to marry the Dauphin. English pressure, as at other times, was of two kinds: military intimidation on one hand, and propaganda about the virtues of Union on the other, the stick and the carrot.

The Complaynt of Scotland was a notable reply to the propaganda. It appeared anonymously but the probable author was Robert Wedderburn, a Catholic priest in Dundee. On internal evidence it was written between 1549 and 1550. The form is an allegorical vision in which Scotland as Dame Scotia addresses her three sons, the nobility, the clergy and the commonality, and urges them to cease this quarrel and work together to defend the independence of Scotland. The most recent editor, A.M. Stewart, describes it as 'a moderate reaction to savage orders executed by the English invaders during their invasion and occupation. It is a document of the resistance, written to combat a massive English propaganda campaign, demanding Union with threats.'[1]

The most famous passage is one dealing with the contrast between the people of the two nations:

(2.3) 'The Grit Difference ... Betwix the Twa Naturis'

There is no thing that is occasioun (O, ye my three
sonnis!) of your adhering to the opinion of Ingland
contrar your native country, bot the grit familiarity
that Inglis men and Scottis hes hed on baitht the
Bordours, [a]ilk ane with otheris, in marchandise,   [a]each
in selling and buying horse and [a]nolt and scheip,   [a]cattle
outfang and infang, ilk ane amang otheris, the
[a]quhilk familiarity is express contrar the lawis and   [a]which
consuetudis baitht of Ingland and Scotland.
    In the dayis of Moses, the Jewis durst nocht
have familiarity witht the Samaritanis, nor witht the
Philistians, nor the Romans witht the Africans, nor
the Greikis witht the Persans, be raisoun that ilk ane
repute otheris to be of ane barbour nature; for every
natioun reputis otheris natiouns to be barbarians,
quhen ther twa naturis and complexiouns are contrar
till otheris; and there is nocht twa natiouns under

the firmament that are mair contrar and different fra
otheris nor is Inglis men and Scottis men, quhoubeit
that thay be withtin ane ile, and nichtbours, and of
ane langage. For Inglis men are subtil, and Scottis
men are facile. Inglis men are ambitious in prosperity,
and Scottis men are humain in prosperity. Inglis men
are hummil quhen thay are subjeckit [a]be force and   [a]by
violence, and Scottis men are furious quhen thay are
violently subjeckit. Inglis men are cruel quhen thay
get victory, and Scottis men are merciful quhen thay
get victory. And to conclude, it is unpossible that
Scottis men and Inglis men can remain in concord
under ane monarchy or ane prince, because ther
naturis and conditiouns are as indefferent as is the
nature of scheip and wolvis ...

'I [a]trou it is as unpossible to gar Inglis men and   [a]am sure
Scottis men remain in gude accord under ane prince,
as it is unpossible that twa Sunnis and twa Munis
can be at one tyme togidder in the [a]lift, [b]be   [a]sky [b]by
raisoun of the grit difference that is betwix ther
naturis and conditiouns. Quharfore, as I haiff before
rehearsit, there suld be na familiarity betwix Inglis
men and Scottis men, because of the grit difference
that is betwix ther twa naturis ...[1]

Quoted in Moray McLaren, *The Wisdom of
the Scots*. London, 1961, pp. 101–2

There is an obvious similarity between the theme of the *Complaynt* and of Sir
David Lindsay's play, *Ane Satyre of the Thrie Estaitis*. In both, the well-being and
good government of Scotland is the issue and the estates of nobility, clergy
and commonality are among the protagonists. Lindsay was a leading figure of
the court of James V, employed several times as an Ambassador. He became
Lord Lyon and as such was concerned not only with protocol and diplomacy,
but with royal ceremonial and entertainment. This did not stop him making
an outspoken attack on the abuses of state and church in his play, which was
performed for the first time in 1552. (After an interval of some 400 years,
it was revived with great success in the Edinburgh International Festival in
1948 and several times since then.) Again, it speaks up for the poor, as in
the dialogue involving the Pauper and the Common-weill:

(2.4)   'The Common-wiel is Crukit'

REX
Schaw me thy name, gude man, I the command.
JOHN
Marie, Johne the Common-weil of fair Scotland.
REX
The Common-weil hes bene amang his fais!
JOHN
Ye, Sir, that gars the Common-weil want clais.
REX
Quhat is the caus the Common-weil is crukit?
JOHN
Becaus the Common-weill hes bene overlukit.
REX
Quhat gars the luke sa with ane dreirie hart?
JOHN
Becaus the Thrie Estaits gangs all backwart.
REX
Sir Common-weill, knaw ye the ᵃlimmers   ᵃscoundrels
   that them leids?
JOHN
Thair canker ᵃcullours, I ken them be the   ᵃspurious arguments
   heads:
As for our reverent fathers of Spiritualitie,
Thay ar led be Covetice and cairles Sensualitie;
And as ye se, Temporalitie hes neid of correctioun,
Quhilk hes lang tyme bene led be publick oppressioun.
Loe, quhair the loun lyis lurkand at his back –
Get up, I think to se thy craig gar ane raip crak!
Loe, heir is Falset and Dissait, weill I ken,
Leiders of the merchants and sillie craft[i]s-men.
Quhat mervell thocht the Thrie Estaits backwart gang.

Quhen sic an vyle cumpanie dwels them amang,
Quhilk hes reulit this rout monie deir dayis,
Quhilk gars John the Common-weil want his clais?
Sir, call them befoir you and put them in ordour,
Or els John the Common-weil man beg on the bordour.
Thou feinyeit Flattrie, the Feind fart in thy face:
Quhen ye was guyder of the Court we gat litill grace!

Ryse up, Falset and Dissait, without ony
    ᵃsunye: ᵃdelay
I pray God nor the Devils dame dryte on thy
    ᵃgrunye.   ᵃcrap on your snout
Behauld as the loun lukis evin lyke a thief:
Monie wicht warkman thou brocht to
    mischief!
My soveraine Lord Correctioun, I mak yow
    supplicatioun,
Put thir tryit ᵃtruikers from Christis   ᵃrogues
    congregatioun!
CORRECTIOUN
As ye have devysit, but doubt it sal be done.
Cum heir, my Sergeants, and do your
    debt sone:
Put thir thrie ᵃpellours into pressoun   ᵃthieves
    strang –
Howbeit ye sould hang them, ye do them na
    wrang!

> SIR DAVID LINDSAY, *Ane Satyre of the Thrie*
> *Estaitis*. Ed. by Roderick Lyall. Edinburgh,
> Canongate 1989, pp. 89–90

George Buchanan is the supreme example of the Scottish wandering scholar, one of those men who for several centuries played an important part in the intellectual life of Scotland and of many countries in Europe. He was educated at Paris and St Andrews and taught at Paris, Bordeaux, where Montaigne was one of his students, and at Coimbra, where he was in trouble with the Inquisition. He wrote poetry and plays in Latin, acquired a European reputation, and was called 'easily the prince of poets of his century'. On his return to Scotland, he sometimes read Livy with Mary, Queen of Scots, after dinner and was the formidable tutor of the future King James VI. He was alienated from Mary by the murder of Darnley.

One of Buchanan's tutors at St Andrews was the philosopher and historian John Mair. In his *History of Great Britain* (1521) Mair said that 'a people may deprive their King and his posterity of all authority, when the King's worthlessness calls for such a course just as at first it had the power to appoint him king',[2] an attitude which is clearly consistent with the Declaration of Arbroath. It is equivalent to saying that sovereignty rests with the whole people, even if at that time they had no normal and effective means of exercising it other than by an uprising. We have never shared the

English view that sovereignty rests with the Crown and Parliament or one
of them. The classic statement of the Scottish case is to be found in an
essay by George Buchanan *De Jure Regni Apud Scotos* (Concerning the law of
Sovereignty among the Scots). Published in 1579, it was probably written
in 1567 or 1568. It is in the form of a dialogue between Buchanan himself
and the young Thomas Maitland, a son of Maitland of Lethington, a leading
statesman of the age. The immediate purpose was to justify the deposition
of Mary to European opinion.

The following extracts are from a translation by the American scholar,
C.F. Arrowood. He says that it is 'one of the most important political treatises
ever written' and that its line of argument was precisely followed by the
American Declaration of Independence:[3]

(2.5)   Buchanan's *de Jure Regni Apud Scotos*

BUCHANAN
In establishing a government, the ancients, I believe, followed
this usage; that if there was, among them, some one of special
eminence, who seemed to excell everyone else in fairness and
foresight, they would confer the political authority upon him.
This is said to be done in colonies of bees.

MAITLAND
That is a credible account of what may have been done.

BUCHANAN
But what if no one of this character is to be found in a state?

MAITLAND
By the law of nature which we mentioned earlier, it is neither
possible nor right for one to assume authority among his
equals; for I believe that it is naturally just for the position
of equals to be alike with respect to the exercise of and
subjection to political authority.

BUCHANAN
But what if the people, wearied by regularly recurring strife
for office, should, as we have indicated before, choose as their
ruler some person who was not gifted with the whole round
of royal virtues, but was distinguished either by superiority of
character, by wealth, or by military achievements? Should we
not as we measure royalty by the highest law, regard him as
truly a king?

MAITLAND
Yes, most emphatically. For it is right that the people confer
the political authority upon whomsoever they will.

* * *

MAITLAND
You seem to be saying that it is reason, from which, as from a fountain, all laws which are of value for the preservation of human society must flow or be derived.
BUCHANAN
Precisely. And if a person posesses wisdom in the highest degree and without flaw, we may say of him that he is a king by nature, and not by virtue of the people's choice. To him we may entrust independent and unlimited power. If, however, no man who completely fills these specifications can be found, we shall call that man king who, having the likeness of a genuine king, approaches most nearly to that highest eminence of character.

* * *

MAITLAND
Do you not believe that the royal authority should be absolute and unlimited?
BUCHANAN
Emphatically, no! For I bear in mind that the ruler is not a king only, but is, as well, a man; mistaken in many cases through ignorance; doing wrong in many cases through wilfulness; acting in many cases under constraint. He is, in fact, an animal, easily moved by every breath of good or ill will; so that I have learned the truth of that exceedingly strong statement from one of the comedies. 'Where there is license, everything goes from bad to worse.' It is for this reason that men of the keenest insight have made the law the King's associate; that it may show him the way when he is ignorant, and bring him back to it when he goes astray. From this, I think, you can see, 'as in a picture', what I regard as the duty of a legitimate king.

It is, therefore, reasonable to stand by the position we have announced from the first, that kings, initially, were set up to preserve justice. If they had been able to have kept their exercise of authority as they had received it – that is, released and made free under the laws – they might have kept it in perpetuity. But, as is always the case in human affairs, matters degenerated, and the authority, which was established to serve the public interest, became an arrogant overlordship. For – since the arbitrary will of kings supplanted the laws,

and men invested with unlimited and undefined powers did
not regulate their conduct by reason but allowed many things
because of partiality, many because of prejudice, and many
because of self-interest – the arrogance of kings made laws
necessary. For this reason, therefore, laws were devised by the
people, and kings were forced to employ the legal authority,
conferred upon them by the people, and not their arbitrary
wills, in deciding cases. The people had been taught by long
experience that it is better to trust their liberty to the laws
than to kings; for the latter can be drawn away from justice
by a great variety of forces, but the former, being deaf to both
entreaties and to threats, pursues the one, unbroken course.

Kings, free in other matters, have their course prescribed
with respect to the exercise of political authority – they
must shape their actions and speech in conformity with the
principles of the laws, and they must apportion rewards and
punishments, those great means of social unity, in accordance
with the laws' sanctions. Finally, as that great authority on
republican government puts it, 'The king should be the law
speaking; the law should be the king mute.'

*   *   *

MAITLAND
What of a case in which a king would not willingly submit to
trial, and could not be compelled to do so?
BUCHANAN
Here he is in a common case with all criminals; for no robber
or poisoner submits to trial of his own accord. But you know,
I think, what the law provides – that anyone may slay a
thief by night, and may slay him by day in self-defense. You
will recall what is done when a criminal cannot be brought
to justice either by his own surrender or by force. Robbers
who are so powerful that they cannot be dealt with by the
ordinary process of law are pursued as in a war with force of
arms. Nor is there any other cause of wars alleged between
nations and between peoples and kings than those injuries
which are decided by the sword when the law cannot settle
the issue.
MAITLAND
This justification of war is generally regarded as valid when
the war is waged against enemies, but the case is far otherwise
with respect to making war against a people's own kings; for

we are under obligation, by the taking of a most sacred oath,
to obey them.
BUCHANAN
We are indeed obligated; but before we take the oath the
kings first promise that they will maintain the law in justice
and goodness.
MAITLAND
Precisely so.
BUCHANAN
There is, then, a mutual compact between king and citizens.
MAITLAND
So it appears.
BUCHANAN
Does not he who first withdraws from the covenant or does
something contrary to the agreement break the covenant and
the agreement?
MAITLAND
He does indeed break it.
BUCHANAN
I think moreover that in case the king has broken the bond
which holds him and his people together, he who first breaks
the agreement forfeits whatever rights belong to him under it.

                        *   *   *

BUCHANAN
You think, then, that tyrants are to be regarded as the most
savage of all monsters; and you think further that the harm
done by tyranny is more contrary to nature than poverty,
sickness, death and the other ills which can befall men in the
course of nature.

                        *   *   *

I think that I have said quite enough to show the justice
of our [the Scottish people's] case; and if I do not satisfy
certain foreigners, I ask them to consider how unfairly they
are persecuting us. For, in view of the fact that there are a
great many rich and powerful nations in Europe, each of
them with its own laws, these hostile critics of Scotland act
most arrogantly when they prescribe for everyone their own
peculiar form of government.
    The Helvetian people form a commonwealth; Germany
calls its constitutional monarchy an empire; I hear that

some German states are ruled by nobles; the Venetians have a government in which all of these features are combined; Russia rejoices in a tyranny. Ours, to be sure, is a poor nation, but for two thousand years now we have held it, free from the domination of foreigners. From the first, we have made our kings constitutional rulers. We have imposed the same laws on them and on ourselves, and the passing centuries have taught the value of the constitutional principle. For this kingdom owes its preservation more to the faithful observance of this principle than to strength of arms.

Would it not be a wicked thing were we to wipe out or to neglect the laws which have proved so valuable through so many centuries? And is it not the height of insolence in those who are scarcely able to maintain their own government to attempt to weaken the stability and order of a foreign country? Are not our institutions advantageous not only to ourselves but to our neighbors also? For what can contribute so much to the maintenance of peace between neighboring nations as well ordered governments? For it is by reason of ungoverned and lawless passion that most wars of aggression are rashly undertaken, wickedly waged, and disgracefully concluded. Furthermore, what can be of more disservice to nations than the bad laws of the nations which touch their borders, the contagion of which, as a general thing, spreads widely?

And why do foreigners attack us only, when each of the nations about them has its own laws and institutions; and there is almost no agreement among them? And why precisely, are they troubled, for we have enacted no new laws, but continue steadfast in our ancient right? Why do they complain, for we are not the only people who enjoy these institutions, nor are we the first to have them nor do we now enjoy them for the first time?

So, our laws do not please certain persons! Perhaps their own laws do not please them either. We do not officiously meddle with the institutions of other nations. Let them leave ours, which have been tested by trial through so many years, to us. Do we disturb their assemblies? In what respect do we cause them trouble?

They say, 'You are divided.'

I can readily answer, 'What is that to you? We are divided at our own risk and at our own loss.'

I can name not a few civil insurrections which were not at all harmful to commonwealths or kingdoms; but I shall not employ that defense. I deny that any people has less internal dissension than we. I deny that any nation has managed its internal disputes with more moderation than we. There have been many contests over questions of the laws, over the powers of government, and over the administration of the kingdom, but the sovereignty has been ever preserved. Nor [in Scotland] has strife been due to an effort to ruin the commons or because of hatred of the princes, but out of love of country and desire to preserve the laws. Have not great armies frequently, within our recollection, stood face to face, and have they not as often dispersed not only without wounds but without harm and without wrangling? Has not the public interest quieted many a private quarrel? Has not the rumor of a foreign invasion composed quarrels between parties within the nation?

Nor have we been less fortunate than moderate in our civil strife; for, always, the party which had the better cause was the more successful. And as we have practiced moderation in our domestic quarrels, so also we have agreed to our mutual advantage.

These matters appear to be enough to suppress the rumors spread by the malicious; to silence the obstinate, and to satisfy the fair-minded. I have thought that we should not be greatly concerned with the laws under which any other nation is governed. I have reviewed briefly our own customs, but more at length than I had planned, or than the matter demanded; for I undertook this task wholly on your account, and, if the way the matter has been dealt with meets with your approval, I am satisfied.

MAITLAND

So far as I am concerned, I am fully satisfied; and if I am able to convince others in the same fashion as you have convinced me, I shall have profited greatly by this discussion, and I shall think my troubles have been greatly lightened.

GEORGE BUCHANAN, *The Powers of the Crown in Scotland.* Trans. by C.F. Arrowood. Austin, 1949, pp. 52–8, 141–50

CHAPTER THREE

From the Reformation to the National Covenant and the first Claim of Right

The Reformation in Scotland was intellectually rigorous and thorough but was free from the atrocity and confusion with which it was sullied in Germany, France, England and Spain. The Protestant revolution was accomplished in Scotland without a single execution on the grounds of religion. The historian, Hume Brown, said of it, 'It is precisely the combination of a fervid temper with logical thinking and temperate action that has distinguished the Scottish people in all the great crises of their history.'[1] The Reformed Kirk's distrust of ornament and frivolity led to a discouragement of music and dance. On the other hand, the emphasis on the equality of all people and on the need for all of them to read and understand the scriptures encouraged education and the habit of thought and debate on metaphysical and moral issues. Sir Walter Scott said in *Rob Roy*, 'The Scotch, it is well known, are more remarkable for the exercise of their intellectual powers, than for the keenest of their feelings; they are, therefore, more moved by logic than by rhetoric, and more attracted by acute and argumentative reasoning on doctrinal points, than influenced by enthusiastic appeals to the heart and to the passions'.[2] The Reformation was partly the consequence and partly the cause of this habit of mind. It was one of the fundamental reasons for the great outburst of new ideas in the Scottish Enlightenment of the 18th Century.

The Presbyterian structure of the Kirk, ruled by committees and assembly and not by hierarchy, was an expression of its egalitarian impulse. The General Assembly of the Church of Scotland was some compensation for the loss of the Scottish Parliament in 1707 and it was far more democratic and representative than the British Parliament until its franchise was extended by the series of Reform Acts in the 19th Century.

Until about the time of the First World War Scotland was a conspicuously religious country. It is now predominantly secular. Even so, and in spite of the pressure of modern consumerism, much of Scottish life is still affected by the Presbyterian attitudes of belief in education, honesty and effort and a distrust of ostentation and self-indulgence. As the old joke has it, 'I may be an atheist but I reserve the right to be a Presbyterian atheist.'

The Reformation in the 16th Century brought to an end the alliance of 300 years with France, one of the longest in European history. Scottish students began to go to universities in Holland rather than France. The whole orientation of Scottish foreign policy changed. Both Scotland and England, unlike France, became Protestant, although with churches which were very different in structure and in ideas.

The *First Book of Discipline* of 1560 was drafted by John Knox to define the creed and structure of the new church and its place in the national life. It included the following ambitious provisions for education:

(3.1)   ## Taught not by Angels but by Men

Seeing that God hath determined that his Church here in
earth shall be taught not by angels but by men ... of necessity
it is that your Honours be most careful for the virtuous
education and godly upbringing of the youth of this Realm. ...
Of necessity therefore we judge it, that every several church
have a Schoolmaster appointed, such a one as is able, at least,
to teach Grammar, and the Latin tongue, if the town be of
any reputation. If it be upland [i.e. rural] where the people
convene to doctrine but once in the week, then must either
the Reader or the Minister there appointed, take care over
the children and youth of the parish, to instruct them in their
first rudiments, and especially in the Catechism, as we have
it now translated in the Book of our Common Order, called
the Order of Geneva. And further, we think it expedient
that in every notable town, and especially in the town of the
Superintendent, [there] be erected a College, in which the
Arts, at least Logic and Rhetoric, together with the Tongues,
be read by sufficient Masters ... (295–6).
    The Grammar Schools and of the Tongues being erected
as we have said, next we think it necessary there be three
Universities in this whole Realm, established in the towns
accustomed. The first in Saint Andrews, the second in
Glasgow, and the third in Aberdeen.
    And in the first University and principal, which is Saint
Andrews, there be three Colleges. And in the first College,
which is the entry of the University, there be four classes or
seiges [i.e. chairs]: the first, to the new Supposts,[2] shall be only
Dialectics; the next, only Mathematics; the third, of Physics

only; the fourth of Medicine. And in the second College, two classes or seiges: the first, in Moral Philosophy; the second in the Laws. And in the third College, two classes or seiges: the first, in the Tongues, to wit, Greek and Hebrew; the second in Divinity (297–8).

A Source Book of Scottish History. Ed. by
W.C. Dickinson, Gordon Donaldson & I.A.
Milne. Edinburgh, 1958, vol. III, pp. 176–7

The *First Book of Discipline* was not fully endorsed at the time and its aspirations were realised only imperfectly and slowly. The ambition to achieve an educated society was well ahead of its time and it was something which the Church and Parliament upheld and worked towards in a series of measures over the next century. Hume Brown said of the *First Book* that it was 'in many respects, the most important of public documents in the history of Scotland ... by defining the ideas and moulding the temper and culture of the prevailing majority of the Scottish people, it has been one of the great formative influences in the national development'.3

The *Second Book of Discipline* of 1578 marks a further stage in the evolution of the Reformed Church. The following extracts define the separation of Kirk and State, and the supremacy of the Kirk in spiritual matters. This has remained a fundamental doctrine of the Church of Scotland and implies a limitation of the sovereignty of the civil power.

(3.2)   The Two Kingdoms

    l. 2.   The kirke ... hes a certane power grantit be God, according to the quhilk it uses a proper jurisdiction and governement, exerciseit to the confort of the haill kirk. This power ecclesiasticall is an authoritie granted be God the Father, throw the Mediator Jesus Christ, unto his kirk gatherit, and having the ground in the Word of God; to be put in execution be them, unto quhom the spirituall government of the kirk be lawfull calling is committit.

    l. 3.   The policie of the kirk flowing from this power is an order or forme of spirituall government, quhilk is exercisit be the members appoyntit thereto be the Word of God; and therefore is gevin immediatly to the office-beararis, be whom it is exercisit to the weile of the haill bodie ...

l. 4. This power and policie ecclesiasticall is different and distinct in the awin nature from that power and policie quhilk is callit the civill power, and appertenis to the civill government of the commonwelth; albeit they be both of God, and tend to one end, if they be rightlie usit, to wit, to advance the glorie of God and to have godlie and gud subjectis.

l. 5. For this power ecclesiasticall flowes immediatlie from God, and the Mediator Jesus Christ, and is spirituall, not having a temporall heid on earth, bot onlie Christ, the onlie spirituall King and Governour of his kirk.

l. 7. Therefore this power and policie of the kirk sould leane upon the Word immediatlie, as the onlie ground thereof, and sould be tane from the pure fountaines of the Scriptures, the kirk hearing the voyce of Christ, the onlie spirituall King, and being rewlit be his lawes.

l. 8. It is proper to kings, princes and magistrates, to be callit lordis, and dominators over their subjectis, whom they govern civilly; bot it is proper to Christ onlie to be callit Lord and Master in the spirituall government of the kirk: and all uthers that bearis office therein aucht not to usurp dominion therein, nor be callit lordis, bot onlie ministeris, disciples and servantis. For it is Christis proper office to command and rewll his kirk universall, and every particular kirk, throw his Spirit and Word, be the ministrie of men.

l. 9. Notwithstanding, as the ministeris and uthers of the ecclesiasticall estait ar subject to the magistrat civill, so aught the person of the magistrat be subject to the kirk spiritually and in ecclesiasticall government. And the exercise of both these jurisdictiones cannot stand in one person ordinarlie. The civill power is callit the Power of the Sword, and the uther the Power of the Keyes.

l. 10. The civill power sould command the spiritual to exercise and doe their office according to the Word of God: the spiritual rewlaris sould requyre the Christian magistrate to minister justice and punish vyce, and to maintaine the libertie and quietness of the kirk within their boundis.

l. 14. ... The ministeris exerce not the civil jurisdictioun, bot teich the magistrat how it sould be exercit according to the Word.

l. 15. ... Finally, as ministeris are subject to the judgement and

punishment of the magistrat in externall things, if they
offend; so aucht the magistratis to submit themselfis to
the discipline of the kirk gif they transgresse in matteris
of conscience and religioun.

*   *   *

III. 5.   In the order of election it is to be eschewit that na person
be intrusit in ony of the offices of the kirk contrar to the
will of the congregation to whom they are appointed, or
without the voce of the elderschip ...

*   *   *

VII. 2.   Assemblies ar of four sortis. For aither ar they of
particular kirks and congregations, ane or ma, or of
a province, or of ane haill nation, or of all and divers
nations professing one Jesus Christ.

VII. 3.   All the ecclesiasticall assemblies have power to convene
lawfully togidder for treating of things concerning the
kirk, and perteining to thair charge. They have power
to appoynt tymes and places to that effect; and at ane
meiting to appoynt the dyet, time and place for anuther.

VII. 10. ... When we speik of the elders of the particular
congregations, we mein not that every particular parish
kirk can or may have their awin particular elderschips,
specially to landwart; bot we think thrie or four, mae or
fewar, particular kirks, may have ane common elderschip
to them all, to judge thair ecclesiasticall causes.

*   *   *

VII. 25. There is ... an uther mair generall kynde of assemblie,
quhilk is of all nations and estaits of persons within the
kirk, representing the universall kirk of Christ; quhilk
may be callit properlie the Generall Assemblie or
Generall Councell of the haill Kirk of God.

A Source Book of Scottish History. Ed. by
W.C. Dickinson, Gordon Donaldson & I.A.
Milne. Edinburgh, 1958, vol. III, pp. 22–4

This doctrine of a Kirk in which Christ was 'the only spiritual King and
Governour', and in which everyone was equal, was unwelcome to kings
like James VI with ideas of divine right and supreme authority. James was

able to develop and express such ideas when he left Scotland in 1603 on his inheritance also of the throne of England. This was a consequence of his descent from James IV and Margaret Tudor, a daughter of Henry VIII of England.

When the marriage of Margaret to James was first proposed some of Henry's court had argued against it on the grounds that it could bring England under the rule of a Scottish prince. Henry told them not to worry. If that happened, it would not be an accession of England to Scotland, but of Scotland to England because the larger country would always dominate the smaller, as England had dominated Normandy.4 Events were to prove that Henry was right.

The flitting of James VI and his court to London in 1603 was disastrous for Scotland. Since the king was then the effective executive head of the government, and in particular of foreign policy and of all appointments to government posts, it meant that Scotland was at a stroke reduced to a state of nominal independence but *de facto* control from London. The king was liberated from the constraints that applied to him in Scotland. In a speech to the English Parliament in 1607, James said: 'Here I sit and govern Scotland with my pen. I write and it is done; and by the Clerk of the Council I govern Scotland now, which others could not do by the sword.'5 The arts and industry lost royal patronage. Scotland was involved in wars conducted by England against our traditional trading partners and our foreign trade was greatly harmed in consequence.

The situation became even worse under James's successors, because they were educated in England and had little understanding of Scotland. The attempts of Charles I to impose the English liturgy and prayer-book on Scotland provoked rebellion which led to the Civil War in both Scotland and England. Its proclamation was the National League and Covenant of 1638, signed with enthusiasm by all ranks of people in all parts of Scotland. This was a long and skilful document, which was revolutionary in intention but only by implication. It proclaimed the defence of both 'true Religion' and the 'King's Majesty'; but it was religion which was placed first and resistance to the king's recent measures was declared in firm and solemn terms. The unstated implication was the doctrine of the Declaration of Arbroath and of George Buchanan that Kings were only tolerable if they upheld the law and carried out the will of the people. The following is the key passage:

(3.3) ## The National Covenant (1638)

In obedience to the Commandment of God, conforme to the practice of the godly in former times, and according to the laudable example of our Worthy and Religious Progenitors,

& of many yet living amongst us, which was warranted also
by act of Councill, commanding a general band to be made
and subscribed by his Majesty's subjects, of all ranks, for two
causes: One was, For defending the true Religion, as it was
then reformed, and is expressed in the Confession of Faith
abovewritten, and a former large Confession established by
sundry acts of lawful generall assemblies, & of Parliament,
unto which it hath relation, set down in publick Catechismes,
and which had been for many years with a blessing from
Heaven preached, and professed in this Kirk and Kingdome,
as Gods undoubted truth, grounded only upon his written
Word. The other cause was, for maintaining the Kings Majesty,
His Person, and Estate: the true worship of God and the
Kings authority, being so straitly joined, as that they had the
same Friends, and common enemies, and did stand and fall
together. And finally, being convinced in our mindes, and
confessing with our mouthes, that the present and succeeding
generations in this Land, are bound to keep the foresaid
nationall Oath & Subscription inviolable, Wee Noblemen,
Barons, Gentlemen, Burgesses, Ministers & Commons under
subscribing, considering divers times before & especially at
this time, the danger of the true reformed Religion, of the
Kings honour, and of the publick peace of the Kingdome: By
the manifold innovations and evills generally conteined, and
particularly mentioned in our late supplications, complaints,
and protestations, Do hereby professe, and before God, his
Angels, and the World solemnly declare, That, with our whole
hearts we agree & resolve, all the dayes of our life, constantly
to adhere unto, and to defend the foresaid true Religion, and
(forbearing the practice of all novations, already introduced
in the matters of the worship of God, or approbation of the
corruptions of the publicke Government of the Kirk, or civil
places and power of Kirk-men, till they be tryed & allowed in
free assemblies, and in Parliaments) to labour by all meanes
lawful to recover the purity and liberty of the Gospel, as it
was stablished and professed before the foresaid Novations.

A Source Book of Scottish History. Ed. by
W.C. Dickinson, Gordon Donaldson & I.A.
Milne. Edinburgh, 1958, vol. III, pp. 100–1

When James II and VII fled from London in 1688, the English Parliament declared that he had abdicated, which was a polite evasion of the fact that he had been deposed by the threat of the rebellion. The Scottish Estates in the Claim of Right of 1689 were more forthright. After listing abuses and violation of the law committed by James, they bluntly dismissed him:

(3.4)   The Claim of Right, 1689

All which are utterly and directly contrary to the known laws, statutes and freedoms of this Realm.

Therefore the Estates of the Kingdom of Scotland, Find and Declare that King James the Seventh being a professed Papist, did assume the Regal power, and acted as King, without ever taking the oath required by law, and hath by the advice of evil and wicked counsellors, invaded the fundamental constitution of the Kingdom, and altered it from a legal limited Monarchy, to an arbitrary despotick Power, and hath exercised the same, to the subversion of the Protestant religion, and the violation of the laws and liberties of the Kingdom, inverting all the ends of Government, whereby he hath forefaulted the right to the Crown, and the Throne is become vacant.

Then follows a long list of arbitrary practices which it declares unlawful and it concludes:

That Prelacy and the superiority of any office in the Church above Presbyters, is, and hath been a great and insupportable grievance and trouble to this Nation, and contrary to the inclinations of the generality of the people, ever since the Reformation (they having reformed from Popery by Presbyters), and therefore ought to be abolished.

That it is the right and privilege of the Subjects to protest for Remeed of law to the King and Parliament, against sentences pronounced by the Lords of Session, providing the same do not stop execution of these sentences.

That it is the right of the subjects to petition the King, and that all imprisonments and prosecutions for such petitioning, are contrary to law.

That for redress of all grievances, and for the amending, strengthening and preserving of the laws, Parliaments ought to be frequently called, and allowed to sit, and the freedom of speech and debate secured to the members.

And they do claim, demand and insist upon all and
sundry the premisses as their undoubted rights and liberties,
and that no declarations, doings, or proceedings, to the
prejudice of the people, in any of the said premisses, ought in
any ways to be drawn hereafter, in consequence or example,
but that all forefaultures, fines, loss of offices, imprisonments,
banishments, pursuits, persecutions, tortures and rigorous
executions be considered, and the parties lesed be redressed.

To which demand of their rights, and redressing of their
grievances, they are particularly encouraged by His Majesty
the King of England, his declaration for the Kingdom of
Scotland, of the ... day of October last, as being the only
means for obtaining a full redress and remedy therein.

Having therefore an entire confidence, that His said
Majesty the King of England, will perfect the deliverance
so far advanced by Him, and will still preserve them from
the violation of their rights which they have here asserted,
and from all other attempts upon their Religion, Laws, and
Liberties.

The said Estates of the Kingdom of Scotland, Do resolve
that WILLIAM and MARY, King and Queen of England, France
and Ireland, Be, and Be Declared King and Queen of Scotland,
to hold the Crown and Royal Dignity of the said Kingdom of
Scotland.

> A *Source Book of Scottish History*. Ed. by
> W.C. Dickinson, Gordon Donaldson &
> I.A. Milne. Edinburgh, 1958, vol. III, pp.
> 202–3; 205–6

This assertion of the 'freedom of speech and debate' in Parliament was
an important advance, but it was unfortunate that the Claim did not go
further. Acts passed by the Parliament were still subject to royal assent
or veto, and official appointments (including the Scottish offices of State,
or as we should now say, Ministers) were made by the Monarch, acting in
practice through and on the advice of his English court. In other words,
the Scottish Parliament was free to debate and decide as it pleased, but
real executive power stayed in London. Scotland, as it had been since
1603, was nominally independent, but hampered and restricted by London
control.

On one of the Acts of the Parliament in 1695, another of the series of
Education Acts, Lord Macaulay commented:

(3.5)   'Superior in Intelligence'

But by far the most important event of this short session
was the passing of the Act for the settling of Schools. By this
memorable law it was, in the Scotch phrase, statuted and
ordained that every parish in the realm should provide a
commodious schoolhouse and should pay a moderate stipend
to a schoolmaster. The effect could not be immediately felt.
But, before one generation had passed away, it began to be
evident that the common people of Scotland were superior
in intelligence to the common people of any other country
in Europe. To whatever land the Scotchman might wander,
to whatever calling he might betake himself, in America or in
India, in trade or in war, the advantage which he derived from
his early training raised him above his competitors. If he was
taken into a warehouse as a porter, he soon became foreman.
If he enlisted in the army, he soon became a serjeant.
Scotland, meanwhile, in spite of the barrenness of her soil and
the severity of her climate, made such progress in agriculture,
in manufactures, in commerce, in letters, in science, in all
that constitutes civilisation, as the Old World had never
seen equalled, and as even the New World has scarcely seen
surpassed.

This wonderful change is to be attributed, not indeed
solely, but principally, to the national system of education.

T.B. MACAULAY, *The History of England.*
London, 1915, vol. VI, p. 2698

CHAPTER FOUR

'Rather a kindly place'

Before coming to more modern times, we might digress to consider the impression which has been put about by some English historians, and sometimes by uninformed Scots as well, that Scotland in the mediaeval past was more unruly and violent than other countries. This is simply untrue, as George Buchanan maintained. (2.5) Gordon Donaldson, the late Historiographer Royal, discussed the point in a lecture which he gave in October 1989. The following is an extract:

(4.1)   A Backward Country

'A backward country', noted for its 'barbarous deeds'
and 'customary turmoil'. With those words Scotland was
introduced to readers of *The Cambridge Modern History* by F. W.
Maitland in 1903. At that time historical thinking in this island
was dominated by the achievements of the great English
constitutional historians like Stubbs, Freeman and Maitland
himself, who created the image of English history as the
history of ordered progress towards a type of parliamentary
democracy to which, it was confidently believed, the rest of
the world would one day conform. Inevitably, therefore, the
institutions of a country like Scotland, which deviated from
the English model, were regarded as second-rate.
        Scottish historians themselves saw things through
English eyes, and capitulated to the English point of view.
For example, Hume Brown, the first Professor of Scottish
History, wrote rather apologetically, and could express little
pride in Scotland's institutional achievements. 'We may look
in vain' in Scottish history, he said in his inaugural lecture,
'for that orderly development which makes the primary
interest of histories such as those of England and Rome'. It
did indeed just occur to him that Scotland's record might

stand comparison with those of some continental countries:
'Scotland during the fifteenth century was certainly not
an Arcadia, but it is equally certain that for its crimes
and oppressions it would be easy to find parallels in the
contemporary histories of France and Germany. Even the
performances of the Wolf of Badenoch are easily left behind
by those of many a robber baron of the Rhine.' But Hume
Brown did not dare to suggest that parallels might be found
without even crossing the English Channel. Hume Brown's
successor, Hannay, did not move very far from Hume Brown's
position, for he was still under the spell of the Victorian
era and the concept of English history as the embodiment
of ordered progress, and he remarked that 'for intellectual
enlightenment we turn first to what has been momentous, to
Greece, to Rome, to England'.

This attitude has still not been shaken off by English
historians, some of whom continue to write of the institutions
of any country other than their own in a patronising and
consciously superior manner. Sir Geoffrey Elton described
the reign of James IV as a 'futile, though fascinating, story'
and its events as 'these romantic but incomprehensible
goings-on'. This, be it noted, of a reign which began only
three years after the close of the Wars of the Roses, which
might well seem futile and incomprehensible without
being either fascinating or romantic. Joel Hurstfield had
only one word to describe Scottish politics – squalid:
'squalid baronial warfare' and 'squalid factional warfare'.
Much of the false image of Scotland's past which was
projected by historians in earlier generations still lingers,
for example in Patrick Riley's recent remark that Scottish
history looks like 'little more than a catalogue of bloody
calamities'.

Too much Scottish history which is being taught or
absorbed today is still Scottish history as seen through
English eyes, Scottish history interpreted from the English
point of view. It is only right that every nation should have
a proper pride in its own achievements, but the particular
form which national conceit takes in England is the idea not
only that English institutions have been and are superior to
the institutions of all other countries, but also that in her
historical development England was always far ahead of
other countries. In English eyes anything that is not English

is peculiar; worse than that, it is backward if not actually
barbarous.

The assumption that Scotland was backward can be
challenged. We ought to have learned by this time that it is
worthwhile at least trying to understand the institutions of
Scotland instead of dismissing them as unworthy of attention
merely because they differ from those of England. It is not
difficult to show that at many points Scotland was more
mature in its outlook than England, was in many ways in
advance of England, and thus to demonstrate that England
was sometimes the backward country.

We may start at the top, with the monarchy. What were
the attitudes of the English and the Scots to their kings and
queens? There is an idea in England that the whole concept
of the divine right of kings, the notion that a particular family
had an inviolable right to the crown, the idea that kings
cannot be lawfully deposed – all the ideas associated with
Jacobitism – were ideas which the Stewart kings brought
with them from Scotland. The English, with their conscious
air of superiority, imply that there was no room in England
for that sort of nonsense and that the sensible English people
taught the Stewarts a lesson and sent them packing. But this
is quite contrary to the facts. It was in England, far more than
in Scotland, that all sorts of half-magical ideas surrounded
the kingship. The belief that a certain disease, The King's Evil
as it was called, could be cured by the king's touch, was an
English idea. The Stewart kings did not 'touch for the Evil',
as the phrase went, until they became kings of England, and
when James VI succeeded to the English throne he was at first
rather sceptical about what he regarded as a quaint English
superstition.

Nor did the Scots believe in the exclusive right to the
throne of one particular family. They were very proud of their
long line of kings, and fondly imagined that there had been
over a hundred of them – their portraits, mostly spurious, can
be seen in the Long Gallery at Holyroodhouse. But the Scots
believed, far more firmly than the English, that the people
could choose their king and set aside a king of whom they
did not approve. The different points of view came out plainly
at the revolution of 1689, when James VII was replaced by
William of Orange. At that time the English declared feebly
that James, by fleeing from the country, had abdicated, which

was simply not true; the Scots, more forthright and more logical, declared that James, by his misdeeds, had forfeited his right to the crown and the throne had become vacant. At that point the Scottish parliament was doing nothing that it had not done, or at least asserted its right to do, in the fourteenth century. It was the Scots who had the more mature point of view.

On the other hand, the Scots did treat their kings with a good deal more consideration than did the English. For some odd reason – possibly because the English, like Alan Breck in *Kidnapped*, have a 'grand memory for forgetting', in this case forgetting things discreditable to themselves – the idea has been put about that the Scots, but not the English, were addicted to murdering their kings. Queen Victoria's complaint that in Scottish history there were 'too many Jameses, and all of them murdered', was a libel. In the fourteenth and fifteenth centuries the Scots murdered only two of their kings – James I and James III; in the same period the English managed to dispose of five of theirs, with two heirs to the throne for good measure. Edward II, Richard II, Henry VI, Edward V and Richard III were all killed by either their subjects or their rivals. Sober arithmetic is against the English claim to superior rectitude here. The English were only following their own brutal old custom when they put to death Mary, Queen of Scots, and Charles I.

During the Wars of the Roses rival kings and rival families were competing for the English crown and one king was almost habitually deposed in favour of another: Plantagenet, Lancastrian, Yorkist and Tudor fell or rose in turn in England. But in Scotland the crown passed regularly, and without a single break, from father to child; for two hundred and fifty years, no less, each Scottish king was peacefully succeeded by his son or daughter. This is a kind of contrast which the English have a grand memory for forgetting: it is nonsense to hold up England as an example of peace and order and to imply that Scotland was, by comparison, backward.

The contrast can be pushed farther. The period in Scottish history which does resemble the Wars of the Roses was away back in the tenth and eleventh centuries: at that time the Scottish throne was contested almost generation by generation, and a king was habitually killed in favour of a rival. Scotland got this kind of thing out of her system quite early, and ceased in the eleventh century to behave towards her kings as England was still doing in the fifteenth. England was centuries behind Scotland.

It is preposterous, too, that Scotland should have a reputation for being disorderly. There were, in truth, far more rebellions in England. There was not a reign between the reign of Edward II and the reign of Elizabeth, except possibly that of Edward III, when there was not at least one rebellion in England, and usually there were more than one. England was a welter of political and social unrest. Yet G.M. Trevelyan wrote about 'a century of peace under the Tudors'. Scotland's record was incomparably superior. She even managed to get through the sixteenth century, so sanguinary in many countries, without any massacres, with very few martyrdoms, and with hardly any executions for treason. Even rebellions were rare and if there were wars of religion they were wars mainly between the English and French, wars on Scottish soil indeed but wars in which little Scottish blood was shed.

In England, too, the many rebellions were suppressed with savage brutality. The leaders were put to death with all the penalties of the barbarous English treason law, including disembowelling while still alive; the Scots very properly regarded such proceedings with scandalised horror; their own traitors were, very occasionally, put away, but it was done decently by beheading. And when it came to beheading the Scots were more humane than the English. English executioners hacked away with an axe and might take half a dozen strokes to finish the job. But in Scotland there was an efficient machine called The Maiden: its sharp blade, aided by a great lump of lead weighing 75 lbs., was guaranteed to shear off the head at one stroke.

Even when England did finally grow out of the Wars of the Roses stage she still did not show real signs of political maturity by learning self-government or political freedom; instead she was subjected to the despotism of the Tudors. Under Henry VIII the king's will was law and the king's will was enforced by something little short of a reign of terror: the executioner's axe and the hangman's rope were seldom idle and all who dared to challenge the crown were dealt with savagely.

But while England was groaning under the brutal tyranny of the Tudors, in Scotland men were at liberty to

form political parties and to bring pressure to bear on the
government. Sometimes the fate of the country was even
decided by a free vote in parliament, though not very often.
But it is also true that a decision was not very often reached
by bloodshed either. More often all that happened was a kind
of demonstration in force when men did gather in arms, but
they seem to have been content with something like counting
heads, and the minority simply withdrew, so that there was a
bloodless *coup d'état* involving a change of government without
much if any violence. It really worked quite well, and Scotland
had party government of a kind in the sixteenth century, when
England was under the Tudor despots.

But the English sneer at all this. If England has political
freedom and party government, that is a good thing. But if
Scotland has it, at a time when England is under a despotism,
then it is a sign of backwardness. England under a tyranny was
orderly and well-disciplined, whereas Scotland, where there
was some liberty, was a welter of confusion. It never seems
to occur to the English historian who takes this attitude that
at the present day the inhabitant of a dictatorship would
consider his stable system far superior to the British, in which
the government is liable to be changed every few years by a
general election.

The Scottish Maiden was less hard-worked than the
English executioners. In England the victims of Henry VIII
and Elizabeth must be numbered by the hundred, and it is
hard to think of a prominent Englishman in that age who
did not end his days on the scaffold. Survivors were rare. In
Scotland it is hard to think of many comparable executions
of notables: there was Lord Home in 1516, the Earl of Morton
in 1581 and the Earl of Gowrie in 1584, and possibly one
should count Kirkcaldy of Grange in 1573, but those are about
all. Now this contrast is not merely a matter of arithmetic –
counting heads, literally: in England a man could not oppose
the government without a very great risk, almost a certainty,
that he would get it in the neck; in Scotland the chances of
success were greater, but, even in the event of bad luck and
failure, death was not likely to be the penalty. One could cite
instance after instance of men who were on the losing side
in Scottish politics, who were active against the government
again and again, and yet who died in their beds at a ripe old
age. Survivors were common. Even when the capital penalty

was not in question practice was more humane in Scotland
than in England: John Knox denounced Mary's marriage plans,
but all he suffered was a dressing-down from the queen in
person, whereas poor John Stubbs, who similarly denounced
Elizabeth's projected marriage to a French prince, had his
right hand cut off. Knox knew that there was more freedom
of speech in Mary Stewart's Scotland than in Elizabeth Tudor's
England.

It can therefore be argued that there was some political
freedom in Scotland, to the extent at least that death was not
the normal penalty for being on the losing side; death was
not the inevitable consequence of unsuccessful opposition. A
comparison of Scotland's record with that of England suggests
that sixteenth-century Scotland was rather a kindly place, and
certainly a safer country to live in than many others.

> GORDON DONALDSON, 'A Backward
> Nation' in *Scotland's History*. Ed. by James
> Kirk. Edinburgh, Scottish Academic Press,
> 1995, pp. 42–7

In his book, *The Union of England and Scotland*, first published in 1896, James
Mackinnon praised the legislative wisdom of the Scottish Parliament before
the Union. His reference to a 'capable critic' is about an essay by Sir
Archibald Alison, published in *Blackwood's Magazine* in 1834. Alison, who
has been described as a mildly liberal Tory, was Advocate-Depute from
1822 to 1830. He wrote extensively both on Scots law and on European
history.

(4.2)   'In the Front Rank of European Nations'

It has been contended, not without reason, that the old
Scottish Parliament had anticipated many of those reforms,
which it has been the endeavour of modern liberalism to
secure for the people. It is certain, at all events, that the old
Scottish statute book contains many Acts, tending to secure
the liberty as well as to foster the well-being of the subject,
which even yet may stand as models of legislative wisdom. If
the object of the unionists had been to amalgamate the legal
systems of the two countries, as well as to unite them under
one parliamentary constitution, the Scottish commissioners
might well have claimed for their system of jurisprudence an
evident superiority, in many points, over that of England. In

their benevolent care of the poor, both from starvation and the litigious oppression of the rich, in the protection of the subject from arbitrary imprisonment, in the recognition of the right of all prisoners to be defended by counsel, in the establishment of an excellent system of popular education, in the humane restriction of the death penalty, the old Scottish Parliament had anticipated legislation which came to the people of England more than a century after the Union.

To the unsympathetic Englishman, Scotland, even as late as the middle of last century, seemed a land of barbarians. The poverty to which the people had been reduced, and for which they held England largely responsible, partially justified the charge. But the institutions of Scotland were certainly not those of a barbarous people. Compared with those of England, or even of Europe at the period of the Union, they justify the assertion that Scotland stood then, in some respects, as it has ever since, in the front rank of the European nations.

In striking contrast to the unwieldiness of the English system of jurisprudence, the sum of the admirable legislative wisdom of the Scottish Parliament, down to the period of the Union, was embodied in three duodecimo volumes. 'And yet,' remarks one who might claim, from special knowledge, to be a capable critic, 'in these little volumes, we hesitate not to say, is to be found more of the spirit of real freedom, more wise resolution and practically beneficent legislation, better provision for the liberty of the subject, and a more equitable settlement of all the objects of the popular party at this time, than is to be found in the whole thirty quarto volumes of the statutes at large, and all the efforts of English freedom, from Magna Charta to the Reform Bill.

In truth, the early precocity of Scotland in legislative wisdom, and the extraordinary provisions made by its native Parliament in remote periods, not only for the well-being of the people, but for the coercion alike of regal tyranny and aristocratic oppression, and the instruction, relief, and security of the poorer classes, is one of the most remarkable facts in the whole history of modern Europe, and one well deserving of the special attention of historians and statesmen, both in this and the neighbouring country.'

JAMES MACKINNON, *The Union of England and Scotland*. London, 1896, pp. 468–9

CHAPTER FIVE

The Treaty of Union

The disadvantages of the semi-autonomy of the shared monarchy reached crisis point at the beginning of the 18th Century. The making of war and peace was a matter of the royal prerogative. The long-established trade with France and the Low Countries had been destroyed by wars in which Scotland had been involved through the joint monarchy without agreement or consultation. William, as King of Scotland, had consented to the Act establishing the company which funded a colony at Darien. As King of England he did his best to sabotage it. Scotland had become a country deprived of the right to safeguard its interest through its own foreign and trade policies. Some solution had to be found. An opportunity was presented by the death in 1700 of the last survivor of the eighteen children of Queen Anne. On her death Scotland could choose a separate succession to the throne, particularly as the English Parliament had decided on the succession of the Hanoverians, again without any consultation with Scotland.

The Parliament elected in 1703 (to the limited extent that Parliaments were then elected) concentrated on this constitutional issue. Andrew Fletcher of Saltoun (who has been known ever since as the Patriot) gave a lucid analysis of the problems in speeches such as the following:

(5.1) Speech by Andrew Fletcher, 28th May 1703

My Lord Chancellor
When our Kings succeeded to the crown of England, the ministers of that nation took a short way to ruin us, by concurring with their inclinations to extend the prerogative in Scotland; and the great places and pensions, conferred upon Scotsmen by that court, made them to be willing instruments in the work. From that time this nation began to give away their privileges one after the other, though they then stood more in need of having them enlarged. And as the collections of our laws, before the union of the crowns, are full of acts to

secure our liberty, those laws that have been made since that time are directed chiefly to extend the prerogative. And that we might not know what rights and liberties were still ours, nor be excited by the memory of what our ancestors enjoyed, to recover those we had lost, in the two last editions of our acts of parliament the most considerable laws for the liberty of the subject are industriously and designedly left out.

All our affairs since the union of the crowns have been managed by the advice of English ministers, and the principal offices of the kingdom filled with such men, as the court of England knew would be subservient to their designs: by which means they have had so visible an influence upon our whole administration, that we have from that time appeared to the rest of the world more like a conquered province than a free independent people.

The account is very short: whilst our princes are not absolute in England, they must be influenced by that nation; our ministers must follow the directions of the prince, or lose their places, and our places and pensions will be distributed according to the inclinations of a king of England, so long as a king of England has the disposal of them: neither shall any man obtain the least advancement, who refuses to vote in council and parliament under that influence. So that there is no way to free this country from a ruinous dependence upon the English court, unless by placing the power of conferring offices and pensions in the parliament, so long as we shall have the same king with England.

The ancient kings of Scotland, and even those of France, had not the power of conferring the chief offices of state, though each of them had only one kingdom to govern, and that the difficulty we labour under, of two kingdoms which have different interests governed by the same king, did not occur. Besides, we all know that the disposal of our places and pensions is so considerable a thing to a king of England, that several of our princes, since the union of the crowns, have wished to be free from the trouble of deciding between the many pretenders. That which would have given them ease, will give us liberty, and make us significant to the common interest of both nations. Without this, it is impossible to free us from a dependence on the English court: all other remedies and conditions of government will prove ineffectual, as plainly appears from the nature of the thing; for who is not sensible of the influence of places and pensions upon all men and all affairs?

If our ministers continue to be appointed by the English court, and this nation may not be permitted to dispose of the offices and places of this kingdom to balance the English bribery, they will corrupt everything to that degree, that if any of our laws stand in their way, they will get them repealed. Let no man say, that it cannot be proved that the English court has ever bestowed any bribe in this country. For they bestow all offices and pensions; they bribe us, and are masters of us at our own cost.

It is nothing but an English interest in this house, that those who wish well to our country, have to struggle with at this time. We may, if we please, dream of other remedies; but so long as Scotsmen must go to the English court to obtain offices of trust or profit in this kingdom, those offices will always be managed with regard to the court and interest of England, though to the betraying of the interest of this nation, whenever it comes in competition with that of England. And what less can be expected, unless we resolve to expect miracles, and that greedy, ambitious, and for the most part necessitous men, involved in great debts, burdened with great families, and having great titles to support, will lay down their places, rather than comply with an English interest in obedience to the prince's commands? Now to find Scotsmen opposing this, and willing that English ministers (for this is the case) should have the disposal of places and pensions in Scotland, rather than their own parliament, is matter of great astonishment; but that it should be so much as a question in the parliament, is altogether incomprehensible: and if an indifferent person were to judge, he would certainly say we were an English parliament.

Every man knows that princes give places and pensions by the influence of those who advise them. So that the question comes to no more than, whether this nation would be in a better condition, if in conferring our places and pensions the prince should be determined by the parliament of Scotland, or by the ministers of a court, that make it their interest to keep us low and miserable. We all know that this is the cause of our poverty, misery, and dependence. But we have been for a long time so poor, so miserable and depending, that we have neither heart nor courage, though we want not the means, to free ourselves.

ANDREW FLETCHER OF SALTOUN, *Selected
Political Writings and Speeches*. Ed. by David
Daiches. Edinburgh, 1979, pp. 70–2

Fletcher's proposal to deal with this situation was that Scotland should either choose a successor to Queen Anne different from the one chosen by England, or, if the joint monarchy was to be continued, that all effective power should be transferred from the Monarch to the Scottish Parliament. For this purpose he proposed twelve limitations on the royal power.

(5.2)   Fletcher's Limitations

1. THAT elections shall be made at every Michaelmas head-court for a new parliament every year; to sit the first of November next following, and adjourn themselves from time to time, till next Michaelmas: That they chuse their own president, and that every thing shall be determined by ballotting, in place of voting.

2. THAT so many lesser barons shall be added to the parliament, as there have been noblemen created since the last augmentation of the number of the barons; and that in all time coming, for every nobleman that shall be created, there shall be a baron added to the parliament.

3. THAT no man have vote in parliament, but a nobleman or elected member.

4. THAT the king shall give the sanction to all laws offered by the estates; and that the president of the parliament be impowered by his majesty to give the sanction in his absence, and have ten pounds sterling a day salary.

5. THAT a committee of one and thirty members, of which nine to be a quorum, chosen out of their own number, by every parliament, shall, during the intervals of parliament, under the king, have the administration of the government, be his council, and accountable to the next parliament; with power in extraordinary occasions, to call the parliament together: and that in the said council, all things be determined by ballotting in place of voting.

6. THAT the king without consent of parliament shall not have the power of making peace and war; or that of concluding any treaty with any other state or potentate.

7. THAT all places and offices, both civil and military, and all pensions formerly conferred by our kings shall ever after be given by parliament.

8. THAT no regiment or company of horse, foot, or dragoons be kept on foot in peace or war, but by consent of parliament.

9. THAT all the fencible men of the nation, betwixt sixty
    and sixteen, be with all diligence possible armed with
    bayonets, and firelocks all of a calibre, and continue
    always provided in such arms with ammunition suitable.
10. THAT no general indemnity, nor pardon for any transgression
    against the publick, shall be valid without consent of
    parliament.
11. THAT the fifteen senators of the college of justice shall
    be incapable of being members of parliament, or of any
    other office, or any pension: but the salary that belongs
    to their place to be increased as the parliament shall think
    fit: that the office of president shall be in three of their
    number to be named by parliament, and that there be no
    extraordinary lords. And also, that the lords of the justice
    court shall be distinct from those of the session, and under
    the same restrictions.
12. THAT if any king break in upon any of these conditions of
    government, he shall by the estates be declared to have
    forfeited the crown.

ANDREW FLETCHER OF SALTOUN, Selected
Political Writings and Speeches. Ed. by David
Daiches. Edinburgh, 1979, pp. 74-5

These ideas were incorporated in an Act of Security passed by the Scottish
Parliament on 13th August 1703. The following is the key clause.

(5.3)   The Act of Security

And further upon the said death of her Majestie without heirs
of her body or a successor lawfully designed and appointed
as above Or in the case of any other King or Queen thereafter
succeeding and deceasing without lawfull heir or successor
the foresaid Estates of Parliament Conveened or Meeting are
hereby Authorized and Impowered to Nominat and Declare
the Successor to the Imperial Crown of this Realm and to settle
the succession thereof upon the heirs of the said successors
body; The said successor and heirs of the successors body
being allwayes of the Royal line of Scotland and of the true
protestant Religion Provideing allwayes that the same be
not successor to the Crown of England unless that in this
present Session of Parliament or any other Session of this or

any ensueing Parliament dureing her Majesties reign there
be such conditions of Government settled and enacted as
may secure the honour and sovereignty of this Crown and
Kingdom, the freedom frequency and power of Parliaments,
the religion liberty and trade of the Nation from English or any
foreigne influence. With power to the said Meeting of Estates
to add such further conditions of Government as they shall
think necessary the same being consistent with and no wayes
derogatory from those which shall be enacted in this & any
other Session of Parliament dureing her Majesties reigne.

> Quoted in Paul H. Scott, *Andrew Fletcher*
> *and the Treaty of Union*. Edinburgh, 1992,
> pp. 230–1

During the debate, the Lord Advocate Stuart of Goodtrees proposed another
clause which was apparently intended as an alternative to the above but the
House accepted it as an addition.

And farther, but prejudice of the Generality aforesaid. It is
hereby specially statuted, enacted and declared, That it shall
not be in the Power of the said meeting of the Estates, to
name the Successor of the Crown of England, to be Successor
to the Imperial Crown of this Realm; nor shall the same
Person be capable in any event to be King or Queen of both
Realms, unless a free Communication of Trade, the Freedom of
Navigation, and the Liberty of the Plantations be fully agreed
to, and established by the Parliament and Kingdom of England,
to the Kingdom and Subjects of Scotland, at the sight, and to
the satisfaction of this, or any ensuing Parliament of Scotland,
or the said meeting of the Estates.

> Quoted in Paul H. Scott, *Andrew Fletcher and*
> *the Treaty of Union*. Edinburgh, 1992, p. 23

Royal assent was refused in 1703, but Parliament passed it again in the following
year and this time it was approved but without Stuart's clause. This omission
may have been made surreptitiously, but it seems to have attracted no notice
or comment at the time. Access to trade with the English colonies was evidently
not the important factor which some later historians have supposed.

The Act of Security was a thoroughgoing declaration of independence
as well as a proposal for the abolition of the royal prerogatives to an extent

which has not yet been achieved in Britain. It had been passed twice by Parliament in defiance of the fact that the Officers of State had been appointed by the Court in London and had been under instructions to obtain only a vote of supply acceptance of the English succession and an early end to the session. Daniel Defoe (who came to Scotland in 1706 as a propagandist and spy for the English government) said in his History of the Union, 'the measures taken in Scotland seemed to be well grounded and their Aims well taken. This effectually Settled and Declar'd the independency of Scotland and put her in a posture fit to be treated with either by England or by any other Nation.'[1] George Ridpath, a Scottish writer of the time, said in a book about the Parliamentary session of 1703 'The Memory of this Parliament will be precious to the Nation so long as it has a being.'[2]

Between the session of 1703 and 1704 Andrew Fletcher published the most important of his works, *An Account of A Conversation Concerning A Right Regulation of Government for the Common Good of Mankind.* It was in the form of a report of a conversation, real or imaginary, held in London on 1st December 1703 between Fletcher, the Earl of Cromarty (one of the few people in Scotland at the time who was genuinely in favour of an incorporating Union) and two prominent members of the English Parliament, Sir Edward Seymour and Sir Christopher Musgrave. It is an argument both for Scottish independence and for peaceful co-operation, not only between Scotland and England, but between all the countries of Europe. In many aspects of his thought, Fletcher was well ahead of his time. He is one of the first advocates of European co-operation to prevent war.

It is important to note that in the language of the time the word 'Union' meant peaceful co-operation, the absence of discord, or agreement for any common purpose. It could therefore describe a relationship between sovereign countries (as it usually does in the extracts which follow). With the Treaty of 1707, 'Union' acquired a particular meaning, which was then described, accurately, as 'an incorporating union'. The following is part of Fletcher's *Account*:

(5.4)   An Account of a Conversation

[We start in mid-conversation. Sir Edward has been complaining about the proceedings in the Scottish Parliament of 1703.]

But pray, Sir, what is it in those young noblemen, or in the proceedings of our parliament in general, that you think deserves so much blame? That they would talk, said he, of such limitations on a successor as tend to take away that dependence which your nation ought always to have upon us, as a much greater and more powerful people.

I said, we are an independent nation, though very much
declined in power and reputation since the union of the
crowns, by neglecting to make such conditions with our kings,
as were necessary to preserve both: that finding by experience
the prejudice of this omission, we cannot be justly blamed
for endeavouring to lay hold on the opportunity put into
our hands, of enacting such conditions and limitations on a
successor, upon the expiration of the present entail, as may
secure the honour and sovereignty of our crown and kingdom,
the freedom, frequency, and power of our parliaments,
together with our religion, liberty, and trade, from either
English or foreign influence.

Sir Edw-rd [sic] all in a fret; hey day, said he, here is a
fine cant indeed, independent nation! honour of our crown!
and what not? Do you consider what proportion you bear to
England? not one to forty in rents of land. Besides, our greatest
riches arise from trade and manufactures, which you want.

This was allowed by me: but I desired to inform him, that
the trade of Scotland was considerable before the union of the
crowns: that as the increase of the English trade had raised
the value of their lands, so the loss of our trade had sunk the
rents in Scotland, impoverished the tenant, and disabled him
in most places from paying his landlord any otherwise than
in corn; which practice has been attended with innumerable
inconveniencies and great loss: that our trade was formerly in
so flourishing a condition, that the shire of Fife alone had as
many ships as now belong to the whole kingdom: that ten or
twelve towns which lie on the south coast of that province,
had at that time a very considerable trade, and in our days are
little better than so many heaps of ruins: that our trade with
France was very advantageous, by reason of the great privileges
we enjoyed in that kingdom: that our commerce with Spain
had been very considerable, and began during the wars
between England and that nation; and that we drove a great
trade in the Baltic with our fish, before the Dutch had wholly
possessed themselves of that advantageous traffic.

Upon the union of the crowns not only all this went to
decay; but our money was spent in England, and not among
ourselves; the furniture of our houses, and the best of our
clothes and equipage was bought at London: and though
particular persons of the Scots nation had many great and
profitable places at court, to the high displeasure of the

English, yet that was no advantage to our country, which
was totally neglected, like a farm managed by servants, and
not under the eye of the master. The great business both of
Scots and English ministers was to extend the prerogative in
Scotland, to the ruin of liberty, property, and trade: and the
disorders which were afterwards occasioned by the civil war,
gave the last and finishing blow to the riches and power of the
nation. Since that time we have had neither spirit, nor liberty,
nor trade, nor money among us.

*   *   *

The Earl said that no considerations whatever ought in such
a degree to diminish the prince's power, which is the very
essence of monarchical government; that no case could exist
by which the essential part of any government could be so
far lessened; and therefore such circumstances of affairs as I
brought for reasons, being only accidents, could not be made
use of to destroy the substance of a government. I told him
I had always thought that princes were made for the good
government of nations, and not the government of nations
framed for the private advantage of princes.

*   *   *

The Earl of Cr-m-rty said, that in his opinion there was an easy
remedy to all these inconveniencies; which was a union of the
two nations. I answered, I was sorry to differ so much from
his lordship, as to think the union neither a thing easy to be
effected, nor any project of that kind hitherto proposed, to
be a remedy to our present bad condition: that the English
nation had never since the union of the two crowns shown any
great inclination to come to a nearer coalition with Scotland;
and that I could not avoid making some remarks upon all the
occasions that had given a rise to treat of this matter during
my time. I have observed that a treaty of union has never been
mentioned by the English, but with a design to amuse us when
they apprehended any danger from our nation. And when their
apprehensions were blown over, they have always shown they
had no such intention.

*   *   *

I am of opinion, said I, that by an incorporating union, as they

call it, of the two nations, Scotland will become more poor
than ever.

Why so?

Because Scotsmen will then spend in England ten times
more than now they do; which will soon exhaust the money of
the nation. For besides the sums that members of parliament
will every winter carry to London, all our countrymen who
have plentiful estates will constantly reside there, no less than
those of Ireland do at this time. No Scotsman who expects
any public employment will ever set his foot in Scotland; and
every man that makes his fortune in England will purchase
lands in that kingdom: our trade, which is the bait that covers
the hook, will be only an inconsiderable retail, in a poor,
remote, and barren country, where the richest of our nobility
and gentry will no longer reside: and though we should allow
all the visionary suppositions of those who are so fond of this
union, yet our trade cannot possibly increase on a sudden.
Whereas the expenses I mentioned will in a very short time
exhaust us, and leave no stock for any kind of commerce.

But, said the Earl, you do not distinguish right, nor
consider where the fallacy of your reasoning lies. You talk of
Scotland and Scots money, and do not reflect that we shall
then be a part of Britain; England will be increased by the
accession of Scotland, and both those names lost in that of
Britain: so that you are to consider the good of that whole
body, of which you then become a citizen, and will be much
happier than you were, by being in all respects qualified to
pretend to any office or employment in Britain, and may trade
or purchase in any part of the island.

But, by your leave, my lord, let me distinguish plainly, and
tell you, that if I make a bargain for the people that inhabit the
northern part of this island, I ought principally to consider the
interest of those who shall continue to live in that place, that
they may find their account in the agreement, and be better
provided for than they are. For if the advantages of getting
employments, trading, and purchasing in any part of the island
are the only things to be considered, all these may be as well
obtained by anyone who would change his country in the
present state of things. And if in the union of several countries
under one government, the prosperity and happiness of the
different nations are not considered, as well as of the whole
united body, those that are more remote from the seat of the

government will be only made subservient to the interest of others, and their condition very miserable.

*   *   *

Here the Earl endeavoured by many arguments to show that our country would be the place, where all manufactures, as well for the use of the whole island, as for exportation, would be made by reason of the cheapness of living, and the many hands that Scotland could furnish. I said the contrary was not only most evident; but that the union would certainly destroy even those manufactures we now have. For example, the English are able to furnish us at an easier rate with better cloth than we make in Scotland: and it is not to be supposed they will destroy their own established manufactures to encourage ours.

*   *   *

But sure you will allow, said the Earl, that a free commerce with England, and the liberty of trading to their plantations, which cannot be expected without a union, must be of incomparable advantage to the Scots nation, unless you will disown one of your darling clauses in the act of security. My lord, said I, the clause you mean is placed there without the condition of a union; and your lordship cannot forget, was brought in by the court as an equivalent for all limitations, and in order to throw out another clause, which declares that we would not nominate the same successor with England, unless sufficient limitations were first enacted. This was done to mislead the commissioners of burghs, who for the most part are for anything that bears the name of trade, though but a sham, as this was. And nothing could be more just than to turn it upon the court by adding both clauses; which sunk your party in the house for a long time after.

For my own part, I cannot see what advantage a free trade to the English plantations would bring us, except a farther exhausting of our people, and the utter ruin of all our merchants, who should vainly pretend to carry that trade from the English. The Earl, who knew the truth of these things, was unwilling to insist any longer upon this ungrateful subject; and therefore proceeding to another argument, said that when we shall be united to England, trade and riches will circulate to the utmost part of the island; and that I could not be ignorant

of the wealth which the remotest corners of the north and
west of England possess.

I answered, that the riches of those parts proceed from
accidental causes. The lead and coal mines, which employ
so much shipping, enrich the north. The western parts of
England, besides mines of tin and lead, have many excellent
harbours lying in the mouth of the Channel, through which
the greatest trade of the world is continually passing. I desired
him to consider that Wales, the only country that ever had
united with England, lying at a less distance from London,
and consequently more commodiously to participate in the
circulation of a great trade than we do, after three or four
hundred years, is still the only place of that kingdom, which
has no considerable commerce, though possessed of one of the
best ports in the whole island; a sufficient demonstration that
trade is not a necessary consequence of a union with England.

*   *   *

[The conversation then turns to Fletcher's ideas about reducing the risk of
war by the creation of a Europe of the Regions]:

But to give you my opinion of this matter, I think mankind
might be best preserved from such convulsions and misery, if
instead of framing governments with regard only to a single
society, as I believe all legislators have hitherto done, we
should constitute such as would be no less advantageous to
our neighbours than ourselves. You talk strangely, said Sir
Chr–, as if our advantage were not frequently inconsistent
with that of our neighbours. I am of opinion, replied I, that the
true interest and good of any nation is the same with that of
any other. I do not say that one society ought not to repel the
injuries of another: but that no people ever did any injustice to
a neighbouring nation, except by mistaking their own interest.

*   *   *

[And he argues for the advantages of small autonomous states]:

That London should draw the riches and government of the
three kingdoms to the south-east corner of this island is in
some degree as unnatural as for one city to possess the riches
and government of the world. And, as I said before, that men
ought to be dispersed over all countries in greater or lesser

numbers according to the fertility of the soil; so no doubt
justice should be administered to all in the most convenient
manner that may be, and no man be obliged to seek it at an
inconvenient distance. And if the other parts of government
are not also communicated to every considerable body of
men; but that some of them must be forced to depend upon
others, and be governed by those who reside far from them,
and little value any interest except their own, studying rather
how to weaken them in order to make sure of their subjection;
I say, all such governments are violent, unjust, and unnatural.

I shall add, that so many different seats of government will
highly encourage virtue. For all the same offices that belong to
a great kingdom must be in each of them; with this difference,
that the offices of such a kingdom being always burdened
with more business than any one man can rightly execute,
most things are abandoned to the rapacity of servants; and
the extravagant profits of all great officers plunge them into
all manner of luxury, and debauch them from doing good:
whereas the offices of these lesser governments extending only
over a moderate number of people, will be duly executed, and
many men have occasions put into their hands of doing good
to their fellow citizens. So many different seats of government
will highly tend to the improvement of all arts and sciences;
and afford great variety of entertainment to all foreigners and
others of a curious and inquisitive genius, as the ancient cities
of Greece did.

I perceive now, said Sir Edw-rd, the tendency of all this
discourse. On my conscience he has contrived the whole
scheme to no other end than to set his own country on an
equal foot with England and the rest of the world.

To tell you the truth, said I, the insuperable difficulty I
found of making my country happy by any other way, led me
insensibly to the discovery of these things, which, if I mistake
not, have no other tendency than to render, not only my own
country, but all mankind as happy as the imperfections of
human nature will admit. For I considered that in a state of
separation from England, my country would be perpetually
involved in bloody and destructive wars. And if we should
be united to that kingdom in any other manner, we must of
necessity fall under the miserable and languishing condition
of all places that depend upon a remote seat of government.
And pray where lies the prejudice, if the three kingdoms were

united on so equal a foot, as for ever to take away all suspicion and jealousy of separation? that virtue and industry might be universally encouraged, and every part contribute cheerfully and in due proportion to the security and defence of this union, which will preserve us so effectually from those two great calamities, war and corruption of manners. This is the only just and rational kind of union. All other coalitions are but the unjust subjection of one people to another.

ANDREW FLETCHER OF SALTOUN, *Selected Political Writings and Speeches*. Ed. by David Daiches, Edinburgh, 1979, pp. 116–20, 129–30, 135–7

The English Parliament had settled the succession to the English throne on the Electress of Hanover and her descendants by the Act of Succession of 1701. They seem to have forgotten about Scotland at the time, but were alerted by the Scottish Act of Security. This was formal notice that the Scots proposed to escape from the subjection which the joint monarchy had imposed on them. The reaction of the English Parliament was to pass an Act 'for the effectual securing of the Kingdom of England from the apparent changes that may arise from several Acts lately passed by the Parliament of Scotland', commonly called the Aliens Act. The first part provided for the authorisation of commissioners nominated by the Queen to 'treat and consult' with Scottish commissioners 'concerning the Union of the two Kingdoms'. The second part was much more aggressive in tone and threatened sanctions. It related not to Union (which I have said was then still a vague term) but to the succession to the throne. Unless Scotland had accepted the same succession as England by 25th December 1705, the Scots would be treated in England as aliens and incapable of inheriting property, and imports from Scotland of the main articles of trade would be prohibited.

The next session of the Scottish Parliament began in July 1705. There was irritation over the English attempt to apply pressure, but little objection to negotiations since there were many outstanding questions between the two countries. Even so, Parliament spent three months debating, and approving, proposals in line with Fletcher's limitations. It was when the House turned to the discussion of the Treaty (which at the time usually meant negotiation rather than the document which might result from it). During this discussion the Duke of Hamilton suddenly proposed, late in the evening when many of his supporters had already left, that the appointment of the Scottish Commissioners should be left to the Queen. It was so adopted.

This was an astonishing *volte face* because Hamilton purported to be the leader of the opposition. As such, he was cheered whenever he appeared on the streets of Edinburgh. This was the first of four separate occasions when he acted against the interests of his own side at crucial moments in the Union debate. Ample evidence has come to light that he was playing a double game, professing to lead the opposition to the Union, but in fact acting in the pay of the English Government. After the vote on the appointment of the Commissioners, he wrote to his contact with the English Ministers to say that he had done her Majesty 'signal service'.[3] This particular service meant that the negotiation of the Treaty in London in 1706 was a fake negotiation with both sides appointed by the English Government and with the Scottish side consisting almost entirely of the Officers of State, appointed, paid and instructed by the same Government.

The so-called negotiations were as might be expected from these circumstances. Even before they started formally, the Scottish Secretary of State, the Earl of Mar, reported in a letter to Edinburgh: 'You see that what we are to treat of is not in our choice, and that we see the inconvenience of treating an incorporating union only.'[4] But that was all that they were allowed to discuss. We have several sources of information about the proceedings. The bare bones are in the official minutes which are admirably brief and lucid and which were printed as an appendix to volume XI of the Acts of the Parliament of Scotland. George Lockhart of Carnwath, the only member of the opposition included in the Scottish team, wrote a vivid account of the transaction.[5] Sir John Clerk of Penicuik was at first opposed to the whole idea because of its unpopularity in Scotland, but he yielded to the pressure of his patron, the Duke of Queensberry. He afterwards did his best to justify the Union both in an essay written many years later (6.6) and in a long history in Latin, a translation of part of which was recently published by the Scottish History Society.

All of the evidence shows clearly that the Treaty was more of an imposed text than the result of anything which could really be described as negotiations. The two teams only met once face to face for real talks. That was when the Scots pleaded with some success for an increase in the pitifully few members that Scotland was to be allocated in the new British Parliament, which was otherwise a continuation of the English Parliament.

The English Government of the time regarded English control of Scotland as a vital national issue. England over a long period was repeatedly at war with France; an independent Scotland, in association with her old ally, might easily threaten England from the north. This could be brought about by a Jacobite restoration in Scotland, as nearly happened in 1745. Faced with this risk, the English Government mounted a very sophisticated operation to achieve an incorporating Union, using methods which are associated more with the 20th century than the 18th: sanctions, military intimidation by moving troops to the Border, bribery, propaganda and a skilful and cynical appeal to the self-interest of the classes represented in the Scottish Parliament.

The articles of the Treaty were signed in London on 22nd July 1706 by the Commissioners of Scotland and England. They do not make easy reading, but because of their importance in the subsequent history of Scotland, they are printed in full as an appendix for reference (pp. 202–20).

The Treaty still had to be ratified by the two Parliaments. It was to go first to the Scottish Parliament because that was where resistance was expected. To avoid public outcry in Scotland, the terms were kept secret until the debate in Parliament began on 3rd October 1706. It continued until 16th January 1707. In contrast, the Treaty was approved by the English House of Commons on 22nd January without opposition or argument.

In the interval between the agreement in London and the opening of the debate in the Scottish Parliament, a pamphlet appeared in Edinburgh with the title *State of the Controversy betwixt United and Separate Parliaments*. As was the custom at the time, it was anonymous. Late in the century, it was attributed on good authority to Fletcher and much of it certainly sounds very like him, but other parts do not. Perhaps it was a work of collaboration, but it is an interesting examination of the pros and cons and is, in many ways as apposite now as it was in 1706. It is entirely in favour of Union, in the sense of an amicable relationship, but strongly in favour of separate Parliaments.

United or Separate Parliaments

(5.5)

It may be here alledged, That all those Dangers and Injuries by which the Scots suffer at the hands of the English, do arise from that State of Separation betwixt the Two Kingdoms, and that the more that this Separation is removed, the less the Danger will be; That an united Parliament makes us One and not Two, all British, and what is done in that Parliament is done for the British, and by the British.

As to which, I do so far agree with the Notion of an Incorporate Union; that both the Jealousies we are under, and the Injuries we receive, do arise from our present State of Separation; and therefore I am for uniting both Nations in all these Interests which are mentioned in this present Treaty, and some more, if so the Wisdom of the Nation shall think fit.

But seeing by the Scheme of this Treaty (and by all other Schemes that ever I heard of) there are some very valuable Interests to be reserved as separate Properties, and

even as distinct Establishments; it seems beyond human
Comprehension, how these separate distinct Interests, and
Establishments, can be regulated and supported by one
Parliament.

There are two Measures, which the Scots in prudence
may take to skreen themselves from the unequal Power of the
English; one is, To purchase their Affections; the other is, To
avoid their Influence.

There is no honourable way for compassing the first, but
by uniting with them, as I have said above; and if this will do
the turn, where is the Necessity or Prudence of dismembring of
a Scots Constitution, through so many Difficulties, Hardships,
and Dangers: If this Union of Interests is not able to purchase
entirely the Affections of the English, but that the English
after such an Union in Interests, may still have an itching to
out-rival the Scots in some of their united Interests, and shall
still find themselves under a Necessity or Duty to suppress or
demolish these Interests which are reserved to the Scots: In
that Case, for the Scots to subject these Interests to an united
Parliament, is so far from being an Expedient to avoid English
Influence, that it is the way to throw themselves head-long into
it; and the Scots deserve no pity, if they voluntarily surrender
their united and separate Interests to the Mercy of an united
Parliament, where the English shall have so vast a Majority.

The English can find access two several ways, to injure the
Scots in their Trade, or other Concerns, By their Influence upon
a Scots Parliament; and, By Law past in an English Parliament.

It is very plain, that they can practise the first of these
means, with a great deal of more ease in an united Parliament,
than in a separate Scots Parliament: It is much easier to
corrupt 45 Scots at *London*, than it is to corrupt 300 at
Edinburgh; and besides, there will be no occasion of corrupting
them, when the Case shall occur, of a difference betwixt the
South-Britons and the North-Britons; for the Northern will
be out-voted, without being corrupted. As the first can be
practis'd with ease, so the Scots may be injured in an united
Parliament with greater safety.

A separate Parliament of *England* (especially if the Terms
of Union are expressly declared) cannot make a Breach in the
Interests of *Scotland*, without eminent danger to themselves;
but in an united Parliament, they have the Concurrence of the
Scots, even though the whole 45 should vote against the Law;

and these 45 Scots Members do serve for no more than as so many Scots Witnesses, to assent to the surrender of such Rights as the English shall please to take from them, and to rise in Judgment against their own Nation, if they should afterwards pretend that any Injury has been done them.

In a word, a Separate English Parliament may perhaps invade the Scots Rights by their Laws; and perhaps a Scots Parliament may find means to move them to repeal those Laws: But in the case of an united Parliament, the Scots do make a formal Surrender of the very Faculty it self, and are for ever left to the Mercy of the English, with respect to all their Interests, both united and separate.

I shall close what I have to say, touching this Dream of being one and not two, by putting the Case, That a Law were offered in the united Parliament, (to make it go down the better) and that it were brought in by one of the 45 Scots Members, for some Regulation in the Church-Government, or for some Regulation of the Civil Judicatures, or touching some matters of Trade; and supposing, that whatever smooth Title this Law might have, yet it did point at no less than to over-turn the Church, or Civil Judicatures in *Scotland*, or to ruine the Trade of *Scotland*; I suppose the other Scots Members should oppose this Law, as being prejudicial to the Scots Rights reserved in the Articles of Treaty; The Answer is very ready and plain, That there is no such thing as Scots or English, they are all British, they are one, and not two; the Law now proposed cannot hurt the Scots no more than the English; if it does hurt, it does hurt to the British, of which the English are a part; and the only way to know whether it does hurt or good to the British, is to put it to the Vote of a British Parliament.

This will be the Issue of that darling Plea, of being one and not two; it will be turned upon the Scots with a Vengeance; and their 45 Scots Members may dance round to all Eternity, in this Trap of their own making.

ANON., *State of the Controversy Betwixt United
and Separate Parliaments* (1706). Reprinted by
the Saltire Society with an Introduction by
P.H. Scott, 1982

CHAPTER SIX

Why did we accept it?

As Sir Walter Scott said, the interests of Scotland were considerably neglected in the Treaty of Union and the nation regarded it as a total surrender of their independence by their false and corrupted statesmen (6.5). The question inevitably arises: why did a country which had invented the concept of national freedom and which had defended it with such determination and courage for more than 300 years apparently tamely surrender its independence in 1707?

The first answer is that the Treaty was not accepted by the people but only by the 110 members of the wholly unrepresentative Parliament who voted for it. It was agreed on all sides at the time that the vast majority of the population were against it. Sir John Clerk, for instance, said in his *Observations* that 'at least three fourths of the kingdom' were opposed (6.6). In his history of the Union he said that not even one per cent approved.

During the debate in the Scottish Parliament on the Treaty from 3rd October 1706 to 16th January 1707 petitions against it poured in from all over the country and from all sections of the population. Not one was in favour. As an example, the following is part of the Address from the Convention of Royal Burghs.

(6.1) Address from the Convention of Royal Burghs

The Humble Address of the Commissioners to the General Convention of the Royal Burrows of this Ancient Kingdom Convened the Twenty-Ninth of October 1706, at Edinburgh, Upon the Great Concern of the Union Prosposed Betwixt Scotland and England, for Concerting Such Measures as Should be Esteemed Proper for Them to Take, With Relation to Their Trade or Other Concerns, Humbly Sheweth,
That, as by the Claim of Right, it is the privilege of all subjects to petition, so at this time being mostly impowered by our constituents, and knowing the sentiments of the people we represent, it is our indispensible duty to signify to your grace,

and [the] Honourable Estates of Parliament that, as we are not against an honourable and safe union with England, consisting with the being of this kingdom and Parliaments thereof, without which we conceive neither our religious nor civil interests and trade, as we now by law enjoy them, can be secured to us and our posterity, far less can we expect to have the condition of the people of Scotland, with relation to these great concerns, made better and improved without a Scots Parliament. And seeing by the articles of union now under the consideration of the Honourable Estates it is agreed that Scotland and England shall be united into one kingdom, and the united kingdom be represented by one and the same Parliament, by which our monarchy is suppressed, our Parliament extinguished and in consequence our religion, character, Claim of Right, laws, liberty, trade and all that is dear to us daily in danger of being encroached upon, altered, or wholly subverted by the English in [a] British Parliament, wherein the mean representation allowed for Scotland can never signify in securing to us the interests reserved by us, or granted to us by the English, and by those articles our poor people are made liable to the English taxes, which is a certain, insupportable burden considering that the trade is uncertain, involved and wholly precarious, especially when regulated as to export and import by the laws of England under the same prohibitions, restrictions, customs and duties. And considering that the most considerable branches of our trade are differing from those of England, and are and may be yet more discouraged by their laws, and that all the concerns of trade and other interests are after the Union subject to such alterations as the Parliament of Great Britain shall think fit, we therefore supplicate your grace and Honourable Estates of Parliament, and do assuredly expect, that you will not conclude such an incorporating union as is contained in the articles proposed, but that you will support and maintain the true reformed Protestant religion and church government, as by law established, the soveraignty and independency of this crown and kingdom and the rights and privileges of Parliament, which have been generously asserted by you in some of the sessions of this present Parliament.

Quoted by George Lockhart of Carnwath
in his memoirs, *Scotland's Ruine*. Ed. by Paul
H. Scott and Daniel Szechi, Aberdeen,
1995, pp. 151–2

But it still remains to be explained why members of the Parliament changed their minds so drastically. These after all were the same men (apart from a few members who had died and were replaced) who had affirmed Scottish independence so robustly in voting for the Act of Security in 1703 and 1704. The usual explanation is that they yielded to bribery and there is no doubt (because much clear evidence has survived) that bribery was deliberate and extensive. Lockhart of Carnwath exposed it in his *Memoirs*, of which a pirated edition was published in 1714, and he uncovered damning evidence in 1711 when he was a member of a commission of the British Parliament. We have seen that James Boswell was aware of it in his remarks in Leipzig in 1764. Burns expressed his feelings in a song:

(6.2)   ## Such a Parcel of Rogues in a Nation

> Fareweel to a' our Scottish fame,
>   Fareweel our ancient glory!
> Fareweel ev'n to the Scottish name,
>   Sae famed in martial story!
> Now Sark rins over Solway sands,
>   An Tweed rins to the ocean,
> To mark where England's province stands –
>   Such a parcel of rogues in a nation!
>
> What force or guile could not subdue
>   Thro' many warlike ages
> Is wrought now by a coward few
>   For hireling traitor's wages.
> The English steel we could disdain,
>   Secure in valour's station;
> But English gold has been our bane –
>   Such a parcel of rogues in a nation!
>
> O, would, or I had seen the day
>   That Treason thus could sell us,
> My auld grey head had lien in clay,
>   Wi' Bruce and loyal Wallace!
> But pith and power, till my last hour,
>   I'll mak this declaration:-
> 'We're bought and sold for English gold' –
>   Such a parcel of rogues in a nation!

ROBERT BURNS, 'Such a parcel of rogues
in a nation', *Poems and Songs*. Ed. by James
Kinsley, London, 1969, pp. 511–2

Other poets expressed the same indignation and regret, such as Robert Fergusson and Iain Lom.

(6.3)   ## Robert Fergusson on the Union

> Or shou'd some canker'd biting show'r
> The day and a' her sweets deflow'r,
> To Holyrood-house let me stray,
> And gie to musing a' the day;
> Lamenting what auld *Scotland* knew
> Bien days for ever frae her view:
> O HAMILTON, for shame! the muse
> Would pay to thee her couthy vows,
> Gin ye wad tent the humble strain,
> And gie's our dignity again:
> For O, waes me! the Thistle springs
> In *domicile* of ancient kings,
> Without a patriot to regret
> Our *palace* and our ancient *state*.

ROBERT FERGUSSON, 'Auld Reekie',
ll. 271–84, *The Poems*. Ed. by Matthew
P. McDiarmid, Edinburgh, Scottish Text
Society, 1956, p. 117

(6.4)   And Iain Lom

Tha *Queensberry* 'n tràth-sa
    Mar fhear-stràice cur thairis,
Eis' a' tarraing gu dìreach
    Mar ghearran dian ann an greallaig;
Is luchd nam putagan anairt
    Làn smear agus geire,
'S nam bu mhise an ceannair'
    Bhiodh 'n ceann d'an amall air deireadh.

Tha Diùc Atholl's Diùc Gòrdon
    Glé chlòiste 's iad dùinte,
Air an sgrìobhadh gu daingeann,
    Ach tha *Hamilton* dùbailt;
Iarla Bhrathainn bhiodh mar ris,
    Cha bhiodh mealladh 'sa' chùis ac',
Toirt a' chrùin uainn le ceannach
    An ceart fhradharc ar sùilean.

Tha Mèinnearach Uaimh ann
    Glé luaineach 'na bhreathal,
'S e mar dhuine gun sùilean
    'G iarraidh iùil air feadh ceathaich;
Ach thig e fathasd le h-ùmhlachd
    Chum an Diùc mas i bheatha,
'S bidh a shannt 's a mhì-dhùrachd
    Anns an smùr gun aon rath air.

Iarla Bhrathainn a Sìòford,
    Cha bhi sìothshaimh ri d' bheò dhuit,
Gum bi ort-sa cruaidh fhaghaid
    Thall a staigh de'n Roinn Eòrpa;
Ach nam faighinn mo raghainn
    Is dearbh gu leaghainn an t-òr dhuit,
A staigh air faochaig do chlaiginn
    Gus an cas e do bhòtainn.

And *Queensberry* there
    taking fistful from bagful,
as he draws tight the string
    as a gelding pulls traces;
they who like clootie dumplings
    well marrowed and larded,
if I harnessed that team
    I'd yoke last in the traces.

Dukes of Atholl and Gordon
    make agreement in secret,
though their names firm in writing,
    but *Hamilton's* two-faced;
but with Brathan his crony,
    their minds were united,
to trade in full view
    crown and sovereign rights.

And Menzies of Weem there
    his brains in a swither,
like a man of poor sight
    seeking guidance through mist;
but he'll come up there creeping
    to the Duke if he's welcome,
though his malice and greed
    get an answer in dust.

No peace, Seaforth of Brahan,
    you'll get in your lifetime,
hot pursuit you will find
    on your tail throughout Europe;
but if I had my way
    I would melt your gold payment,
pour it into your skull
    till it reached to your boots.

> *The Poetry of Scotland.* Ed. by Roderick
> Watson. Edinburgh, 1995, pp. 228–9.
> Translation by William Neill

Note: Hamilton's betrayal of the side he professed to lead was, in the words of the English historian, G.M. Trevelyan, 'the instrument, under Heaven, of the almost miraculous passage of the Union'.[1] Queensberry

and Seaford were the two principal officers of State who managed the
Union Parliament.

Sir Walter Scott in his *Tales of a Grandfather* (1828) wrote a frank account
of the Union transaction which clearly drew on the evidence uncovered by
Lockhart of Carnwath:

(6.5)   Walter Scott's View of the Union:
          'A Total Surrender of Independence'

But these Scottish commissioners, or a large part of them, had
unhappily negotiated so well for themselves, that they had
lost all right of interfering on the part of their country. We
have already explained the nature of the equivalent, by which
a sum of four hundred thousand pounds, or thereabouts,
advanced at this time by England, but to be repaid out of the
Scottish revenue within fifteen years, was to be distributed
in the country, partly to repay the losses sustained by the
Darien Company, partly to pay arrears of public salaries in
Scotland, most of which were due to members of the Scottish
Parliament: and finally, to satisfy such claims of damage
arising out of the Union as might be brought forward by any
one whose support was worth having.

The distribution of this money constituted the charm
by which refractory Scottish members were reconciled
to the Union. I have already mentioned the sum of thirty
thousand pounds, which was peculiarly apportioned to the
commissioners who originally laid the basis of the treaty. I
may add there was another sum of twenty thousand pounds,
employed to secure to the measures of the court the party
called the Squadróne Volánte. The account of the mode in
which this last sum was distributed has been published; and it
may be doubted whether the descendants of the noble lords
and honourable gentlemen who accepted this gratification
would be more shocked at the general fact of their ancestors
being corrupted, or scandalised at the paltry amount of the
bribe. One noble lord accepted of so low a sum as eleven
guineas; and the bargain was the more hard, as he threw his
religion into the bargain, and from Catholic turned Protestant
to make his vote a good one.

Other disgraceful gratuities might be mentioned, and
there were many more which cannot be traced. The treasure
for making good the equivalent was sent down in waggons

from England, to be deposited in the castle of Edinburgh; and never surely was so valuable an importation received with such marks of popular indignation. The dragoons who guarded the wains were loaded with execrations, and the carters, nay, even their poor horses, were nearly pelted to death, for being accessary in bringing to Edinburgh the price of the independence of the kingdom.

The public indignation was the more just, that this large sum of money in fact belonged to the Scottish nation, being the compensation to be paid to them for undertaking to pledge their revenue for a part of the English national debt. So that, in fact, the Parliament of Scotland was bribed with the public money belonging to their own country. In this way, Scotland herself was made to pay the price given to her legislators for the sacrifice of her independence.

The statesmen who accepted of these gratuities, under whatever name disguised, were marked by the hatred of the country, and did not escape reproach even in the bosom of their own families. The advantage of their public services was lost by the general contempt which they had personally incurred. And here I may mention, that while carrying on the intrigues which preceded the passing of the Union, those who favoured that measure were obliged to hold their meetings in secret and remote places of rendezvous, lest they should have been assaulted by the rabble. There was a subterranean apartment in the High Street (No. 177), called the Union Cellar, from its being one of their haunts; and the pavilion in the gardens belonging to the Earl of Moray's House, in the Canongate, was distinguished by tradition as having been used for this purpose.

Men, of whom a majority had thus been bought and sold, forfeited every right to interfere in the terms which England insisted upon; and Scotland, therefore, lost that support which, had these statesmen been as upright and respectable as some of them were able and intelligent, could not have failed to be efficacious. But, despised by the English, and detested by their own country; fettered, as Lord Belhaven expressed it, by the golden chain of equivalents, the Unionists had lost all freedom of remonstrance, and had no alternative left save that of fulfilling the unworthy bargain they had made.

Owing to all these adverse circumstances, the interests of Scotland were considerably neglected in the treaty of Union;

and in consequence the nation, instead of regarding it as an identification of the interests of both kingdoms, considered it as a total surrender of their independence, by their false and corrupted statesmen, into the hand of their proud and powerful rival. The gentry of Scotland looked on themselves as robbed of their natural consequence, and disgraced in the eyes of the country; the merchants and tradesmen lost the direct commerce between Scotland and foreign countries, without being, for a length of time, able to procure a share in a more profitable trade with the English colonies, although ostensibly laid open to them. The populace in the towns, and the peasants throughout the kingdom, conceived the most implacable dislike to the treaty; factions, hitherto most bitterly opposed to each other, seemed ready to rise on the first opportunity which might occur for breaking it; and the cause of the Stewart family gained a host of new adherents, more from dislike to the Union than any partiality to the exiled prince.

A long train of dangers and difficulties was the consequence, which tore Scotland to pieces with civil discord, and exposed England also to much suffering. Three rebellions, two of which assumed a very alarming character, may, in a great measure, be set down to the unpopularity of this great national act; and the words, 'Prosperity to Scotland, and no Union,' is the favourite inscription to be found on Scottish sword blades betwixt 1707 and 1746.

SIR WALTER SCOTT, *Tales of a Grandfather*
(1828), Chapter LX

Some historians have sought to excuse the bribery on the grounds that management and patronage were a normal part of the 18th-Century machinery of government but it is clear from contemporary comments that this was on an unusual scale and intensity. The Earl of Glasgow, for instance, said in a letter to his English paymasters that 'the Union had certainly broken'[1] if it had become known, and, of course, it was the independence of the country that was at stake, not merely the smooth transaction of routine parliamentary business.

The financial inducements were more subtle and persuasive than the mere handing over of cash or pensions. The Treaty itself had many sweeteners, not for the country as a whole, but for those who were going to vote on it in the Scottish Parliament. The Scottish peers were to be given all the privileges of English peers except that only sixteen of them would have seats in the House of Lords. Heritable jurisdictions, the rights and privileges of the burghs and of the Scottish law courts were all preserved. The independence of the Church of Scotland was guaranteed in a separate Act which required each successive Monarch to swear to it. Above all there was the Equivalent (Article XV of the Treaty), a sum of £398,085 and 10 shillings to be granted to Scotland in exchange for accepting the burden of part of the English national debt and of the English excise duty. A first charge on this money was to repay to the investors in the Darien Company their original investment plus five per cent per year from the time when it was made. Very many members of the Scottish Parliament had invested most of such wealth as they had in the Company and thought that it had been lost for ever. This was therefore a very powerful inducement.

Were there any more respectable motives than financial self-interest? In the middle of the 19th Century, when Macaulay was writing his *History of England*, he was puzzled by the problem of the acceptance of the Union by the Scottish Parliament when it was 'notoriously unpopular' in Scotland. The Scottish historian, John Hill Burton, suggested to him that an explanation was to be found in a desire for access to trade with England and its plantations.[3] This was a plausible, convenient and face-saving theory and it became so firmly established as the orthodox view that it still persists. It has, however, no basis in fact. The evidence shows clearly that considerations of trade were not a significant factor.

Andrew Fletcher in his *An Account of a Conversation* and the Convention of Royal Burghs, which was closely connected with the trading interest (5.5 and 6.1), both argued that the immediate effects of the Union would be harmful to Scottish trade. They were right. Daniel Defoe, as an English propagandist for the Union, had argued that it would be beneficial for the Scottish economy. When he described the condition of Scotland in his *Tour Thro the Whole Island of Great Britain* in 1727 he admitted that 'this is not the case, but rather the contrary'.[2] Sir John Clerk of Penicuik was made a Baron of the Court of Exchequer as his reward for supporting the Union and this meant that he was concerned with questions of economics and foreign trade. He did his best to justify the Union in his Latin *History* and in two essays, but the best that he could say in 1730 about its effects on trade was that it had not made things worse but had left them much the same.[3] Adam Smith discussed the question in a letter in 1760, at a time when most people in Scotland were reconciled to the Union as an inescapable fact. He said that it was no wonder that at the time 'all orders of men conspired in cursing a measure so hurtful to their immediate interest ... Even the merchants seemed to suffer at first. The trade to the Plantations was, indeed, opened to them. But that was a trade which they knew nothing about: the trade they were acquainted with, that to France, Holland and the Baltic, was laid under embarrassments which almost totally annihilated the two first and most important branches of it.'[4]

Clerk, however, had an alternative explanation: those who voted for the Union did so because they knew that the only available alternative was invasion by England and the imposition of worse terms. Scotland was then in no position to resist. England had an experienced and strong army under Marlborough, one of the most accomplished generals of his time. Scotland had hardly any defence forces at all. Clerk said in his *History*, that when the Act of Security demonstrated that the Scots were no longer prepared to tolerate the damaging consequences of the joint monarchy it became a necessary policy for England 'either to destroy us or to force us into union on well-defined terms'. In a *Testamentary Memorial* which he left for his family he wrote: 'England as being at least four times more numerous in people than Scotland wou'd have found little difficulty in subduing us ... and in treating us ignominiously and cruelly as a conquered province.'[5] This realistic explanation was played down after the Union because it was discreditable to both sides. The Scots did not want to admit that they surrendered without a struggle, and the English did want to be seen as the bully with the big stick. The following is an extract from Clerk's *Observations on the Present Circumstances of Scotland* of 1730:

(6.6)   ## Clerk's Observations: The Union: An Alternative to Conquest

> But the wiser projectors of this affaire cou'd not but see, first, that it wou'd be absolutely against the interest of England if African or Indian goods were imported free or at very lou duties into Scotland because it would require an army of men to stope their importations in a clandestine way by land into England; secondly that it was absolutly against the interest of England to suffer Scotland to grou rich in a seperat state because it was more than probable that this increase of wealth would sometime or other be made use of to the prejudice of England (long animosities between the tuo nations made this so very probable that it had been perfectly chymerical to have thought otherways); thirdly, these projectors cou'd not but knou that it was the easiest thing in nature for the English at any time to ruine our trade, so soon as they thought we were in a faire way of makeing any advances to pouer either by sea or land, consequently that the whole projected trade was to the last degree precarious.

*   *   *

In these circumstances we were at the time of the Union.
In short, we drove a most pernicious trade abroad in all its
branches and at home we had the misfortune to neglect our
manufactories and to aim at very feu things that were for the
advantage of our country. The most beneficial branch of all
our exportations being that of black cattle into England stood
prohibited and we had lost much blood and treasure in the
prosecution of our African and Indian Schemes.

Sober people were, houever, content to sit doun under
all these losses and misfortunes and in a kind of glade
poverty live on what remain'd. But here a melancholy scene
presented itself, for so long as the Succession to the Croun
of Great Britain remain'd unsettled and that Her Majesty
Queen Anne was not likely to live long, many in Scotland
expected such a scene of misfortunes as had been felt
dureing the Civil Wars in the reign of King Charles the First
and in the end that the whole country would fall under the
Dominion of England by right of conquest. The Union of the
tuo Kingdoms was then thought of as the best expedient
to preserve the honour and liberties of Scotland and like
ways the peace of the whole island, for as the councils of
Britain wou'd then be united, the Succession wou'd naturally
devolve on one and the same person. This was the principal
motive both in Scotland and England for bringing about the
Union.

There were indeed other reasons which had great
influence with many of this country, such as the prohibition
of our black cattle in England, a general mismanagement and
decay of trade, want of money to engadge in other projects
and an inability for enlarging our trade or improving our
manufactories, and (which was worse) a moral certainty that
England wou'd never allow us to grou rich and pouerfull in a
separat state.

It was likeways a very strong motive for some to favour
the scheme of Union when they considered what had been
more than once complained of in our Parliaments – to wit,
that we were in a state of absolute bondage to England, tho'
under the appearance of national liberty supported by our
oun Parliaments and Privy Councils.

*   *   *

I need not acquaint you hou the treaty was managed in
England, nor hou the Union was caried on in the Parliament
of Scotland, for you knou most of the steps that were taken
and you cannot but knou likeways that the Articles were
confirmed in the Parliament of Scotland contrary to the
inclinations of at least three-fourths of the Kingdom.

SIR JOHN CLERK OF PENICUIK,
'Observations on the Present Circumstances
of Scotland', in *Miscellany X*. Edinburgh,
Scottish History Society, 1965, pp. 190–2

CHAPTER SEVEN

The Enlightened Century

The 18th Century in Scotland was one of contrasts: the humiliation of the Union and an evident determination to compensate for the loss of political power by achievement of other kinds; the bold attempts in 1715 and 1745 to restore the Stewarts and dissolve the Union, followed by the destruction of Highland society which led to depopulation during the Clearances; the 'sudden burst of genius' (7.4) in the abstract thought of the Scottish Enlightenment and in the very different revival of the vernacular poetic tradition.

In October 1745, during the Jacobite occupation of Edinburgh, Prince Charles issued a proclamation. In this he promised to dissolve the Union and came close to the spirit of Fletcher's Limitations by appearing to promise automatic royal assent to Acts of Parliament:

(7.1) Prince Charles's Proclamation, October 1745

Charles Pr: of Wales, and Reg^t of ye kingdoms of England, Scotland, France, & Ireland, & the dominions thereto belonging, Unto all his Maj's Subjects of qt degree Soever, Greeting. As soon as we, conducted by the Providence of God, arrived in Scotland, and were Joined by a handful of our Royal father's Subjects, our first care was, to make publick his most gracious Declaration; And in consequence of ye large powers by him vested in us in quality of Reg^t, We also emited our own Manifesto explaining and enlargeing the promises formerly made, according as we came to be better acquainted wth the inclinations of the people of Scotland. Now that it has pleased God, so far to smile upon our undertaking, as to make us Master of the ancient kingdom of Scotland, We Judged it proper, in this publick manner, to make manifest what ought to fill yhe hearts of all his Maj's Subjects, of what nation or Providence soever, with comfort and Satisfaction.

We yrfore hereby in his Maj's name declare, That his Sole
intention is, To reinstate all his Subjects, in the full enjoyment
of their religion, laws, & liberties; & that our present attempt
is not undertaken to enslave a free people, but to redress
and remove the encroachments made upon them; Not to
impose upon any a religion which they dislike, but to Secure
them all in the enjoyment of those which are respectively, at
present, established among them, either in England, Scotland,
or Ireland; And, if it shall be deemed proper, that any farther
Security be given to the established Church or Clergy, We
hereby promise in his name, that he shall pass any law that
his Parl^t shall see necessary for that purpose. In consequence
of the rectitude of our Royal father's intentions, we must
further declare his Sentiments with respect to the National
Debt. That it has been contracted under an unlawful Gov^t,
no body can disown; no more than that it is now a most
heavy load upon the Nation. Yet, in regard, that it is, for the
greatest part, due to those very subjects qm he promises to
protect, cherish, & defend, he is resolved to take the advice
of his Parl^t concerning it; In wch he thinks, he acts the part of
a Just Prince, who makes the good of his people ye rule of his
Actions.

Furthermore, we in his name declare, that the Same
rule laid doun for his funds, shall be followed w^t respect
to every law or Act of Parl^t Since the Revolution; And in so
far, as in a free & legal Parl^t they shall be approved, he will
confirm them. With respect to the pretended Union of the
two Nations, the King cannot possibly ratify it, Since he has
had repeated remonstrances agt it from each kingdom; And
Since it is incontestible, that the principal point then in view
was, the exclusion of the Royal family from their undoubted
right to the crown; For which purpose the grossest corruptions
were openly used to bring it about. But whatever may be
hereafter devised for the Joint benefit of both Nations, ye King
will most readily wth ye request of his Parl^t to establish it [sic].

And now that we have in his Maj's name given the most
ample Security for your religion, liberties, and laws, that
the power of a British Soveraign can grant. We hereby for
ourselvs, as Heir apparent to the crown, ratify and confirm the
Same in our own name, before almighty God, upon the faith
of a Christian, & ye honour of a Prince.

Let me now expostulate this weighty matter with you

my father's Subjects, & let me not omit this first publick
opportunity of awakening your understandings, & of
dispelling that cloud which the assiduous pains of ill designing
men have all along, but chiefly now, been endeavouring
to cast on the truth. Do not the pulpits & congregations
of the Clergy, as well as your weekly papers, ring with the
dreadful threats of Popery and slavery, tyranny and arbitrary
power, which are now ready to be imposed on you, by the
formidable power of France and Spain? Is not my Royal Father
represented, as a blood-thirsty tyrant, breathing out nothing
but destruction to all those who will not immediatly embrace
an odious religion? Or, have I myself been better used? But
listen only to the naked truth. I, with my own money hired
a small vessel, ill provided with money, arms, or friends. I
arrived in Scotland attended by 7 persons only, I published
the King my father's Declaration, and proclaimed his title,
with pardon in one hand, and liberty of conscience in the oy^r,
and the most solemn promises to grant whatever a free Parl^t
shall propose for the happiness of a people.

I have, I confess, the greatest reason to adore the
goodness of almighty God, who has, in so remarkable a
manner, protected me, & my small army, thro' the many
dangers to which we were, at first, exposed; And who
has led me in the way to victory, & to the Capital of this
ancient kingdom, amidst the acclamations of the King my
father's Subjects. Why then is so much pains taken, to Spirit
up the minds of the people agt this my undertaking? The
reason is obvious. It is, least the real sense of the Nation's
present sufferings, should blot out the remembrance of past
misfortunes; And of ye Outcries formerly raised agt the Royal
family. Whatever miscarriages might have given occasion to
them, they have been more than atoned for Since; And the
Nation has now an opportunity of being Secured ag^t the like
for the future.

That my family has suffer'd exile during these 57 years,
every body knows. Has the Nation, during that period of time,
been the more happy & flourishing for it? Have you found
reason to love & cherish your Governours, as the fathers of
the people of great Britain & Ireland? Has a family, upon
whom a fraction unlawfully bestowed the diadem of a rightful
Prince, retained a due Sense of so great a Trust & favour?
Have you found more humanity & condescention, in those

who were not born to a crown, than in my Royal Forefathers?
Have their ears been open to the cries of ye people? Have
they, or do they consider only the interest of these Nations?
Have you reapt any other benefit from them, than an immense
load of debts? If I am answer'd the affirmative, Why have their
Govt been so often railed at in all your publick Assemblies?
Why has the Nation so long been crying out redress agt the
abuses of Parl^t? upon the account of their long duration? the
multitude of Place-men, which occasions their venality? The
introduction of penal laws? And, in general, ag^t the miserable
Situation of the kingdom, at home and abroad? All these, &
many more, inconveniencies, must now be removed, unless
the people of great Britain be already so far corruptted, as
that they will not accept of freedom when offer'd to them,
Seeing the King, on his restoration, will refuse nothing y^t a
free Parl^t can ask, for the Security of the religion, laws, and
liberties of the people.

The fears of the Nation, from the powers of France &
Spain, appear Still more vain and groundless. My expedition
was undertook, unsupported by either. But, indeed, when
I see a foreign force brought by my enemies ag^t me; And
when I hear of Dutch, Danes, Hessians, and Swiss, the
Elector of Hannover's Allies, being called over, to protect
his Gov^t ag^t the King's Subjects; Is it not high time for the
King my father to accept also of the assistance of those,
who are able, and who have engaged, to Support him?
But will the world, or any man of Sense in it, infer from
thence, That he inclines to be a tributary Prince, rather than
an independent Monarch? Who has the better chance to
be independent on foreign Powers? He, who with the aid
of his own Subjects, can wrest the Gov^t out of the hands
of an Intruder? Or he, who cannot, without assistance
from abroad, Support his Gov^t, tho' establish'd by all
the Civil power, and Secured by a strong military force,
ag^t the undisciplined part of those he has ruled over for
many years?

Let him, if he pleases, try the experiment. Let him Send
off his foreign hirelings, & put the whole upon the issue of
a battle. I will trust only to the King my father's Subjects,
who were, or shall be, engaged in mine and their countrie's
cause. But notwithstanding all the opposition he can make,
I still trust the Justice of my cause, the valour of my troops,

& the assistance of the Almighty, to bring my enterprise to a glorious issue.

It is now time to conclude, and I shall do it wth this reflexion. Civil wars are ever attended with rancour and ill-will, which party-rage never fails to produce in the minds of those, whom different interests, principles, or views, set in opposition to one another. I therefore earnestly require it of my friends, to give as little loose as possible to Such passions. This will prove the most effectual means to prevent the Same in the enemies of our Royal Cause. And this my Declaration will vindicate, to all posterity, the Nobleness of my Undertakeing, & the generosity of my intentions. Given at our Palace of Holyroodhouse the 10th day of Octo^r 1745. C.P.R. By his Highness's command, I: Murray.

> ANON., *History of the Rebellion in the Years 1745 and 1746*, a contemporary account which was published by the Roxburghe Club in 1944.

The trouble with this was, of course, that Charles and his father aimed at the English as well as the Scottish throne. If they had succeeded, Scotland would have been exposed again to the problem of nominal independence which the Act of Security had attempted to solve. Perhaps there was a hint here of a possibility of the Fletcher solution, especially as the Proclamation was drafted by Sir James Stuart of Goodtrees, said to be one of the most brilliant men of his generation. He was the heir of the Stuart of Goodtrees who, although Lord Advocate in the Parliament of 1703 to 1707 had drafted a clause in the Act of Security and a protestation against the Union. This James Stuart was a Presbyterian but he has been described by John Sibbald Gibson as the driving intellect of the Scottish Jacobites.[1] This is an eloquent example of the contrary pressure which confused the issues and made it difficult for conscientious people to decide their allegiance. The Jacobites were associated with arbitrary monarchy and hostility to Presbyterianism but also with traditional Scottish values and the restoration of the Parliament. The Hanoverians represented the Union and new mercantile values but also greater religious tolerance and the increase of Parliamentary over royal power inherent in the Revolutionary Settlement of 1688–9. Many people were torn in two directions.

The ruthless suppression of the Highlands after the '45 had several far-reaching consequences. In the Highlands itself, it destroyed the traditional form of society and undermined Gaelic culture. This helped to create the conditions which led to the massive loss of population in the Clearances. No doubt, the previous way of life was far from idyllic and there was already pressure on it from over-population and economic decline. Even so, the result was not unlike the consequences which Calgacus attributed to the Romans, 'They make a desolation and they call it peace.'

Since the Jacobite rising had been an attempt to overthrow the Union, its defeat and the brutality which followed tended to persuade Scotland as a whole that resistance was no longer possible. The complex of emotions which this involved discouraged, for a time, controversy, or even thought, about the Scottish situation. It was a strong influence towards conformity and a quiet life.

On the other hand, the aftermath of the '45 had paradoxically also a beneficial result. In the past, the Lowland Scot had usually regarded the Highlander with fear and distrust. In place of this, the Highlands became a symbol of oppression and suffering imposed by the British state. This awoke in the Lowlander a feeling of sympathy and a shared Scottishness, a process completed by the influence of Walter Scott. R.L. Stevenson comments on this:

(7.2)   R.L. Stevenson, The Foreigner at Home

The division of races is more sharply marked within the borders of Scotland itself than between the countries. Galloway and Buchan, Lothian and Lochaber, are like foreign parts; yet you may choose a man from any of them, and, ten to one, he shall prove to have the headmark of a Scot. A century and a half ago the Highlander wore a different costume, spoke a different language, worshipped in another church, held different morals, and obeyed a different social constitution from his fellow-countrymen either of the south or north. Even the English, it is recorded, did not loathe the Highlander and the Highland costume as they were loathed by the remainder of the Scots. Yet the Highlander felt himself a Scot. He would willingly raid into the Scottish lowlands; but his courage failed him at the border, and he regarded England as a perilous, unhomely land. When the Black Watch, after years of foreign service, returned to Scotland, veterans leaped out and kissed the earth at Port Patrick. They had been in Ireland, stationed among men of their own race and language, where they were well liked and treated with affection; but it was the soil of Galloway that they kissed at the extreme end of the hostile lowlands, among a people who did not understand their speech, and who had hated, harried, and hanged them since the dawn of history. Last, and perhaps most curious, the sons of chieftains were often educated on the continent of Europe. They went abroad speaking Gaelic; they returned speaking, not English, but the broad dialect of Scotland. Now, what idea had they in their minds when they thus, in thought, identified themselves with their ancestral enemies? What was the sense in which they were Scottish and not English, or Scottish and not Irish? Can a bare name be thus influential on the minds and affections of men, and a political aggregation blind them to the nature of facts? The story of the Austrian Empire would seem to answer, No; the far more galling business of Ireland clenches the negative from nearer home. Is it common education, common morals, a common language or a common faith, that join men into nations? There were practically none of these in the case we are considering.

The fact remains: in spite of the difference of blood and language, the Lowlander feels himself the sentimental countryman of the Highlander. When they meet abroad, they fall upon each other's neck in spirit; even at home there is a kind of clannish intimacy in their talk. But from his compatriot in the south the Lowlander stands consciously apart. He has had a different training; he obeys different laws; he makes his will in other terms, is otherwise divorced and married; his eyes are not at home in an English landscape or with English houses; his ear continues to remark the English speech; and even though his tongue acquire the Southern knack, he will still have a strong Scots accent of the mind.

R.L. STEVENSON, 'The Foreigner
at Home', in *Memories and Portraits*
(1887)

The Lowlands as well as the Highlands have suffered a drastic loss of population through emigration. In every census since 1801 Scotland's proportion of the population of Britain has declined. At the time of the Union, Scotland had about 18 per cent of the population of England; in the census of 1991 it had fallen to 9.2 per cent, a striking symptom of relative economic and social decline. In his book *Invisible Country* in 1984, James Campbell said: 'Throughout the entire country there

is the sense that what took place in the Highlands during the earlier part of the last century is a clue to what happened to modern
Scotland.'

There was another effect of the ruthlessness of the British Government
after the '45. In 1706 Robert Wodrow had said in a letter: 'I have a great
many melancholy thoughts of living to see this ancient Kingdom made
a province, but lost irrevocably, and this is the most dismall aspect one
incorporating union has to me, that it puts matters past help.'² The defeat
at Culloden and its aftermath convinced Scotland that Wodrow was right
about this. The last chance of escape from the Union had gone. It was
reasonable to conclude that we had to make the best of a situation which
we could not change.

A country which had just lost its independence, and suffered a civil
war and the brutal repression which followed, might seem an unlikely
place to experience an outburst of creative energy. The American, H.W.
Thompson, is not alone in comparing the Scotland of this period to the
Athens of Pericles as he does in his biography of Henry Mackenzie:

(7.3)   A Golden Age

A Golden Age of Scotland lay between the Jacobite rising of
'45 and the passage of the Reform Bills of 1832 – between
the birth of Henry Mackenzie in 1745 and his death in 1831.
Within Mackenzie's crowded lifetime of eighty-six years
Scotland produced the greatest of sceptical philosophers,
David Hume; the best loved of song-poets, Robert Burns; the
king of romancers, Sir Walter Scott; the two chief masters of
modern biography, James Boswell and John Gibson Lockhart;
the most virile of British portrait-painters, Sir Henry Raeburn;
the greatest British architect of his century, Robert Adam.
At the same time, the dynasty of the Doctors Monro made
Edinburgh's Medical College the most respected in the
world; Adam Smith founded the modern science of Political
Economy, James Hutton did as much for Geology, and Joseph
Black revolutionized Chemistry. Nor was this all; the world's
roads were rebuilt according to the methods of John Loudon
McAdam; the world's industry was remade by the steam-
engine of James Watt; the world's annals of military glory
shone with new lustre at the exploits of the most famous of
regiments, the Black Watch. Nearly all that makes the name of
Scotland great is of that Golden Age; to discover comparable
achievements by so small a nation in so short a time we

should need to go back from the Age of Mackenzie to the Age of Pericles.

HAROLD W. THOMPSON, *Henry Mackenzie,*
A Scottish Man of Feeling. Edinburgh,
1931, p. 1

Thompson exaggerates in two aspects. Scotland had great achievements in philosophy, poetry, music and architecture long before the 18th Century and he also forgets the Florence of the Renaissance. Even so, he is certainly right in celebrating a remarkable record of accomplishment. Dugald Stewart, Professor of Moral Philosophy at Edinburgh from 1785 to 1810 and Adam Ferguson's successor in the chair, was one of the first writers to comment on the phenomenon which we now know as the Scottish Enlightenment:

(7.4) ## The Sudden Burst of Genius

It deserves to be remarked, as a circumstance which throws considerable light on the literary history of Scotland during the latter half of the eighteenth century, that, from time immemorial, a continual intercourse had been kept up between Scotland and the Continent. To all who were destined for the profession of law, an education either at a Dutch or French university was considered as almost essential. The case was nearly the same in the profession of physic; and, even among the Scottish clergy, I have conversed, in my youth, with some old men who had studied theology in Holland or in Germany. Of our smaller country gentlemen, resident on their own estates (an order of men which, from various causes, has now, alas! totally vanished), there was scarcely one who had not enjoyed the benefit of a university education; and very few of those who could afford the expense of foreign travel, who had not visited France and Italy. Lord Monboddo somewhere mentions, to the honour of his father, that he sold part of his estate to enable himself (his eldest son) to pursue his studies at the University of Groningen. The constant influx of information and of liberality from abroad, which was thus kept up in Scotland in consequence of the ancient habits and manners of the people, may help to account for the sudden

burst of genius, which to a foreigner must seem to have
sprung up in this country by a sort of enchantment, soon after
the Rebellion of 1745.

> DUGALD STEWART, *Collected Works*. Ed. by
> Sir William Hamilton. Edinburgh, vol. I,
> pp. 550–1

No doubt the influx of information and of liberality from abroad contributed; but, in John MacQueen's words, 'the Scottish Enlightenment was the
natural, almost the inevitable, outcome of several centuries of Scottish and
European intellectual history'.3 The centuries of emphasis on education and
the encouragement by the Kirk of logical thought on metaphysical questions
were also involved. The Scottish educational tradition was democratic in
two senses: it was available to all and it regarded all aspects of thought
and enquiry as valid and interdependent. Its spirit is well expressed in the
comment of Amyat on the Edinburgh of the Enlightenment:

(7.5)   'A Noble Privilege'

Mr Amyat, King's Chymist, a most sensible and agreeable
English gentleman, resided in Edinburgh for a year or two. He
one day surprised me with a curious remark. There is not a
city in Europe, said he, that enjoys such a singular and such
a noble privilege. I asked, What is that privilege? He replied,
Here I stand at what is called the *Cross of Edinburgh*, and
can, in a few minutes, take fifty men of genius and learning
by the hand. The fact is well known; but to a native of that
city, who has all his days been familiarized with it, and
who has not travelled in other countries, that circumstance,
though very remarkable, passes unnoticed: Upon strangers,
however, it makes a deep impression. In London, in Paris,
and other large cities of Europe, though they contain many
literary men, the access to them is difficult; and, even after
that is obtained, the conversation is, for some time, shy and
constrained. In Edinburgh, the access of men of parts is not
only easy, but their conversation and the communication of
their knowledge are at once imparted to intelligent strangers
with the utmost liberality. The philosophers of Scotland have
no nostrums. They tell what they know, and deliver their
sentiments without disguise or reserve. This generous feature

was conspicuous in the character of Mr Hume. He insulted
no man, but, when the conversation turned upon particular
subjects whether moral or religious, he expressed his genuine
sentiments with freedom, with force, and with a dignity which
did honour to human nature.

WILLIAM SMELLIE, *Literary and Characteristical*
Lives. Edinburgh, 1800, pp. 161–2

So soon after the '45, it is perhaps not surprising that the *literati* of the
Scottish Enlightenment, men such as David Hume, Adam Smith and Adam
Ferguson, seem at first glance largely to ignore Scotland. That was still
dangerous ground. They speculated freely about everything, but usually
not about Scotland. One of the key figures, William Robertson, did write
a *History of Scotland;* but that was an exception. In their books the *literati*
drew most of their examples from classical Greece and Rome, or even from
contemporary North America, but hardly ever from Scotland. There are,
however, many indications that they regretted the loss of independence.

Although Hume was for a time British Chargé d'Affaires in Paris and an
Under Secretary of State in the Foreign Office, he was no enthusiast for the
British establishment. His letters often refer to the 'Barbarians who inhabit
the Banks of the Thames'.4 He wrote a *History of England* but it was not,
unlike the work of many English historians, a panegyric on the supposed
ancient origins of their constitution. On the contrary, it was an exposure
of repeated corruption by 'ignorance, superstition and zealotry'.5 There
are references in his essays which show that he shared Andrew Fletcher's
preference for a diversity of small independent countries. Like Fletcher, he
draws a parallel with ancient Greece:

(7.6)   A Cluster of Little Principalities

GREECE was a cluster of little principalities, which soon
became republics; and being united both by their near
neighbourhood, and by the ties of the same language
and interest, they entered into the closest intercourse of
commerce and learning. There concurred a happy climate, a
soil not unfertile, and a most harmonious and comprehensive
language; so that every circumstance among that people
seemed to favour the rise of the arts and sciences. Each city
produced its several artists and philosophers, who refused to
yield the preference to those of the neighbouring republics;

their contention and debates sharpened the wits of men; a
variety of objects was presented to the judgement, while each
challenged the preference to the rest; and the sciences, not
being dwarfed by the restraint of authority, were enabled
to make such considerable shoots as are even at this time
the objects of our admiration. After the ROMAN *christian*
or *catholic* church had spread itself over the civilized world,
and had engrossed all the learning of the times, being really
one large state within itself, and united under one head, this
variety of sects immediately disappeared, and the PERIPATETIC
philosophy was alone admitted into all the schools, to the
utter depravation of every kind of learning. But mankind
having at length thrown off this yoke, affairs are now returned
nearly to the same situation as before, and EUROPE is at
present a copy, at large, of what GREECE was formerly a
pattern in miniature. We have seen the advantage of this
situation in several instances. What checked the progress
of the CARTESIAN philosophy, to which the FRENCH nation
showed such a strong propensity towards the end of the last
century, but the opposition made to it by the other nations
of EUROPE, who soon discovered the weak sides of that
philosophy? The severest scrutiny which NEWTON's theory
has undergone proceeded not from his own countrymen,
but from foreigners; and if it can overcome the obstacles
which it meets with at present in all parts of EUROPE, it will
probably go down triumphant to the latest posterity. The
ENGLISH are become sensible of the scandalous licentiousness
of their stage, from the example of the FRENCH decency and
morals. The FRENCH are convinced that their theatre has
become somewhat effeminate by too much love and gallantry,
and begin to approve of the more masculine taste of some
neighbouring nations.

> DAVID HUME, 'Of the Rise of the Arts and
> Sciences' in *Selected Essays*. Ed. by Stephen
> Copley and Andrew Edgar, Oxford, 1993,
> pp. 64–5

In his essay, 'Idea of a Perfect Commonwealth', Hume said that 'a small
commonwealth is the happiest government in the world within itself,
because every thing lies under the eye of the rulers'.[6]

Similarly, Adam Smith in *The Wealth of Nations* refers to the Greek colonies as an example of the advantages of independence to manage their own affairs and of the disadvantages of central control in the colonies of Rome:

(7.7)   The Advantages of Independence

The progress of many of the ancient Greek colonies towards wealth and greatness seems accordingly to have been very rapid. In the course of a century or two, several of them appear to have rivalled, and even to have surpassed their mother cities. Syracuse and Agrigentum in Sicily, Tarentum and Locri in Italy, Ephesus and Miletus in Lesser Asia, appear by all accounts to have been at least equal to any of the cities of ancient Greece. Though posterior in their establishment, yet all the arts of refinement, philosophy, poetry, and eloquence seem to have been cultivated as early, and to have been improved as highly in them as in any part of the mother country. The schools of the two oldest Greek philosophers, those of Thales and Pythagoras, were established, it is remarkable, not in ancient Greece, but the one in an Asiatic, the other in an Italian colony. All those colonies had established themselves in countries inhabited by savage and barbarous nations, who easily gave place to the new settlers. They had plenty of good land, and as they were altogether independent of the mother city, they were at liberty to manage their own affairs in the way that they judged was most suitable to their own interest.

The history of the Roman colonies is by no means so brilliant. Some of them, indeed, such as Florence, have in the course of many ages, and after the fall of the mother city, grown up to be considerable states. But the progress of no one of them seems ever to have been very rapid. They were all established in conquered provinces, which in most cases had been fully inhabited before. The quantity of land assigned to each colonist was seldom very considerable, and as the colony was not independent, they were not always at liberty to manage their own affairs in the way that they judged was most suitable to their own interest.

ADAM SMITH, *The Wealth of Nations.*
London, Everyman's Library, 1971, vol. II,
pp. 64–5

By the time that he was writing *The Wealth of Nations* (first published in 1776), Adam Smith, like many people, was reconciled to the Union. By then the economy was recovering mainly because of new technologies in farming and industry. Even so, Smith still had doubts about the effects of the Union on trade. He says that 'of all the commercial advantages' of the Union (without specifying what they were) the 'rise in the price of cattle was perhaps the greatest'. On the other hand: 'The wool of Scotland fell very considerable in its price in consequence of the union with England, by which it was excluded from the great market of Europe, and confined to the narrow one of Great Britain.'7

Adam Fergusson's *Essay on the History of Civil Society* (1767) is one of the first classic works in the literature of sociology. He too believed in the advantages of a small independent nation:

(7.8)   Of National Felicity

> Great and powerful states are able to overcome and subdue the weak; polished and commercial nations have more wealth, and practise a greater variety of arts, than the rude: but the happiness of men, in all cases alike, consists in the blessings of a candid, an active, and strenuous mind. And if we consider the state of society merely as that into which mankind are led by their propensities, as a state to be valued from its effect in preserving the species, in ripening their talents, and exciting their virtues, we need not enlarge our communities, in order to enjoy these advantages. We frequently obtain them in the most remarkable degree, where nations remain independent, and are of a small extent.

> ADAM FERGUSSON, *An Essay on the History*
> *of Civil Society* (1767). Ed. by Duncan
> Forbes, Edinburgh, 1966, p. 59

I have already mentioned the interest of James Boswell in the Declaration of Arbroath. Although he admired England and pined for the pleasures of London, he was opposed throughout his life to the Union. Consistently with this, he was a supporter of the Americans in their war of independence and, at the other end of the scale, for the independence of Corsica. He visited Corsica and became a friend of the leader of the independence movement, General Paoli. In his book about the island he quotes the Declaration of Arbroath on its title page and writes about liberty in his Introduction. It clearly echoes the Declaration, Barbour and Buchanan:

(7.9)   Boswell on Liberty

Liberty is so natural, and so dear to mankind, whether as
individuals, or as members of society, that it is indispensibly
necessary to our happiness. Every thing worthy ariseth from it.
Liberty gives health to the mind, and enables us to enjoy the
full exercise of our faculties. He who is in chains cannot move
either easily or gracefully; nothing elegant or noble can be
expected from those, whose spirits are subdued by tyranny,
and whose powers are cramped by restraint.

There are those who from the darkest prejudice, or most
corrupt venality, would endeavour to reason mankind out
of their original and genuine feelings, and persuade them
to substitute artificial sentiment in place of that which is
implanted by GOD and Nature. They would maintain, that
slavery will from habit become easy, and, that mankind are
truly better, when under confinement and subjection to the
arbitrary will of a few.

Such doctrine as this, could never have gained any
ground, had it been addressed to calm reason alone. Its
partisans therefore have found it necessary to address
themselves to the imagination and passions; to call in the aid
of enthusiasm and superstition; in some countries to instill a
strange love and attachment to their sovereigns; and in others
to propagate certain mystical notions, which the mind of man
is wonderfully ready to receive, of a divine right to rule; as if
their sovereigns had descended from heaven. This last idea
has been cherished for ages, from the 'Cara Deum suboles,
The beloved offspring of the Gods', among the Romans, to
those various elevated and endearing epithets, which modern
nations have thought proper to bestow upon their sovereigns.

But whatever sophisms may be devised in favour of
slavery, patience under it, can never be any thing but 'the
effect of a sickly constitution, which creates a laziness
and despondency, that puts men beyond hopes and fears;
mortifying ambition, and other active qualities, which
freedom begets; and instead of them, affording only a dull
kind of pleasure, of being careless and insensible.'

There is no doubt, but by entering into society, mankind
voluntarily give up a part of their natural rights, and bind
themselves to the obedience of laws, calculated for the
general good. But, we must distinguish between authority,

and oppression; between laws, and capricious dictates; and keeping the original intention of government ever in view, we should take care that no more restraint be laid upon natural liberty, than what the necessities of society require.

Perhaps the limits between the power of government, and the liberty of the people, should not be too strictly marked out. Men of taste reckon that picture hard, where the outlines are so strong, as to be clearly seen. They admire a piece of painting, where the colours are delicately blended, and the tints, which point out every particular object, are softened into each other, by an insensible gradation. So in a virtuous state, there should be such a mutual confidence between the government and the people, that the rights of each should not be expressly defined.

But flagrant injustice, on one side or other, is not to be concealed; and, without question, it is the priviledge of the side that is injured, to vindicate itself.

I have been led into these reflections from a consideration of the arguments by which ingenious men in the refinement of politics have endeavoured to amuse mankind, and turn away their attention from the plain and simple notions of liberty.

Quoted in Moray McLaren's *The Wisdom of the Scots*. London, 1961, pp. 250–1

J.G. Lockhart, the son-in-law and biographer of Walter Scott, deplored the neglect by the *literati* of the national history and the national modes of feeling, as opposed to the intellect:

(7.10)   'The Richer and Warmer Spirit'

Again, although the history of Scotland has not been throughout filled with splendid or remarkable events, fitted to show off the national character in the most luminous and imposing points of view, yet few persons will refuse to consider the Scots as a nation remarkable – most remarkable – for natural endowments. It would be difficult to say in what elements adapted to make a nation shine in literature they are at all deficient. Now, when the character of a nation has once fully developed itself in events or in literature, its posterity are too apt to consider its former achievements or writings as an adequate expression or symbol of what exists in themselves, and so to remain contented without making any farther exertions – and this, I take it, is one of the main causes of what appears externally in the history of nations, to be barrenness, degeneracy, and exhaustion of intellectual power, – so that it may perhaps be one of the advantages which Scotland possesses over England and many other countries, that she has not yet created any sufficient monuments of that 'mightiness for good or ill' that is within her.

If a remainder of her true harvest is yet to be reaped – if any considerable body of her yet unexpended force is now to make its appearance in literature, it will do so under the most favourable circumstances, and with all appliances to boot, which the present state of intellectual cultivation in Europe can furnish, both in the way of experience, and as objects for examination and reflection. The folly of slighting and concealing what remains concealed within herself, is one of the worst and most pernicious that can beset a country, in the situation wherein Scotland stands. Although, perhaps, it is not now the cue of Scotland to dwell very much on her own past history (which that of England has thrown too much into the shade), yet she should observe what fine things have been made even of this department, by the great genius of whom I have spoken above – and learn to consider her own national *character* as a mine of intellectual wealth, which remains in a great measure unexplored. While she looks back upon the history of England, as upon that of the country to which she has suspended and rendered subordinate her fortunes, yet she should by no means regard English *literature*, as an expression of her mind, or as superseding the examination of what intellectual resources remain unemployed within her own domains of peculiar possession.

The most remarkable literary characters which Scotland produced last century, showed merely (as I have already said) the force of her intellect, as applied to matters of reasoning. The generation of Hume, Smith, &c., left matters of feeling very much unexplored, and probably considered Poetry merely as an elegant and tasteful appendage to the other branches of literature, with which they themselves were more conversant. Their disquisitions on morals were meant to be the vehicles of ingenious theories – not of convictions of sentiment. They employed, therefore, even in them, only the national intellect, and not the national modes of feeling.

The Scottish literati of the present day have inherited the ideas of these men, and acted upon them in a great measure – with scarcely more than the one splendid exception of Walter Scott. While all the rest were contenting themselves with exercising and displaying their speculative acuteness, this man had the wisdom – whether by the impulse of Nature, of from reflection, I know not – to grapple boldly with the feelings of his countrymen. The habits of self-love, so much pampered and indulged by the other style, must have opposed some resistance to the influence of works such as his – I mean their more solid, and serious and abiding influence upon the characters and minds of those who read them; but these are only wreaths of snow, whose cold flakes are made to be melted when the sun shines fairly upon them. His works are altogether the most remarkable phenomenon in this age of wonders – produced among a people, whose taste had been well nigh weaned from all those ranges of feeling, on which their main inspiration and main power depend – they have of themselves been sufficient to create a more than passionate return of faith and homage to those deserted elements of greatness, in all the better part of his countrymen. I consider him, and his countrymen should do so, as having been the sole saviour of all the richer and warmer spirit of literature in Scotland.

J.G. LOCKHART, *Peter's Letter to his Kinsfolk*
(1819). Ed. by William Ruddick, Edinburgh,
1977, pp. 146–8

Walter Scott's contribution to the revival of the national consciousness and self-confidence is certainly, to use the favourite word of one of his characters, prodigious. But he was not alone. Alexander Gray, a rare combination of economist and poet, said 'what Scotland owes to Burns and Scott is beyond all computation'.[8] Not only Burns, but also his predecessors in the revival of Scots poetry, Ramsay and Fergusson, all helped to prevent Scotland from disappearing under enlightened abstraction and universalism and less enlightened anglicisation. They not only expressed national feelings but consciously collected and responded to the poetry of the Scottish past. In the Highlands too the 18th Century was a great period of poetry with major poets such as Alasdair MacMaighstir Alasdair, Duncan Ban Macintyre and Rob Donn.

Robert Burns expressed his feelings about Scotland in his letters as well as in his verse:

(7.11)   What are the Boasted Advantages?

[TO MRS DUNLOP]

Ellisland, 10th April, 1790.

I have just now, my ever honored friend, enjoyed a very high luxury, in reading a paper of the Lounger. You know my national prejudices. I have often read and admired the Spectator, Adventurer, Rambler, and World; but still with a certain regret, that they were so thoroughly and entirely English. Alas! have I often said to myself, what are all the boasted advantages which my country reaps from the union, that can counterbalance the annihilation of her Independance, and even her very name! I often repeat that couplet of my favorite poet, Goldsmith –

'– States of native liberty possest,

Tho' very poor, may yet be very blest.'9

Nothing can reconcile me to the common terms, 'English ambassador, English court,' &c. And I am out of all patience to see that equivocal character, Hastings, impeached by 'the Commons of England'.

ROBERT BURNS, *Letters*. Ed. by J. De Lancey
Ferguson, Oxford, 1931, vol. II, p. 18

(7.12)   'Scots, Wha Hae'

[TO GEORGE THOMSON]

My dear Sir,   [*About* 30 August 1793]

You know that my pretensions to musical taste, are merely a few of Nature's instincts, untaught & untutored by Art. – For this reason, many musical compositions, particularly where much of the merit lies in Counterpoint, however they may transport & ravish the ears of you, Connoisseurs, affect my simple lug no otherwise than merely as melodious Din. – On the other hand, by way of amends, I am delighted with many little melodies, which the learned Musician despises as silly & insipid. – I do not know whether the old air, 'Hey tutti taitie,' may rank among this number; but well I know that,

with Fraser's Hautboy, it has often filled my eyes with tears.
– There is a tradition, which I have met with in many places
of Scotland, that it was Robert Bruce's March at the battle
of Bannock-burn. – This thought, in my yesternight's evening
walk, warmed me to a pitch of enthusiasm on the theme of
Liberty & Independance, which I threw into a kind of Scots
Ode, fitted to the Air, that one might suppose to be the
gallant ROYAL SCOT's address to his heroic followers on that
eventful morning.—

> Robert Bruce's march to BANNOCKBURN—
>   To its ain tune—
> Scots, wha hae wi' WALLACE bled,
> Scots, wham BRUCE has aften led,
> Welcome to your gory bed,—
>   Or to victorie.—
> Now's the day, & now's the hour;
> See the front o' battle lower;
> See approach proud EDWARD's power,
>   Chains & Slaverie.—
> Wha will be a traitor-knave?
> Wha can fill a coward's grave?
> Wha sae base as be a Slave?
>   —Let him turn & flie:—
> Wha for SCOTLAND's king & law,
> Freedom's sword will strongly draw,
> FREE-MAN stand, or FREE-MAN fa',
>   Let him follow me.—
> By Oppression's woes & pains!
> By your Sons in servile chains!
> We will drain our dearest veins,
>   But they *shall* be free!
> Lay the proud Usurpers low!
> Tyrants fall in every foe!
> LIBERTY's in every blow!
>   Let us DO – or DIE!!!

So may God ever defend the cause of Truth and Liberty, as he
did that day! – Amen!

RB

P.S. I shewed the air to Urbani, who was highly pleased with

it, & begged me to make soft verses for it; but I had no idea
of giving myself any trouble on the subject, till the accidental
recollection of that glorious struggle for Freedom, associated
with the glowing ideas of some other struggles of the same
nature, *not quite so ancient*, roused my rhyming Mania. –
Clarke's set of the tune, with his bass, you will find in the
Museum; though I am afraid that the air is not what will
entitle it to a place in your elegant selection. – However, I am
so pleased with my verses, or more properly the Subject of
my verses, that although Johnson has already given the tune a
place, yet it shall appear again, set to this Song, in his next &
last Volume.—

RB

ROBERT BURNS, *Letters*. Ed. by J. De
Lancey Ferguson, Oxford, 1931, vol. II,
pp. 195–6

Burns wrote not only the classic poetic statement of Scottish independence,
but also of Scottish egalitarianism:

(7.13)   A Man's a Man for a' That

Is there for honest poverty
    That hings his head, an a' that?
The coward slave, we pass him by –
    We dare be poor for a' that!
For a' that, an a' that,
    Our toils obscure, an a' that,
The rank is but the guinea's stamp,
    The man's the gowd for a' that.

What though on hamely fare we dine,
    Wear hoddin grey, an a' that?
Gie fools their skills, and knaves their wine –
    A man's a man for a' that.
For a' that, an a' that,
    Their tinsel show, an a' that,
The honest man, tho' e'er sae poor,
    Is king o' men for a' that.

Ye see you birkie ca'd 'a lord,'
    Wha' struts, an stares, an a' that?
Tho' hundreds worship at his word.

He's but a cuif for a' that.
For a' that, an a' that.
His ribband, star, an a' that.
The man o' independent mind,
He looks an laughs at a' that.

A prince can mak a belted knight.
A marquis, duke, an a' that!
But an honest man's aboon his might –
Guid faith, he mauna fa' that!
For a' that, an a' that.
Their dignities, an a' that.
The pith o' sense an pride o' worth.
Are higher rank than a' that.

Then let us pray that come it may
(As come it will for a' that),
That Sense and Worth o'er a' the earth,
Shall bear the gree an a' that.
For a' that, an a' that,
It's comin' yet for a' that,
That man to man, the world, o'er
Shall brithers be for a' that.

ROBERT BURNS, 'Such a parcel of rogues
in a nation', in *Poems and Songs*. Ed. by
James Kinsley, London, 1969, pp. 602–3

In the postscript to his letter to George Thomson, Burns mentions struggles for freedom, 'not quite so ancient'. He was thinking of the trial of Thomas Muir of Huntershill on 30th August 1793, the probable date also of the letter. Muir was sentenced to fourteen years' transportation to Australia for sedition, but he escaped in an American ship and reached France. Here he addressed a Memorial to the Foreign Minister, Talleyrand, in which he deplored the Union and its effects. The charge against Muir was that, as a member of the Friends of the People, he was an advocate of social and economic reform and of Scottish independence, views very similar to those of Burns himself. He was a victim of the Government panic that revolutionary ideas might spread from France. The fate of Muir and others was the reason why Burns, especially when he became a Government official as an exciseman, found it prudent towards the end of his life to profess opinions very different from those in which he really believed.

Another member of the Friends of the People was Lord Daer. He was a son of the Earl of Selkirk, and was introduced to Burns by Dugald Stewart. He wrote to Charles Grey, the future Lord Grey of the Reform Bill on 17th January 1793:

(7.14)   'A Conquered Province'

Scotland has long groaned under the chains of England and knows that its connection there has been the cause of its greatest misfortunes. Perhaps you may shrug your shoulders at this and call it Scot's prejudice, but it is time at moments like these when much may depend on suiting measures to the humour of the people, that you Englishmen should see this rather as it is or at least be aware of how we Scotsmen see it. We have existed a conquered province these two centuries. We trace our bondage from the Union of the Crown and find it little alleviated by the Union of the Kingdoms. What is it you say we have gained by the Union? Commerce, Manufactures, Agriculture. Without going deep into the principles of political economy or asking how our [sic] Government or any country can give these to any nation, it is evident in this case that the last Union gave us little assistance in these except removing a part of the obstacles which your greater power had posterior to the first union thrown around us. But if it did more what would that amount to, but to the common saying that we bartered our liberty and with it our morals for a little wealth?

You say we have gained emancipation from feudal tyranny. I believe most deliberately that had no Union ever taken place we should in that respect have been more emancipated than we are. Left to ourselves we should probably have had a progression towards Liberty and not less than yours. Our grievances prior to the accession of the Stewarts to your throne were of a kind which even had that event not taken place, must before this time have been annihilated. Any share of human evil that might have awaited us we are ignorant of; whereas we feel what we have undergone. Even to the last of our separate parliaments they were always making laws for us and now and then one to remedy a grievance. And a people acquiring knowledge must have compelled a separate legislature to more of these.

Since the parliaments were united scarcely four acts have been passed in as many score of years affecting Scots law or merely the incongruities which must arise betwixt old laws and modern manners. As our courts of law found something of this to be necessary they instead of applying to the parliament at London have taken upon themselves with a degree of audacity which can hardly be made credible to a stranger, to make under pretence of regulating of court Little Laws (acts of parliament as they call them) materially affecting the liberty of the subject.

Kept out of view by your greater mass so as never to make our concerns be the principal objects even to our own representatives, at a distance so as not to make our cries be heard in the capital which alone awes an arbitrary government; our laws and customs different so as to make our grievances unintelligible; our law establishment distinct so as to deprive us of the benefit of those constant circuits from the capital which by rendering the learned and spirited defender of the laws, dwelling at the source of actual power, acquainted with the lesser transactions of the remotest corner of the country, provides perhaps the greatest remedy to a half free state against some of the bad consequences of an extended territory. Our civil establishment distinct, so as to isolate the petty tyranny of office; even our greed and national vanity working to retain all these offices to natives so as still more to leave you (our then only protectors, although oppressors) ignorant of our internal situation.

We have suffered the misery which is perhaps inevitable to a lesser and remote country in a junction where the Governing powers are united but the Nations are not united. In short, thinking we have been the worse of every connection hitherto with you, the Friends of Liberty in Scotland have almost universally been enemies to Union with England. Such is the fact, whether the reasons be good or bad.

LORD DAER, in *The Scottish Historical*
Review, vol. 35, 1956, pp. 34–5

In 1792 James Thomson Callender published a pamphlet, *The Political Progress of Britain*, which the Government attempted to suppress. Copies were seized and a warrant issued for Callender's arrest, but he escaped to America. The pamphlet attacks the impotence of forty-five Scottish members in a British Parliament of 513, but its principal target is the imperial and war-making policy of Britain in which Scotland had been involved by the Union.

(7.15)   The Impotence of Scottish MPs

THE people of Scotland are, on all occasions, foolish enough
to interest themselves in the good or bad fortune of an
English minister; though it does not appear that we have
more influence with such a minister, than with the cabinet of
Japan. To England we were for many centuries a hostile, and
we are still considered by them as a foreign, and in effect a
conquered nation. It is true, that we elect very near a twelfth
part of the British House of Commons; but our representatives
have no title to vote, or act in a separate body. Every statute
proceeds upon the majority of the voices of the whole
compound assembly: What, therefore, can forty-five persons
accomplish, when opposed to five hundred and thirteen?
They feel the total insignificance of their situation and behave
accordingly. An equal number of elbow chairs, placed once
for all on the ministerial benches, would be less expensive to
government, and just about as manageable.

JAMES THOMSON CALLENDER, *The*
Political Progress of Britain. 1792, pp. 3–4,
9–10, 41

(7.16)   British Wars and Colonial Expansion

WITHIN the last hundred years of our history, Britain has
been five times at war with France, and six times at war with
Spain. During the same period, she has been engaged in two
rebellions at home, besides an endless catalogue of massacres
in Asia and America. In Europe, the common price which we
advance for a war, has extended from one to three hundred
thousand lives, and from sixty to an hundred and fifty millions
Sterling. From Africa, we import annually between thirty and
forty thousand slaves, which rises in the course of a century
to at least three millions of murthers. In Bengal only, we
destroyed or expelled within the short period of six years,
no less than five millions of industrious and harmless people;
and as we have been sovereigns in that country for about
thirty-five years, it may be reasonably computed that we
have strewed the plains of Indostan, with fifteen or twenty
millions of carcases. If we combine the diversified ravages of
famine, pestilence, and the sword, it can hardly be supposed
that in these transactions less than fifteen hundred thousand

of our countrymen have perished; a number equal to that of
the whole inhabitants of Britain who are at present able to
bear arms. In Europe, the havock of our antagonists has been
at least not inferior to our own, so that this quarter of the
world alone has lost by our quarrels, three millions of men
in the flower of life; whose descendants, in the progress of
domestic society would have swelled into multitudes beyond
calculation. The persons positively destroyed must, in whole,
have exceeded twenty millions, or two hundred thousand acts
of homicide *per annum*. These victims have been sacrificed to
the balance of power, and the balance of trade, the honour
of the British flag, the universal supremacy of parliament, and
the security of the Protestant succession. If we are to proceed
at this rate for another century, we may, which is natural to
mankind, admire ourselves, and our achievements, but every
other nation in the world must have a right to wish that an
earthquake or a volcano may first bury both islands together
in the centre of the globe; that a single, but decisive exertion
of Almighty vengeance may terminate the progress and the
remembrance of our crimes.

*   *   *

We have adopted a fancy, that frequent hostilities are
unavoidable. Yet the Swiss, a nation of soldiers, and placed
in the midst of contending tyrants, have hardly been thrice
at war in the course of three centuries. The reason is, that
their governments are founded on wisdom, benevolence, and
integrity; while ours breathe only maxims of a less amiable
nature.

JAMES THOMSON CALLENDER, *The*
Political Progress of Britain (1792). pp. 3, 4,
9, 10, 41

Other victims of the Government's panic were the Radicals in Glasgow,
provoked by *agents provocateurs* into an attempt at rising in April 1820. They
reacted, in the words of a history of the episode, 'not only against the
appalling social conditions but against their country's union with England
which they considered the main reason for all their ills'. Forty-seven men
were arrested and tried for treason. James Wilson, John Baird and Andrew
Hardie were executed.

CHAPTER EIGHT

Walter Scott's Letters of Malachi Malagrowther

Throughout his life Walter Scott was deeply disturbed by the erosion of the character and distinctiveness of Scotland through the Union with England. This was the emotional impulse which drew him both to collect the Border ballads (similarly to Burns's collection of folk songs) and to capture the past of Scotland in his historical novels. His biographer, J.G. Lockhart, records an episode in 1806, when Scott was thirty-five, which shows the strength of his feelings:

(8.1) 'Nothing of What Makes Scotland Scotland Shall Remain'

But he was, in truth, earnest and serious in his belief that the new rulers of the country were disposed to abolish many of its most valuable institutions; and he regarded with special jealousy certain schemes of innovation with respect to the courts of law and the administration of justice, which were set on foot by the Crown Officers for Scotland. At a debate of the Faculty of Advocates on some of these propositions, he made a speech much longer than any he had ever before delivered in that assembly; and several who heard it have assured me that it had a flow and energy of eloquence for which those who knew him best had been quite unprepared. When the meeting broke up, he walked across *the Mound*, on his way to Castle Street, between Mr Jeffrey and another of his reforming friends, who complimented him on the rhetorical powers he had been displaying, and would willingly have treated the subject-matter of the discussion playfully. But his feelings had been moved to an extent far beyond their apprehension: he exclaimed, 'No, no – 'tis no laughing matter; little by little, whatever your wishes may be, you will destroy and undermine, until nothing of what makes Scotland Scotland

shall remain.' And so saying, he turned round to conceal his
agitation – but not until Mr Jeffrey saw tears gushing down
his cheek – resting his head until he recovered himself on the
wall of the Mound. Seldom, if ever, in his more advanced age,
did any feelings obtain such mastery.

> J.G. LOCKHART, *Memoirs of the Life of Sir
> Walter Scott Bart.* (1837–8). London, 1900,
> vol. I, p. 460

Scott's fullest statement of his views on the relationship between Scotland
and England is in the three *Letters of Malachi Malagrowther* which he published
in the *Edinburgh Weekly Journal* in February and March 1826. The title was
a facetious reference to the supposed descendant of a character in his
novel, *The Fortunes of Nigel*, but his purpose was entirely serious. He was
responding to a crisis. Not for the first or last time, the British Government
was proposing to impose on Scotland a solution to an English problem. The
London money market had crashed after a period of wild speculation and
the Government intended to introduce restraint by forbidding the banks
to issue notes of less than £5 in value. This might have been sensible in
England where the banks had a record of instability and issued notes of
purely local validity. It would have been a disaster in Scotland where the
banks were sound and their £1 notes the basis of all economic activity.

Scott's defence of the Scottish banks was so persuasive and influential
that the Government abandoned the measure. But Scott's purpose was
much wider that this alone. He wanted to raise the whole question of the
British Government's interference in purely Scottish matters and their evident attempt to convert everything in Scotland to the English model. He said
that this had been disturbing him for years and that he would sleep quieter
in his grave for having so fair an opportunity for speaking his mind.

The result was a powerful statement of the case made by Andrew
Fletcher, and echoed by Hume, Smith and Ferguson, that the autonomy
of small countries is desirable. Scott argued that diversity is preferable
to uniformity and centralisation; that Scottish national characteristics are
valuable in themselves and should not be abandoned without good cause;
that London is already over-burdened and should refrain from interfering
in Scottish affairs. It is the first manifesto of modern Scottish nationalism.

(8.2)   Affairs Entirely and Exclusively Proper
to Scotland

A spirit of proselytism has of late shown itself in England for
extending the benefits of their system, in all its strength and

weakness, to a country, which has been hitherto flourishing and contented under its own. They adopted the conclusion, that all English enactments are right; but the system of municipal law in Scotland is not English, therefore it is wrong. Under sanction of this syllogism, our rulers have indulged and encouraged a spirit of experiment and innovation at our expense, which they resist obstinately when it is to be carried through at their own risk.

For more than one half of last century, this was a practice not to be thought of. Scotland was during that period disaffected, in bad humour, armed too, and smarting under various irritating recollections. This is not the sort of patient for whom an experimental legislator chooses to prescribe. There was little chance of making Saunders take the patent pill by persuasion – main force was a dangerous argument, and some thought claymores had edges.

This period passed away, a happier one arrived, and Scotland, no longer the object of terror, or at least great uneasiness, to the British Government, was left from the year 1750 under the guardianship of her own institutions, to win her silent way to national wealth and consequence. Contempt probably procured for her the freedom from interference, which had formerly been granted out of fear; for the medical faculty are as slack in attending the garrets of paupers as the caverns of robbers. But neglected as she was, and perhaps *because* she was neglected, Scotland, reckoning her progress during the space from the close of the American war to the present day, has increased her prosperity in a ratio more than five times greater than that of her more fortunate and richer sister. She is now worth the attention of the learned faculty, and God knows she has had plenty of it. She has been bled and purged, spring and fall, and *talked* into courses of physic, for which she had little occasion. She has been of late a sort of experimental farm, upon which every political student has been permitted to try his theory – a kind of common property, where every juvenile statesman has been encouraged to make his inroads.

✳   ✳   ✳

What I *do* complain of is the general spirit of slight and dislike manifested to our national establishments, by those of the sister country who are so very zealous in defending their own;

and not less do I complain of their jealousy of the opinions of
those who cannot but be much better acquainted than they,
both with the merits and deficiencies of the system, which
hasty and imperfectly informed judges have shown themselves
so anxious to revolutionize.

*   *   *

The inquiries and result of another Commission are too much
to the purpose to be suppressed. The object was to investigate
the conduct of the Revenue Boards in Ireland and Scotland.
In the former, it is well known, great mismanagement was
discovered; for Pat, poor fellow, had been playing the loon
to a considerable extent. In Scotland, *not a shadow of abuse
prevailed.* You would have thought, Mr Journalist, that the Irish
Boards would have been reformed in some shape, and the
Scotch establishments honourably acquitted, and suffered to
continue on the footing of independence which they had so
long enjoyed, and of which they had proved themselves so
worthy. Not so, sir. The Revenue Boards, in both countries,
underwent exactly the same regulation, were deprived
of their independent consequence, and placed under the
superintendence of English control; the innocent and the
guilty being treated in every respect alike. Now, on the side of
Scotland, this was like Trinculo losing his bottle in the pool –
there was not only dishonour in the thing, but an infinite loss.
    I have heard two reasons suggested for this indiscriminating
application of punishment to the innocent and to the
culpable.
    In the first place, it was honestly confessed that Ireland
would never have quietly submitted to the indignity offered
to her, unless poor inoffensive Scotland had been included in
the regulation.

*   *   *

This gratification of his humours is gained by Pat's being
up with the pike and shilelah on any or no occasion. God
forbid Scotland should retrograde towards such a state –
much better that the Deil, as in Burns's song, danced away
with the whole excisemen in the country. We do not want
to hear her prate of her number of millions of men, and her
old military exploits. We had better remain in union with
England, even at the risk of becoming a subordinate species of

Northumberland, as far as national consequence is concerned, than remedy ourselves by even hinting the possibility of a rupture. But there is no harm in wishing Scotland to have just so much ill-nature, according to her own proverb, as may keep her good-nature from being abused; so much national spirit as may determine her to stand by her own rights, conducting her assertion of them with every feeling of respect and amity towards England.

*   *   *

The Scottish Members of Parliament should therefore lose no time – not an instant – in uniting together in their national character of the Representatives of Scotland. Their first resolution should be, to lay aside every party distinction which can interfere with the present grand object, of arresting a danger so evident, so general, so imminent. It may be at first an awkward thing for Whig and Tory to draw kindly together; for any of the natural Scottish spirit which is left among us has been sadly expended in feeding a controversy in which we must always play a subordinate part, and these party distinctions have become far too much a matter of habit to us on both sides to be easily laid aside.

*   *   *

There has been in England a gradual and progressive system of assuming the management of affairs entirely and exclusively proper to Scotland, as if we were totally unworthy of having the management of our own concerns. All must centre in London. We could not have a Caledonian Canal, but the Commissioners must be Englishmen, and meet in London; – a most useful canal they would have made of it, had not the lucky introduction of steam-boats – *Deus ex machina* – come just in time to redeem them from having made the most expensive and most useless undertaking of the kind ever heard of since Noah floated his ark! We could not be intrusted with the charge of erecting our own kirks (churches in the Highlands), or of making our roads and bridges in the same wild districts, but these labours must be conducted under the tender care of men who knew nothing of our country, its wants and its capabilities, but who, nevertheless, sitting in their office in London, were to decide, without appeal, upon the conduct of the roads in Lochaber! – Good

Heaven, sir! to what are we fallen? – or rather, what are we
esteemed by the English? Wretched drivellers, incapable of
understanding our own affairs; or greedy peculators, unfit to
be trusted? On what ground are we considered either as the
one or the other?

But I may perhaps be answered, that these operations
are carried on by grants of public money; and that, therefore,
the English – undoubtedly the only disinterested and
public-spirited and trust-worthy persons in the universe –
must be empowered exclusively to look after its application.
Public money forsooth!!! I should like to know whose pocket
it comes out of. Scotland, I have always heard, contributes
FOUR MILLIONS to the public revenue. I should like to know,
before we are twitted with grants of public money, how much
of that income is dedicated to Scottish purposes – how much
applied to the general uses of the empire – and if the balance
should be found to a great amount on the side of Scotland,
as I suspect it will, I should like still farther to know how the
English are entitled to assume the direction and disposal of
any pittance which may be permitted, out of the produce of
our own burthens, to revert to the peculiar use of the nation
from which it has been derived? If England was giving us
alms, she would have a right to look after the administration
of them, lest they should be misapplied or embezzled. If she
is only consenting to afford us a small share of the revenue
derived from our own kingdom, we have some title, methinks,
to be consulted in the management, nay, intrusted with it.

✳   ✳   ✳

Is any real power derived by centering the immediate and
direct control of everything in London? Far from it. On the
contrary, that great metropolis is already a head too bulky
for the empire, and, should it take a vertigo, the limbs
would be unable to support it. The misfortune of France,
during the Revolution, in all its phases, was, that no part of
the kingdom could think for itself or act for itself; all were
from habit necessitated to look up to Paris. Whoever was
uppermost there, and the worst party is apt to prevail in a
corrupted metropolis, were, without possibility of effectual
contradiction, the uncontrolled and despotic rulers of France
– *absit omen!*

Again, would the British empire become stronger, were

it possible to annul and dissolve all the distinctions and peculiarities, which, flowing out of circumstances, historical events, and difference of customs and climates, make its relative parts still, in some respects, three separate nations, though intimately incorporated into one empire?

*   *   *

For God's sake, sir, let us remain as Nature made us, Englishmen, Irishmen, and Scotchmen, with something like the impress of our several countries upon each! We would not become better subjects, or more valuable members of the common empire, if we all resembled each other like so many smooth shillings. Let us love and cherish each other's virtues – bear with each other's failings – be tender to each other's prejudices – be scrupulously regardful of each other's rights. Lastly, let us borrow each other's improvements, but never before they are needed and demanded. The degree of national diversity between different countries, is but an instance of that general variety which Nature seems to have adopted as a principle through all her works, as anxious, apparently, to avoid, as modern statesmen to enforce, anything like an approach to absolute 'uniformity'.

SIR WALTER SCOTT, *The Letters of Malachi
Malagrowther* (1826). Ed. by P.H. Scott,
Edinburgh, 1981, pp. 9–11, 13–14, 15–18,
72, 136–8, 142–4

The 19th Century

In the 19th Century religion, and that then meant mainly Presbyterianism, was still a major element in Scottish life. In the words of Sydney and Olive Checkland: 'It was a central theme with its own powerful identity and a baffling complexity. It came from a remote but still compelling past.'¹ Sydney Smith, a clergyman of the Church of England and a famous wit and letter writer, spent four years in Edinburgh from 1798. In one of his first letters from there he notes the power of religion in Scottish life:

(9.1) The Most Remarkable Nation in the World

To Mrs Beach   15th July 1798
    The best way of giving you a just idea of the Scotch is to
shew you in what they principally differ from the English.
In the first place (to begin with their physical peculiarities)
they are larger in body than the English, and the women in
my opinion (I say it to my shame) handsomer than English
women; their dialect is very agreeable. The Scotch certainly
do not understand cleanliness. They are poorer than the
English, they are a cautious, and a discreet people. – They are
very much in earnest in their religion, tho' less so than they
were. In England I maintain that (except amongst Ladies in the
middle class of life) there is no religion at all. The Clergy of
England have no more influence over the people at large than
the Cheesemongers of England have. In Scotland the Clergy
are extreemly active in the discharge of their functions, and
are from the hold they have on the minds of the people a very
important body of men. The common people are extreemly
conversant with the Scriptures, are really not so much pupils,
as formidable critics to their preachers; many of them are
well read in controversial divinity. They are perhaps in some
points of view the most remarkable nation in the world, and

no country can afford an example of so much order, morality, oeconomy, and knowledge amongst the lower classes of Society. Every nation has its peculiarities, the very improved state of the common people appears to me at present to be the phoenomenon of this country, and I intend to give it a good deal of my attention. – Adieu my dear Madam and believe me your very sincere friend

SYDNEY SMITH

SYDNEY SMITH, *Letters*. Ed. by N.C. Smith,
Oxford, 1953, vol. I, pp. 21–2

The national Church from the Reformation of 1560 onwards was clearly a major influence in the evolution of Scottish characteristics. I have mentioned the effect on intellectual attitudes and the value attached to education. It also encouraged egalitarianism, moral seriousness, industriousness and a concern for social justice. Walter Scott said in *The Heart of Midlothian* that 'the habits and principles of the nation are a sort of guarantee for the character of the individual' and that this 'conviction if undeserved would long since have been confuted by experience'.[2] Of course, these qualities like everything else had their negative side. They implied a tendency to disapprove not only of ostentation, but of many of the graces and pleasures of life. Still, like Dr Johnson's friend who aspired to philosophy, cheerfulness kept breaking in.

Because of the dominant role of the Kirk, the Disruption of 1843, when it split in two, was a devastating event. The 'Ten Years' Conflict', which led to it, was a direct consequence of the Union. In the debate on the Treaty in 1706, the support or at least the acquiescence of the Kirk had been secured by an Act which guaranteed that it would 'continue without alteration to the people of this land in all succeeding generations'. This was an Act of particular solemnity requiring each sovereign and his successors to swear to uphold it. In violation of this undertaking, the British Parliament passed the Patronage Act of 1712 which, on the English model, gave the landowners a role in the appointment of ministers. This was contrary to the Presbyterian doctrine, stated in the *Second Book of Discipline*, that the congregations alone had the right to decide.

The moderate wing in the Kirk preferred to accept the civil power and avoid confrontation with it. The Court of Session, to whom several cases were referred, upheld the right of Parliament to legislate. To the Evangelicals in the Kirk, the State had no right to interfere in religious affairs and the Patronage Act had therefore no validity. This view prevailed in the General Assembly of 1842, which passed a Claim, Declaration, and

Protest, generally known, for the second time in Scottish history, as a Claim
of Right:

(9.2)   The 2nd Claim of Right, 1842

CLAIM, DECLARATION, AND PROTEST, BY THE GENERAL
ASSEMBLY OF THE CHURCH OF SCOTLAND.

The General Assembly of the Church of Scotland, taking
into consideration the solemn circumstances in which, in the
inscrutable providence of God, this Church is now placed, and
that, notwithstanding the securities for the government thereof
by general assemblies, synods, presbyteries, and kirk-sessions,
and for the liberties, government, jurisdiction, discipline,
rights, and privileges of the same, provided by the statutes of
the realm, by the constitution of this country, as unalterably
settled by the Treaty of Union, and by the oath 'inviolably to
maintain and preserve the same', required to be taken by each
sovereign at accession, as a condition precedent to the exercise
of the royal authority – which securities might well seem, and
had long been thought, to place the said liberties, government,
jurisdiction, discipline, rights, and privileges of this Church
beyond the reach of danger or invasion – these have been
of late assailed by the very courts to which the Church was
authorized to look for assistance and protection, to an extent
that threatens their entire subversion, with all the grievous
calamities to this Church and nation which would inevitably
flow therefrom, did, and hereby do, solemnly and in reliance
on the grace and power of the Most High, resolve and agree on
the following Claim, Declaration, and Protest: That is to say:-

WHEREAS it is an essential doctrine of this Church, and a
fundamental principle in its constitution, as set forth in the
Confession of Faith thereof, in accordance with the word and
law of the most holy God, that 'there is no other Head of the
Church but the Lord Jesus Christ'; and that while 'God, the
supreme Lord and King of all the world, hath ordained civil
magistrates to be, under him, over the people, for his own
glory and the public good, and to this end, hath armed them
with the power of the sword'; and while 'it is the duty of
people to pray for magistrates, to honour their persons, to pay
them tribute and other dues, to obey their lawful commands,
and to be subject to their authority for conscience sake', 'from

which ecclesiastical persons are not exempted'; and while the
magistrate hath authority, and it is his duty, in the exercise
of that power which alone is committed to him, namely, the
'power of the sword', or civil rule, as distinct from the 'power
of the keys' or spiritual authority, expressly denied to him,
to take order for the preservation of purity, peace, and unity
in the Church, yet 'The Lord Jesus, as King and Head of his
Church, hath therein appointed a government in the hand
of Church officers distinct from the civil magistrate': which
government is ministerial, not lordly, and to be exercised in
consonance with the laws of Christ, and with the liberties of
his people:

The Claim then set out the objections to the Patronage Act as contrary to
the constitution of the Church and then concludes:

THEREFORE the General Assembly, while, as above set forth,
they fully recognise the absolute jurisdiction of the civil courts
in relation to all matters whatsoever of a civil nature, and
especially in relation to all the temporalities conferred by the
State upon the Church, and the civil consequences attached
by law to the decisions, in matters spiritual, of the Church
courts, DO, in name and on behalf of this Church, and of the
nation and people of Scotland, and under the sanction of the
several statutes, and the Treaty of Union herein before recited,
CLAIM, as of RIGHT, that she shall freely possess and enjoy
her liberties, government, discipline, rights, and privileges,
according to law, especially for the defence of the spiritual
liberties of her people, and that she shall be protected therein
from the foresaid unconstitutional and illegal encroachments
of the said Court of Session, and her people secured in their
Christian and constitutional rights and liberties.
    AND they DECLARE that they cannot, in accordance with the
Word of God, the authorized and ratified standards of this
Church, and the dictates of their consciences, intrude ministers
on reclaiming congregations, or carry on the government
of Christ's Church, subject to the coercion attempted by the
Court of Session as above set forth; and that, at the risk and
hazard of suffering the loss of the secular benefits conferred by
the State, and the public advantages of an Establishment, they
must, as by God's grace they will, refuse so to do; for, highly as
they estimate these, they cannot put them in competition with

the inalienable liberties of a Church of Christ, which, alike by
their duty and allegiance to their Head and King, and by their
ordination vows, they are bound to maintain, 'notwithstanding
of whatsoever trouble or persecution may arise.'

ROBERT BUCHANAN, *The Ten Years' Conflict.*
Glasgow, 1841, vol. 2, Appendix I

This was a clear indication that a substantial part of the Church of Scotland
could not in their consciences accept patronage. It was also a challenge to
the English doctrine of Parliamentary Sovereignty under which Parliament
could legislate as it pleased on any matter, including the internal arrange-
ments of the Kirk. The Government decided to take no action and said so
in a letter of 4th January 1843. Accordingly, at the next General Assembly
on 18th May 470 of the 1,200 ministers walked out after making a protest.
It ended with these words:

(9.3)   Protest by Commissioners to the General
Assembly on 18th May 1843

And, finally, while firmly asserting the right and duty of the
civil magistrate to maintain and support an establishment
of religion in accordance with God's word, and reserving to
ourselves and our successors to strive by all lawful means,
as opportunity shall, in God's good providence, be offered,
to secure the performance of this duty agreeably to the
Scriptures, and in implement of the statutes of the kingdom
of Scotland, and the obligations of the Treaty of Union as
understood by us and our ancestors, but acknowledging that
we do not hold ourselves at liberty to retain the benefits of
the Establishment while we cannot comply with the conditions
now deemed to be thereto attached – we PROTEST, that in the
circumstances in which we are placed, it is and shall be lawful
for us, and such other commissioners chosen to the Assembly
appointed to have been this day holden, as may concur
with us, to withdraw to a separate place of meeting, for the
purpose of taking steps for ourselves and all who adhere to us
– maintaining with us the Confession of Faith and standards
of the Church of Scotland, as heretofore understood – for
separating, in an orderly way, from the Establishment; and
thereupon adopting such measures as may be competent to

us, in humble dependence on God's grace and the aid of the Holy Spirit, for the advancement of His glory, the extension of the gospel of our Lord and Saviour, and the administration of the affairs of Christ's house, according to His holy word; and we do now for the purpose foresaid withdraw accordingly, humbly and solemnly acknowledging the hand of the Lord in the things which have come upon us, because of our manifold sins, and the sins of this Church and nation; but, at the same time, with an assured conviction, that we are not responsible for any consequences that may follow from this our enforced separation from an Establishment which we loved and prized – through interference with conscience, the dishonour done to Christ's crown, and the rejection of His sole and supreme authority as King in His Church.

ROBERT BUCHANAN, *The Ten Years' Conflict*.
Glasgow, 1841, vol. 2, Appendix II

In his *Journal* Lord Cockburn said of this event:

(9.4) One of the Rarest Occurrences in Moral History

For the present the battle is over. But the peculiar event that has brought it to a close is as extraordinary, and in its consequences will probably prove as permanent, as any single transaction in the history of Scotland, the Union alone excepted. The fact of above 450 clerical members of an Establishment, being above a third of its total complement, casting it off, is sufficient to startle any one who considers the general adhesiveness of Churchmen to their sect and their endowments. But when this is done under no bodily persecution, with no accession of power, from no political motive, but purely from dictates of conscience, the sincerity of which is attested by the sacrifice not merely of professional station and emoluments but of all worldly interests, it is one of the rarest occurrences in moral history. I know no parallel to it. There have been individuals in all ages who have defied and even courted martyrdom in its most appalling forms, but neither the necessity of such a fate nor its glory have been within the view of any one in modern times, and we must appreciate recent sacrifices in reference

to the security of the age for which these clergymen were
trained. Such a domestic catastrophe never entered into
their calculations of the vicissitudes of life. Whatever,
therefore, may be thought of their cause, there can be no
doubt or coldness in the admiration with which all candid
men must applaud their heroism. They have abandoned
that public station which was the ambition of their lives,
and have descended from certainty to precariousness, and
most of them from comfort to destitution, solely for their
principles. And the loss of the stipend is the least of it.
The dismantling of the manse, the breaking up of all the
objects to which the hearts and the habits of the family
were attached, the shutting the gate for the last time of the
little garden, the termination of all their interest in the
humble but respectable kirk – even all these desolations,
though they may excite the most immediate pangs, are not
the calamities which the head of the house finds it hardest
to sustain. It is the loss of station that is the deep and
lasting sacrifice, the ceasing to be the most important man
in the parish, the closing of the doors of the gentry against
him and his family, the altered prospects of his children,
the extinction of everything that the State had provided
for the decent dignity of the manse and its inmates. And
in some views these self-immolations by the ministers are
surpassed by the gallantry of the 200 probationers who have
extinguished all their hopes at the very moment when the
vacancies of 450 pulpits made their rapid success almost
certain.

   Yet these sacrifices have been made by churchmen, and not
by a few enthusiastic ones; and with no bitterness; with some
just pride, but with no boasting; no weak lamentations, but
easily, contentedly, and cheerfully. I have conversed with many
of them, especially of the obscure country ministers, who are
below all idea of being ever consoled by the fame and large
congregations which may support a few of the city leaders,
and their gentleness and gaiety is inconceivable. But the truth
is, that these men would all have gone to the scaffold with the
same serenity. What similar sacrifice has ever been made in
the British empire? Among what other class, either in Scotland
or in England, could such a proceeding have occurred? The
doctors? the lawyers? Oxford? the English Church? the Scotch
lairds? It is the most honourable fact for Scotland that its

whole history supplies. The common sneers at the venality of
our country, never just, are now absurd.

HENRY COCKBURN, *Journal*, Edinburgh,
1874, vol. II, pp. 29–32

The Ministers who walked out in this bold and dramatic fashion established the Free Church and set about duplicating all the services of the
Church they had left. With funds collected from their congregations they
began to build churches, halls and schools all over Scotland. This was an
impressive undertaking which reinvigorated religious life but it was also a
massive distraction of effort. The Church and education (and the two went
together) had been the major influence and unifying force in the Scottish
nation. The Church of Scotland had been responsible both for elementary
education and the welfare of the poor. Precisely at a time of increasing social
problems caused by rapid industrialisation, the response of the Church was
weakened by this split and its consequences. The long tradition of a national
educational system under a national Church was lost, and the ability to resist
anglicisation was impaired.

These effects of the Disruption contributed to what George Davie, in his
book *The Democratic Intellect*, called a failure of intellectual nerve (10.11).
From about the time of the Disruption to about the end of the 19th
Century Scotland seemed to be losing its distinctive character and declining
into a complacent provincialism. After the defeat of Napoleon in 1815,
Britain (which predominantly means England) became for about 100 years
the leading world power, and its influence was more difficult to resist.
The worldwide Empire was embraced by the Scots as a substitute for
accomplishment at home. They regarded it as a partnership in which they
played an important role and as a force for moral and social progress.

It is true that Scotland still had autonomy of a kind. Administration
was largely in the hands of Scottish Boards; the law and education were
still staffed by Scots; Scotland was a major country industrially and the
industry was still largely owned and directed by Scots. William Donaldson
in his book, *Popular Literature in Victorian Scotland*, has shown that, if Scottish
literature and the Scots language was making little appearance in books, it
still had a vigorous life in the newspapers, of which more than 200 separate
titles appeared every week.

But there was a fundamental weakness about all of this. In the words of
Bruce Lenman, 'Scotland had become the most undemanding and subservient of British provinces ... a state whose masters regarded Scottish politics
as an exercise in buying individuals to ensure that Scottish problems were
not even raised'. [3] Scotland had a legal system, but no power to amend

the laws to meet changing circumstances. There were wretched conditions of poverty, and a massive loss of population through emigration; but no legislature to focus attention on the problems and seek a solution. The Government's response to the Claim of Right of 1842 was only one example of Westminster's indifference to any purely Scottish problem.

In Lockhart's phrase, Walter Scott had 'rehoisted the old signal of national independence'[4] in 1826. The next move was in 1852 when the National Association for the Vindication of Scottish Rights was formed. It issued a pamphlet, *Justice for Scotland*, which, like Scott in the *Malachi* letters, appealed to the Treaty of Union for defence against the infringement of it by the British Parliament. 'Scotland, so long as she trusted herself, governed herself, acted for herself and developed her own resources, was a nation full of life and energy and enterprise ... It is only when the affairs of one nation are managed by the men of another or by an unpatriotic clique within itself that it is neglected or misruled ... The Union had left us in undisturbed possession of our national laws and our national religion ... It enabled Scotland to a large extent to govern itself. But there was a flaw in it ... We allowed our representatives to be swamped ... There was no means of ensuring that the same consideration be shown by Parliament to matters which are purely Scottish as to those which relate exclusively to England.'[5]

On 2nd November 1853 the Association held a public meeting of over 2,000 people in Edinburgh. A number of resolutions were passed in the spirit of the pamphlet, but again without proposing the end of the Union. At the zenith of British power, and before the majority of people had the vote, that would have been too ambitious. Three of the resolutions were:

(9.5) The National Association for the Vindication of Scottish Rights

1. That the Treaty of Union ... asserts the individuality and provides for the preservation of the National laws and institutions of Scotland. That any attempt to subvert or place those institutions under English control, and under the pretence of a centralising economy to deprive her of the benefit of local action, is an infraction of the true spirit of this Treaty, injurious to her welfare, and should be strenuously resisted.

2. For the better administration of the public business of this part of the United Kingdom, and for securing to Scotland the practical benefits of a united legislative, that the office of Secretary of State be restored.

3. That the representation of Scotland in Parliament be increased.

> SIR REGINALD COUPLAND, *Welsh*
> *and Scottish Nationalism*. London, 1954,
> pp. 285–6

One of the moving spirits in the Association and probably the author of the pamphlet was W.S. Aytoun, a poet and essayist and professor of rhetoric and *belles lettres* at Edinburgh. He was a Tory of the old Scottish school which was entirely different from the modern variety. In Scotland the Tory party had begun as the party of the opponents to the Union and of the Jacobites and it was to this tradition that Aytoun belonged. Perhaps for this reason, Lord Cockburn, who was a Whig, disapproved of the Association but he agreed with many of its opinions. In the following passage from his *Journal* he uses the word 'empire' to mean the United Kingdom (so did Walter Scott and it was the general usage of the time). It was part of the Whig philosophy to believe that the interests of Scotland, or of any of the other constituent nations, should be sacrificed to the supposed interests of the whole. That was why they assisted the process of the anglicisation of Scotland and that was one of the reasons why Walter Scott strongly disagreed with them.

(9.6) The Regret and Occasional Anger of Scotchmen

10th July 1853. We have all been surprised by a proclamation from a set of people of whose organised existence we have never heard, and who announce themselves as 'the National Association for the Vindication of Scottish Rights'. Eighty-six persons are named, with the Earl of Eglinton at their head, as those who are to carry the fiery cross over the land. The names are respectable, yet I have seldom seen greater nonsense.

There are three changes which a sensible Scotchman may naturally lament.

1st, The now almost complete abolition of every official thing connected with our ancient monarchy and political state, which is not necessary for modern purposes. All the phylacteries of our royalty have been trimmed. We have lost nearly every paid office of dignity or show which had nothing but its antiquity and ancient Scotch nativity to defend it. This may be lamented; but it can scarcely be blamed. It is only with great caution that a wise man can say that public money should be given for what is not necessary for the public. Yet it is undoubtedly true that there are some things that are useful for the public, though not necessary, and the difficulty lies in distinguishing between these two. In some instances – such as in the recent abstraction of its last pittance from our Privy Seal, the contemptuous spirit has too much prevailed. But, on the whole, it has perhaps been as much restrained as the times allowed.

2d, The centralisation of everything in London. This has been carried quite far enough. For example, after transferring Scotch administration as familiarly into England as if Scotland was incapable of administering its own affairs, our Board of Northern Lights, the best and cheapest Board for this object in the world, and immeasurably beyond its English or Irish rivals, has of late had some narrow escapes from being sunk in the overgrown mass of the Trinity House of London. Our own 'Gazette', too, was lately within an inch of being abolished in favour of the 'London Gazette'. Still, notwithstanding such exceptions, the tendency of all Governments to bring subordinate power as near themselves as they can is natural, and, to a great extent, irresistible; so that it is in vain for what has become but a limb of the general body to attempt to retain all the authority that it used to possess when in a prior age it formed a body of its own.

3d, The occasional disregard, if not contempt, by England, of things dear to us, merely because they are not English. One, and a very serious, example of this, consists in the superiority which is constantly claimed, especially from high places, for the law of England over the law of Scotland; and this even in the settlement of matters both of right and of policy, which ought to depend entirely on Scotch law. The House of Lords, both as a Senate and as a Court of Appeal, is deeply tainted with this vice. A direct attempt is making [sic] at this moment to assimilate the laws of the two countries by abolishing ours; and Brougham is said to abet this. If they were to adopt our law, the assimilation would certainly be for their advantage; but the attempt to swamp the most rational law in the world in the quagmire of a system, the absurdities of which it required the whole life of Bentham to expose, and which have since been attested by the sweepings away by innumerable committees and statutes, could not be even proposed, except under that bigotry which rarely fails to make Englishmen very unjust to everything not their own.

Our Solomon, King Jamie, tried to get the two kingdoms united just about a hundred years before the thing was actually effected. He seems to have tried to cajole each people into it by telling each that he would take care that the benefits should be all on its side. In his speech to his Parliament at Whitehall, 31st March 1607, he says, – 'You have here all the great advantage by the Union. Is not here the personal residence of the King? His whole Court and family? Is not here the seat of justice and the fountain of Government? *Must they not be subjected to the laws of England, and so, with time, become but as Cumberland and Northumberland, and those other remote and northern shires?*' Jamie was nearer the truth than he fancied. Another century produced a union of kingdoms, and a century more effaced the deeper lineaments of national habits; and the century that is passing away has every chance of leaving Scotland but an English county.

As against these tendencies the regret and occasional anger of Scotchmen is by no means unnatural. I feel my own indignation often roused. But though particular examples may justify this, it is useless and wrong to attempt to resist the general current. These are the feelings of every small and once independent nation, with rights and habits of its own, that has been absorbed into a larger and more powerful country; and the regret or discontent are the deeper when, like Scotland, the absorbed community has relics and a history of its own to which it still clings. Offensiveness in the manner, or in the extent, of the swamping ought to be blamed and checked; but it is in vain, and though practicable would be absurd, to prolong anything hurtful to the general interest of the empire, merely because it is either Scotch, or Irish, or English.

But this grand association informs us that we are degraded by intolerable wrongs, and talks of Bannock-burn. Most of its grievances resolve into a claim for more public money. The badness of the post-office at Glasgow is a national grievance. So is the fact that the red coats of the Edinburgh letter-carriers are made in London. And the revenues that we send every year to England, amounting to nearly six millions of pounds sterling, is all spent on English objects (such as the army and navy); and while England has great Government docks, etc., Scotland has none. I wish them all success in their attempts to loose the public purse-strings, but I fear that their folly will rather throw discredit on the reasonable portion of our demands. The best part of their case, if they knew it, is furnished by the contrast between the large sums given, not merely to England, but to thankless and rebellious Ireland for literature and science, and the shabby allowances to Scotland for similar objects.

But it is not this that can preserve the memory of Old Scotland. It can only live in the character of the people, in its native literature, and in its picturesque and delightful language. The gradual disappearance of the Scotch accent and dialect is a national calamity which not even this magniloquent association can arrest.

> HENRY COCKBURN, *Journal*. Edinburgh, vol.
> ll, pp. 291–6

Elsewhere in his *Journal*, Cockburn regrets the decline in the use of our 'picturesque and delightful language'. A hundred years earlier, James Boswell had also predicted and lamented the demise of Scots. So did R.L. Stevenson, some forty years after Cockburn. It's nae deid yet, for a' that.

(9.7) 'Our Picturesque and Delightful Language'

Every year makes me the more afraid that henceforth Burns' glory must contract, not extend; and this solely because the sphere of the Scotch language, and the course of Scotch feelings and ideas, is speedily and rapidly abridging, even in Scotland. The lower orders still speak Scotch, but even among them its flavour is not so fresh and natural as it was fifty years ago, particularly in towns. There are more English words, and less of the Scotch accent and idiom. This is the necessary consequence of the increased habit of reading English books, and of listening to English discourses, and of greatly increased English intercourse. When I was a boy no Englishman could have addressed the Edinburgh populace without making them stare, and probably laugh. We looked upon an English boy at the High School as a ludicrous and incomprehensible monster. Now, these monsters are so common that they are no monsters at all; indeed, there are Scotch schools (the Edinburgh Academy, for example) from which Scotch is almost entirely banished, even in the pronunciation of Greek and Latin; and the sound of an English voice in a popular assembly of the lowest description is received with great favour. Still, however, Scotch is pretty deeply engrained into the people, but among the gentry it is receding shockingly. Among families spending £700 or even £500 a year, it seems to me that there is a majority of the modern children to whom, in his Scotch poems, Burns is already a sealed book. I could name dozens of families, born, living, and educated in Edinburgh, which could not produce a single son or daughter capable of understanding even *The Mouse* or *The Daisy*. English has made no encroachment upon me; yet, though I speak more Scotch than English throughout the day, and read Burns aloud, and recommend him, I cannot get even my own children to do more than pick up a queer word of him here and there. Scotch has ceased to be the vernacular language of the upper classes, and this change will go on increasing with the increasing intercourse which rolls the language of the greater people over our surface. Railways and steamers, carrying the southern into every recess, will leave no asylum for our native classical tongue. I see no other remedy except to treat it as a dead language. I would teach it as a regular branch of education. Burns, Scott, and Wilson, besides many others, have made this as reasonable as to teach some continental languages which the want of opportunities of speaking make the half-learners quite sure soon to forget. Scotch cannot be obliterated without our losing the means of enjoying some of the finest productions of genius, and of understanding the habits and characters of one of the most picturesque of European nations, and of losing an important key to the old literature, even of the south. Above all, we lose *ourselves*. Instead of being what we are, we become a poor part of England.

HENRY COCKBURN, *Journal*. Edinburgh,
1874, vol. II, pp. 88–9

If George Davie spoke of a 'failure of intellectual nerve', he also said that the distinctive national inheritance ... has more than once been saved 'by a sudden burst of reviving energy' (10.11). Such a burst saved us again at the end of the last century. Political development and the establishment of new cultural institutions coincided with a resurgence of literature and the other arts. In the 1880s the Scottish Home Rule Association was formed and the conference of the Scottish Liberal Party adopted for the first time the policy of Home Rule for Scotland; the office of Secretary of State for Scotland was restored; the Scottish National Portrait Gallery, the Scottish Text Society and the Scottish History Society were founded: R.L. Stevenson wrote *Kidnapped* and *The Master of Ballantrae*; William McTaggart was painting some of his finest pictures; Greig and Duncan collected 3,500 folk songs in Aberdeenshire alone. By 1895, Patrick Geddes was able to write in his periodical, *Evergreen*, of a Scots Renaissance, long before the term was applied to the movement associated with Hugh MacDiarmid. Geddes himself was a leader in this revival, devoted to the cause of escaping from the 'intellectual thralldom of London' and restoring the old sympathies between Scotland and continental Europe.[6]

In 1889, the first of a long series of Home Rule Bills was presented to the House of Commons. Keir Hardie, one of the founders of the Labour Party, wrote in his paper, *Labour Leader*:

(9.8)   ## Keir Hardie on Home Rule

Dr Clark deserves credit for pushing on his Scottish Home Rule resolution to a division in Parliament. True, the only member who showed any true appreciation of what Home Rule would ultimately lead to was Cunninghame-Graham. Dr Hunter's nice picture of a Scottish Parliament composed of smug, bald, pot-bellied shopkeepers is too laughable to be taken seriously. With Mr Graham we say in all seriousness, 'God forbid.' Of course the G.O.M. was cautious, and threw the onus to the people of Scotland. In this he is perfectly right. I believe the people of Scotland desire a Parliament of their own, and it will be for them to send to the next House of Commons a body of men pledged to obtain it.

KEIR HARDIE, *Labour Leader*. April 1889

In the same issue Hardie defended his socialism in terms which show the clear relationship between it and the Scottish egalitarian tradition:

(9.9)   ## Keir Hardie on Socialism

We have just enough Socialism to protect the strong and give them power to oppress the weak. If a workman steals five shillings from the pocket of his employer, he gets sixty days in jail; if an employer steals a thousand a year from the wages of the workers, he is made an elder in the kirk, created a Bailie, and invited to deliver lectures against Socialism. If a pirate attacks a merchant ship and carries off the merchandise, the power of the British Navy is at once employed to catch the

depredator, and hang him up at the yard arm; if the merchant
gets his goods to land, and cheats his customers by selling
them at fifty per cent. above their true value, we point to
him as an example of a successful business man. If a wealthy
man puts a thousand pounds into the purchase of a piece of
land, the whole civil and military power of the State is at his
disposal in helping him to compel his tenants to pay rent so as
to give him a return for his money; if an agricultural labourer
has put fifty years of his life into the cultivation of that same
piece of land, making it yield of its increase sufficient to
provide for the requirements of ten men like himself, he may
have lived on meal and water all the time, and in the end be
turned out to die like a dog in a ditch, and there is no law
to interfere on his behalf. We State Socialists protest against
all this. We say it is not the strong who need protection. We
ask for such legislation as will protect the worker in the full
enjoyment of the whole of the wealth produced by him. . . .We
don't believe it possible to reconcile the antagonistic interests
of the capitalist and the worker.

A few generations hence and all that will be left of the
landlord tribe will be a preserved specimen in a museum with
patent leather shoes, tight-fitting clothes, a stand-up collar,
a vacant grin on its countenance, an eye glass and a coronet,
and having for an inscription – 'This monster used to roam
the earth and swallow up the home happiness of the common
people, but not being found worth his keep was allowed to die
out. It took too much to feed him.'

KEIR HARDIE, *Labour Leader*. April 1889

James Mackinnon, whom I have already quoted (4.2), ended his book on the
Union with an account of the Home Rule movement as it stood in 1896.
Many of his points are still being made 100 years later.

(9.10)   ## The Case for Home Rule in 1896

The general object of the Home Ruler is intelligible enough.
While maintaining the integrity of the empire, he aims at
securing a separate legislature and executive for Scotland, for
the management of Scottish affairs. He undertakes to foster
Scottish nationality, and maintain her national rights. That is
to say, he desires to return, at the end of nearly two centuries,

to the position maintained by the Scottish anti-unionists in
1707. Like them, he is of the opinion that a federal, instead
of an incorporating union is the only form of union that is
compatible with the interest of Scotland, and the maintenance
of Scottish nationality. This contention involves, of course,
a radical modification of the Union; but it is not open to
the objection that it would tend to obliterate more and
more Scotland's distinctive institutions. On the contrary, it is
dictated by the desire to restore the most distinctive national
institution of all, the old Scottish Parliament, for the legislation
of purely Scottish questions.

As was formerly remarked, there is no reason – very much
less reason now than during the Union controversy – why
the project should be regarded as dangerous, or necessarily
impracticable. Take the case of two countries, situated
as Scotland and England are. Both are possessed of ripe
experience in the arts of legislature and government. Both
have a vast interest at stake in maintaining that mighty
empire, on which the sun never sets. Both are endued with
intense national sentiment, along with a common pride in
the achievements of the great men of both nations, who have
contributed to build up that wider nation of imperial Britain.
Both are impressed with the conviction, that the united
Parliament is overburdened with the weight of imperial and
national questions. The necessity of sub-division of legislative
labour is forcing itself upon the attention of all parties.
Tentative endeavours have already been made, with good
results in this direction. There can be nothing revolutionary,
in the bad sense of that word, in agreeing to devolve on two,
or, if Wales be included in this distribution of responsibility,
say three, national Parliaments, the work that is at present so
unsatisfactorily performed by one unwieldy body in London.

Is there any insuperable obstacle in the way of retaining
one imperial legislative body for the despatch of imperial
business? There may be more practical difficulties than there
seem to be on paper, but they have been solved by other
great empires before now. In the case of Germany, to take the
most recent example, we have a great State which has risen to
unity by the adoption of the principle of combining national
or local legislatures (*Landtage*) with an imperial Parliament
or *Reichstag*. Is Germany worse governed or less united than
Great Britain, because its component States enjoy what goes

in this country under the party name of Home Rule? We leave
the case of Ireland out of consideration, as being subject to
the objection that the experiment of Irish Home Rule is at
present inexpedient and dangerous, owing to the peculiar
circumstances of religious division in that country; though the
case of Germany might again be cited to prove that the danger
is capable of being surmounted. We confine ourselves merely
to the case as between two countries, in which the danger of
internal friction and civil war is non-existent. If imperial unity
is compatible with the sub-division of local legislative labour
in an empire, formerly divided by religious and historical
contentions, and whose larger States were but yesterday at war
with each other, how much more so in the case of two peoples,
whose international animosities have been obliterated in the
long interval of two centuries of mutual friendship!

A priori, then, the case for national legislatures in Great
Britain is not incompatible with the larger patriotism, which
we cherish as citizens of the greatest empire that the world
has ever witnessed. Taking now the special circumstances of
Scotland, let us ask, what the men who advocate Scottish
Home Rule have to say on its behalf? They affirm that a
national Parliament at Edinburgh could meet the demands
of Scottish legislation more efficiently than is done by the
British House of Commons. If they can prove this part of their
case – and perfervid arguments, of a few months' or years'
standing, should not be allowed a premature sway – they have
unquestionably gained the day.

What, then, do they complain of in support of their
contention? They complain that Scottish legislation is jostled
out of the running in the race for supremacy with English, Irish,
and imperial measures. The history of the last half-century
has admittedly tended to substantiate the complaint. They
object that Scotsmen are put to an enormous expense by the
necessity of constant deputations to London, by the cost of
private bill legislation, and by appeals to the House of Lords.
This position is incontrovertible. They maintain that a large
proportion of this expense is incurred to no purpose, by the
opposition of English members to Scottish measures. There is
less ground for this grievance, and at any rate Englishmen are
entitled to some extent to retort that they have the same fault
to find in regard to the action of Scottish members, who may
join with the Irish and an English minority to swamp the public

voice of England. They say that the money thus expended
is carried out of the country to enrich an army of English
parliamentary agents, and that it might be spent both more
patriotically and practically in the Scottish capital. The Scots,
it may be answered, get a return for their money in the shape
of the measures which Parliament passes. This fact ought not
to be overlooked; but the answer is, that the business could be
better done, and done more cheaply in Scotland.

One fact is certain, unless more radical measures are
adopted in the direction of Home Rule, than have hitherto
been attempted, for remedying what are admitted to be
reasonable grievances, Scotsmen will not continue to acquiesce
in the present unsatisfactory *régime*. Men will not pay large
sums for an effete order of things, merely because that order is
a part of the constitution, established two hundred years ago.
They may reasonably conclude that expediency, apart from
a mere doctrinaire patriotism, suggests the establishment of
a national legislative Council, as the logical sequence of the
County Council.

This is not the sum of the Home Ruler's contention.
He complains that Scotland is overtaxed in comparison
with England and Ireland, and that Scotland receives an
inadequate return out of the British exchequer. The Home Rule
literature abounds in calculations intended to prove this. The
weakness of these calculations consists in the fact that they
are indefinite, and therefore, to a certain extent, unreliable.
Our perfervid Home Ruler is not at all nervous in dealing with
hundreds of millions; and some of these calculations run wild
in their appalling results. They will, at least, serve to amuse
the future historian, when investigation has produced definite,
or approximately definite, figures. There is, all the same,
room for the conviction that, apart from taxation for imperial
purposes, which must always be equal throughout the whole
of Great Britain, Scotland ought to be less heavily burdened
in proportion to wealth and population than is the case at
present.

One recent writer, who seems to keep himself within the
range of probability, estimates the sum with which Scotland is
overtaxed, at £1,100,000 per annum. It must not be forgotten,
however, that, as far as the Scottish revenue is derived from
income and property, this fact is simply an evidence that
Scotland has proportionally overshot both England and

Ireland in wealth. There is a good deal more force in the complaint, that, although the Scottish contribution to the imperial revenue is relatively so high, she does not derive the benefit she is entitled to claim in the matter of allowances. The proportion of the expenditure for the civil service ought to be higher. She may lay claim to a larger share of the expense of maintaining the army and navy. She ought to have larger sums spent on her public institutions. Aberdeen University, for instance, has been petitioning during recent years for a Government grant to help to defray the cost of building extensions. Her petition was more than once politely refused on the plea of budget necessities. The plea is not defensible, in view of Scotland's generosity to the exchequer, in relative comparison with England or Ireland. Were it a petition backed by half a dozen English dukes, for some English public object, would not the funds be forthcoming, out of the abundance of the Scottish revenue?

St Andrews wants, say, a chair of English Literature, or of General History. Have not Scotsmen a right to demand a Government endowment for objects so palpably patriotic, even from the English point of view, out of the surplus of Scottish money, spent, perhaps, on some petty scheme in Africa or New Guinea? Scotland, it is said, is so orderly, and so well served by her official class, that it is unnecessary to spend more on her military and civil services. Scotland is certainly peaceable, and the Government services are in a state of efficiency. But it is a question whether she is not practically defenceless, in case of a threatened invasion, and whether the Government might not have reason to curse their short-sightedness, as in 1708, 1715, and 1745, in leaving her without adequate fortifications, – and at least one central and thoroughly-equipped naval station. She may not unreasonably demand a Government subsidy out of the large sum which, according to even the most moderate calculations, has to be placed to her credit; for the purpose of carrying out the great project, whose commercial and strategic importance is self-evident, of a deep-sea canal uniting the two estuaries of the Forth and Clyde.

Finally, the argument based on nationality is a strong one. It is the unfortunate tendency of combination with a stronger people, that the weaker is in danger of being absorbed, and its nationality depreciated. The political status of Scotland

declined the moment her king accepted the crown of England.
In the diplomatic world she became practically non-existent,
and so unfairly were her interests represented at foreign courts
by the English ambassadors, under the regal union, that the
demand arose for separate Scottish representatives at the
European capitals. With the inauguration of the legislative
union, her national existence, in a political sense, ceased. This
alternative she was compelled to accept as the price of free
trade. England, it must be remembered, accepted the same
alternative as the price of legislative unity. In the concert of
the European nations, Great Britain alone remained, greater
and stronger from the fact that her king was the sovereign
of an united kingdom. Englishmen, however, have practically
ignored the fact. They accept the treaty, and at first admitted
the fact. Only a few months after the completion of the Union,
we find Lord Haversham apologising in the House of Lords
for inadvertently using the name England in place of Great
Britain. The English members of both Houses of Parliament
now seldom use any other when speaking of the United
Kingdom, or even of the vast British empire. They have carried
the tendency so far as to insert the name of England for Great
Britain in an important treaty with a foreign State. They might,
with as much reason, have made use of the term Scotland; but
then every Englishman from Land's End to the Tweed would
have been furious, and the error promptly rectified. As it was,
Scotland had to be content quietly to pocket the assumption
of her domineering sister. This constant use of the term is
entirely unconstitutional. Were it nothing more reprehensible
than an error of taste, it would only be another illustration of
the self-conscious character of the Englishman in such matters;
and the sturdy Scot might let it pass in silence, as an evidence
of supercilious thoughtlessness, rather than an intentional
insult. But it is more than that – it is a transgression both of
history and of the constitution, and shows that the conditions
of the treaty of Union are becoming, to the Englishman, in
an important respect, a dead letter. It is well to remind him
that Scotland parted with its separate political existence on
equal terms with England; and that the Union by no means
obliterated Scottish nationality, as it by no means effaced that
of England.

   To write and speak of the laws, the church, the universities,
or other institutions of England, is strictly correct, and entirely

constitutional; it is no less so to speak of those of Scotland: for the legal, ecclesiastical, and educational institutions of both countries were preserved as a distinct national inheritance to the respective peoples. To speak of the English army, the English navy, the English Parliament, or, in the sense in which it is frequently done, the English people, is both bad history and bad constitutional law. A protest on this matter usually excites a laugh on the other side of the border, and even among Scotsmen, who have learned to speak of themselves as 'Englishmen'. In the face of history, the laugh should be the other way; and no piece of arrogance or ignorance, whichever it be, better deserves the ridicule. The subject may appear trifling to our self-conscious compatriots; but they should have the good sense to remember, that the Scotsman has as much right, on national and historical grounds, to the quality of self-consciousness, as the Englishman; and that the assumption that his nationality may be ignored with a laugh is as irritating to the Scottish, as it would be to the English patriot.

There is no doubt that this ungraceful English custom inclines many Scotsmen to look with favour on a measure of Home Rule, which, by reinstating the old Scottish Parliament, would be a much-needed bulwark of Scottish nationality, against this insidious tendency to ignore it. Englishmen ought to know that they cannot obliterate Scottish nationality by perpetually harping on that of England, and attempting to dazzle Scottish eyes with the glamour of English greatness as such. The true Scotsman, with his immemorial history, with the grandeur of his eternal hills, contrasting with 'the tame beauties' of England, and the deeds of his ancestors, to remind him of his cherished past, will never submit to be patronised as an Englishman.

If there had been a suspicion of such a result in the mind of the Scottish unionists, there never would have been an incorporating union, which meant to them, and still means to their posterity, the conjunction of two peoples in their international and imperial interests, not the obliteration of their respective nationality. Mere sentimental and imprac-ticable rhetoric! retorts our unsympathetic English reader. What has become of your Scottish nationality; he demands in a tone of supercilious compassion, after two centuries of association with Old England? To all such we venture to present a not very arduous lesson in history, followed by a delightful trip to certain parts of Scottish scenery. Let them study the treaty of Union; and then pay a visit to Holyrood, to Iona, to Abbotsford, to Dunfermline, Stirling, Linlithgow, and Scone; and perhaps the secret of Scottish nationality will at last dawn on their nebulous brains. Let them then meditate on the contributions made, since the Union, by Scotsmen to the literature, the science, the political thought, the civilisation of the world, and the fact will become still more patent. A people that can claim the national continuity of a long series of great men, whose deeds might make any people proud of its national inheritance, will never consent to part with the symbol of so much that is inspiring and ennobling in its history – a symbol imprinted in the records of a hoary past, and inscribed on its national monuments.

The growing intensity of this sense of the past and of its claims is one of the signs of the age. The history, art, architecture, literature, political and social institutions of byegone ages, are calling forth a quickened interest. The effort to restore our ancient ecclesiastical buildings, which has become a passion, and which has so successfully been realised in several notable cases; the no less laudable efforts to preserve the archaeological remains of past centuries from destruction or oblivion; the praiseworthy enterprise of the Scottish History Society, and the numerous learned clubs, both literary and antiquarian; the establishment of clan societies; the never-failing appreciation of the patriotic strains of a Burns or a Scott; in a word, the strong instinct of home and country, which inspires the Scot all over the world, bear witness to the fact that the consciousness of the past has not been stifled by the altered conditions of the present.

> JAMES MACKINNON, *The Union of England*
> *and Scotland*. Aberdeen, 1907, pp. 516–24

A succession of Home Rule bills followed, all of them talked out, although supported by a majority of Scottish members. These hopes, and the promise of the Scottish Renaissance at the end of the century, were frustrated by the First World War. Scotland suffered losses out of all proportion to its population. Lewis Grassic Gibbon wrote of this at the end of his novel *Sunset Song*: 'It was the old Scotland that perished then, and we may believe that never again will the old speech and the old songs, the old curses and the old benedictions, rise but with alien effort to our lips.'

CHAPTER TEN

The 20th Century up to the Referendum of 1979

By the 1920s and 30s it seemed to many people that Lewis Grassic Gibbon's prediction was coming true, that the old Scotland, or any Scotland at all, was dying. Many books were written to analyse and regret the loss of a nation which has been a creative force in European civilisation. One of these books was Edwin Muir's *Scottish Journey*, published in 1935:

(10.1) ## 'Urgently in Need of Independence'

Scotland is, like all countries, a confusing conglomeration, containing such strange anachronisms as Edinburgh, a great expanse of cultivated and a greater of fallow land, and a number of different races. In the course of my journeyings I came in contact with these various Scotlands, passing from one into another without rhyme or reason, as it seemed to me; but what Scotland is I am still unable to say. It is Edinburgh, certainly, and Airdrie, and Glasgow, and Kirriemuir, and the Kailyard, and the rich agricultural areas of the South, and the depopulated glens of Sutherland, and the prosperous islanded county of Orkney. It has a human north and south, east and west, as well as a geographical; but though they have been clamped within a small space for a long time, one feels they have never met. Then there is the rivalry between Edinburgh and Glasgow, ridiculous in essence, jocular in expression, and acrid in spirit; there are the various classes, of which I found the working – or rather the workless – class by far the most honestly admirable; there are the Socialists, the intellectuals – mostly anti-Calvinistic, but sentimental compared with their fore-runners – the Catholics, the Orangemen, the Fascists, the Nationalists, the hikers, and the churchgoers. Most of these might be found in any other country, though the proportions would be different; the intellectuals, the hikers and the Fascists

would be more numerous, the Socialists and the churchgoers
fewer. Finally, cutting across these classifications, come the
Highlanders and the Lowlanders. No two sets of people could
be more temperamentally incompatible. I shall have to say
something about these various divisions in Scottish life in the
course of this book, and perhaps when I have done that some
picture of Scotland will emerge. But I should like to put here
my main impression, and it is that Scotland is gradually being
emptied of its population, its spirit, its wealth, industry, art,
intellect, and innate character. This is a sad conclusion; but it
has some support on historical grounds. If a country exports
its most enterprising spirits and best minds year after year,
for fifty or a hundred or two hundred years, some result will
inevitably follow.

*   *   *

The effect of all such innovations as the movies and the
wireless is to make the place people stay in of less and less
importance. Immediate environment has no longer, therefore,
the shaping effect that it used to have; the inhabitants
of all our towns, great and small, Scottish and English, are
being subjected more and more exclusively to action from a
distance, and, which is more important, to the same action
from the same distance. This is a great revolution, and in
part, no doubt, a beneficial one. But the freedom which the
radio offers has the illusoriness of spiritualistic messages; it
breaks a path into a new dimension of space, but the voice
that reaches us from that world is the voice of everyman,
everyman carefully groomed, on his best behaviour, at his
most civil, invisible and invulnerable; the perfect, discreetly
distilled extract of everyman. Such a phenomenon has never
been known in history before our day, and what effect the
utterances of this extraordinary ghost will eventually have
upon us is past imagination. It will probably be an improving
effect; but one can safely say that it is not likely to encourage
variety and originality of character, as the older state of
things did, before the appearance of the popular newspaper.
For variety and originality of character are produced by an
immediate and specific environment; and that, in modern life,
counts for less and less; it is being disintegrated on every side,
and seems to be, indeed, a life-form of the past. It would be
idle to regret this process, since it is inevitable.

This great change is nevertheless disquieting to many people; and it was mainly to combat it, I think, that the Scottish National Party came into existence. Though Scotland has not been a nation for some time, it has possessed a distinctly marked style of life; and that is now falling to pieces, for there is no visible and effective power to hold it together. There is such a visible and effective power to conserve the life of England; and though in English life, too, a similar change of national characteristics is going on, though the old England is disappearing, there is no danger that England should cease to be itself. But all that Scotland possesses is its style of life; once it loses that it loses everything, and is nothing more than a name on a map. The question arises whether that style of life is worth conserving, and therefore whether something should be done to conserve it. That is a question which can be decided ultimately only by the Scots people themselves, though for its effectual solution the understanding and help of England are needed. It would be foolish to claim that the Scottish style of life is inherently better than the English; in most ways it is less admirable; but it is a style with laws of its own, which it must obey if it is to achieve anything of genuine worth.

Everybody knows that the Scotsman who tries to be English takes on the worst English qualities and exaggerates them to caricature. And the vowel-clipping, flag-wagging, Empire-trumpeting Scotsman is, I think, not a fantastic example of what the Scottish race in general might become if it were submitted unconditionally to English influence. For the Scottish character has a thoroughness, or in other words an inability to know where to stop, which is rarely found in Englishmen, who make a virtue of compromise. When Scotsmen become English they do it with this thoroughness; they work out the English character, which has the vaguest connection with logic, to its logical conclusion, to something, in other words, which only formally resembles it, and is in spirit completely different. They do this on insufficient knowledge and with the aggressive confidence which is one of the curses of the Scottish character, and produce with elation a botched copy of a warped original. This process is called Anglicisation, and it is going on rapidly among the upper classes in Scotland. It is clearly harmful to both countries, and it is bound to become more harmful as it continues.

The great mass of Scotsmen and women have not reached

this stage. They are not conscious of English influence, and they have certainly no wish to become English. The possession of an accent approximately English is certainly regarded by them as a mark of social and intellectual superiority. But that is mainly because English is the language of the schools, the universities, the pulpits, the business world, the Press, and finally of the Bible itself, which, though it is not read now as widely as in the past, has had a deep influence on Scottish ways of thought, even about English, and has, through centuries of usage, engendered a reverence for that tongue. The ability to speak English is an accomplishment, however, and little more; and though it may bring with it a slight contempt for colloquial Scots, as a language suitable only for humble needs, it does not involve any wish or any intention of becoming English or denying the Scottish tradition. And besides, English as it is spoken in Scotland is very different from English, and certainly very full of Scottish character.

What makes the existence of the mass of the people in Scotland so unsatisfactory, apart from their economic plight (which is the only urgent question: I shall come to it later), is not the feeling that they are being subjected to English influence, but rather the knowledge that there is no Scottish influence left to direct them. They are not English, and they are ceasing to be Scottish for lack of encouragement. They live in the sort of vacuum which, one imagines, exists in the provincial towns of Austrian Italy, or of German Poland: in places that have lost their old life and have not yet found a new one. A certain meaninglessness and despondency hangs round such places; they are out of things; they do not know the reason for their existence; and people emigrate from them readily, without knowing why. The increasing centralisation of all vital energies in London has turned Scotland more and more into a place of this kind. A hundred years ago it still led a life of its own; it no longer does so, except in remote regions, and an impalpable atmosphere of dejection is spread over it.

It was, then, to make way against this internal ailment that the Scottish Nationalist movement came into existence. To some people the very name of Nationalism is hateful; it is over-weening and dangerous in a great nation, and niggling

in a small one; trying either to set up a world empire, or
to establish a provincial caucus. No doubt Nationalism is
the symptom of a morbid state, since it springs either from
inflated pride, as it did in England's Jingo days, or from a sense
of oppression, or from a mixture of both, as in present-day
Germany. When it springs from pride it is a general danger;
but when it is caused by a local injustice it loses its virulence
once the injustice is removed. The unfortunate thing for
Scotland is that it is not an obviously oppressed nation, as
Ireland was, but only a visibly depressed one searching for
the source of its depression. Glencoe and Culloden are things
of the distant past, useful perhaps for a peroration or the
refrain of a song, but with no bearing on the present state
of things, since everybody can see the English and the Scots
living side by side in peace. In such circumstances Nationalism
becomes an argument supported by reason on the one side
and met with scepticism on the other. Yet in spite of that
Scotland is as urgently in need of independence as Ireland
was. More urgently, indeed, for if she does not get it she
will lose her national consciousness, as Ireland would never
have done.

*   *   *

What stands in the way of Home Rule for Scotland is simply
apathy, the apathy of England, but chiefly the apathy of
Scotland. Consequently the Scottish Nationalist movement
at its present stage is mainly a movement to rouse Scotland
from its indifference, an attempt to quicken national life and
bring about an internal regeneration. There are faint signs
that it is beginning to succeed, but its success is slow, and
the great mass of the population are still sunk in indifference.
They are quick to resent any insult to Scotland, but do not
see the necessity of taking any action to stop their country's
decline, for, being already half denationalised, they are almost
unconscious of the danger.

EDWIN MUIR, Scottish Journey (1935),
Edinburgh, 1979, pp. 2, 3, 24–30

In 1961, Moray McLaren in *The Wisdom of the Scots* was still regretting an
acceptance of the mediocre:

The Spirit of Mediocrity

The genius of the Scottish people has always been opposed by
one quality, one thing particularly inimical to it – mediocrity.
When that genius has triumphed it has done so individually
and in the face of mediocrity. When mediocrity does get a
grip upon the people of Scotland its effects are particularly
mischievous – because inimical to their true spirit.

The story of Scotland's achievements in thought, in
dreaming, in poetry, in writing, in wisdom and in the action that
may come from these things is the story of men individually,
originally, yet with the national spirit animating them,
triumphing over, scorning out of existence one thing –
mediocrity. The true Scot of history and tradition may have
had many bad qualities, but he was never a mediocrity. Not
one name mentioned in this large anthology of wisdom, even
of those whom we have held up for dislike or qualified praise,
is the name of a mediocrity.

Yet today the curse of Scotland is not, as is commonly
supposed, whisky or the nine of diamonds, or even after-dinner
public speaking, but mediocrity. It is particularly pernicious
and prevalent with us because essentially so unlike us. How has
this come about? There are a number of reasons, but most of
them stem from something that happened two hundred and
fifty-three years ago.

The consent to the Act of Union in 1707 was the most
mediocre thing that the rulers of Scotland ever did. This is not
the place in which to bandy about political arguments. It is
enough to state that the action was a compromise, therefore
repugnant to the Scottish genius, and was mediocre. If we had
resisted the Union the results might or might not, in your view,
have been disastrous. If we had surrendered completely and
had become Scotlandshire, a northern extension of England,
the action might have been tragic, but neither course would
have been mediocre. There is nothing mediocre in suicide or
in a determination to live. But about the most mediocre thing
you can do is to sell yourself slowly out of existence and be
cheated even of your pieces of silver in doing so.

Ever since 1707 the spirit of mediocrity in Scotland
has grown and spread. Deep down in men's hearts there is
the knowledge that this is unnatural to them, and it is this
knowledge that is responsible for those gaucheries which

display what we now call the Scottish inferiority complex. It is lamentable.

MORAY MCLAREN, *The Wisdom of the Scots.*
London, 1961, pp. 314–15

But even while Edwin Muir and others were writing these despondent books, there were stirrings of reviving energy. In 1932 John Buchan, Conservative MP for the Scottish Universities, novelist, poet and historian, the future Lord Tweedsmuir and Governor General of Canada, spoke in the House of Commons:

(10.3)   # Every Scotsman Should be a
              Scottish Nationalist

It is easy enough to pull to pieces any scheme put forward for Scottish Home Rule. Whenever the proposer of a novelty is forced to come down to particulars, he is in a difficult position. But when you have driven your most stately coach-and-four through those schemes you have not solved the problem. It is to the fundamentals of that problem that I would ask this House to turn its attention for a very few minutes. I would ask especially two questions: What is the exact nature of this sentiment of dissatisfaction which is behind the Scottish movement? What element of substance and of value is there in that sentiment?

First, let me say that many arguments brought against Scottish Home Rule are merely foolish. We are told sometimes that a Scottish Parliament would be a fiasco and that it would be a kind of enlarged, noisy, incompetent town council. What earthly warrant is there for that view? The Scottish people, with a long tradition of democracy in their bones, are at least as capable of running a parliament successfully as any other race. Moreover, we all know that there is in Scotland to-day a great deal of public spirit and administrative ability which, for various reasons, cannot find an outlet in this Parliament, but might, in a domestic legislature.

Let us get rid also, once for all, of the absurd argument that because Scotsmen are successful in England and in the Empire and take a large part in their maintenance, it does not matter what happens to Scotland. It is not with what Scotsmen outside are doing that we are concerned, but with

Scotland herself. That argument misses the whole point. Many
people believe, rightly or wrongly, that there is a danger
of Scotland sinking to the position of a mere Northern
province of England. Finally, there is the argument, not so
often put into words, but which I think lies at the back of
the minds of a good many people. It is what I would call the
genteel argument. They think that Scotland is, after all, only
a province, that Scottish affairs are provincial, and that it is
out of date and a little vulgar to fuss too much about minor
local attachments. I do not think we need bother about that
class of person, the class who are quick to discard honest local
loyalties, and who would fail to be citizens of the world, but
are only waifs.

I believe that every Scotsman should be a Scottish
Nationalist. If it could be proved that a separate Scottish
Parliament were desirable, that is to say that the merits were
greater than the disadvantages and dangers, Scotsmen should
support it. I would go further. Even if it were not proved
desirable, if it could be proved to be desired by any substantial
majority of the Scottish people, then Scotland should be
allowed to make the experiment, and I do not believe that
England would desire for one moment to stand in the way.

I turn to my first question, as to the nature of and the
reason for this feeling that something must be done, and done
soon, if Scotland is not to lose its historic individuality. All
is not well with our country. Our population is declining; we
are losing some of the best of our race stock by migration and
their place is being taken by those who, whatever their merits,
are not Scottish.

*   *   *

The main force clearly in the movement is what might be
called the cultural force, the desire that Scotland shall not
lose her historic personality. I am afraid that people in
cultural movements are always apt to run to machinery for
a solution. Machinery will never effect a cultural revival. I
would remind the House that the greatest moment in Scottish
literary and artistic history was at the end of the eighteenth
century when Scotland was under the iron heel of Henry
Dundas. To imagine that a cultural revival will gush from the
establishment of a separate legislature is like digging a well
without making an inquiry into the presence of water-bearing

strata. Still institutions do play a part in cultural life, and machinery cannot be disregarded. I would ask the House to consider whether, inside the present system, it is not possible to devise reforms which will not only be defensible on the grounds of greater efficiency, but will do much to satisfy a legitimate national pride, and to intensify that consciousness of individuality and idiom, which is what is meant, or at least is what I mean, by national spirit.

*   *   *

We want a Scottish policy. We have never had one; we have only had a policy tacked on to English policies in a Clause or two which my hon. Friends must have thought to be peppered with unintelligible jargon. While agriculture, education, health and other branches have many points in their problems which are common to English problems, they have many which are individual and idiomatic. The mere fact that Scotland is constitutionally to a large degree a distinct unit gives us a chance of planning ahead in Scotland in a way that is not possible for any other part of Britain. The Scottish National Development Council is an excellent thing, but it will never succeed without a big backing from Parliament. Our ancient system of education has in some ways declined, and we want the opportunity to plan ahead to improve it, realising that it is something wholly different from the system in England. I want to see Scottish Members, over and above their particular party affiliations, regarding themselves as a Scottish party who will treat Scottish matters purely from the point of view of Scotland's interest. We shall quarrel among ourselves; we shall differ violently; but we shall always differ on Scottish lines.

*   *   *

But the problem is insistent, and must be faced. I believe that the kind of reforms which I have tried to sketch, and which my right hon. Friend has sketched, would meet what is sane and honest in the present movement – and there is in that movement a great deal that is both honest and sane. In the future it may be necessary to go further; I do not know; I have no gift of prophecy. But if we assert our national individuality, and give it a visible form in our administration, at any rate we are creating a foundation on which can be built any structure which the needs of the future may require.

May I be allowed to say one word to my friends who
regard this whole question as trivial – trivial compared
with the great economic problems with which we are faced
to-day? I do not deny for a moment the gravity of these other
problems, but, believe me, this question is not trivial; it goes to
the very root of the future not only of Scotland but of Britain
and of the Empire. Britain cannot afford, the Empire cannot
afford, I do not think the world can afford, a denationalised
Scotland. In Sir Walter Scott's famous words,
    'If you un-Scotch us, you will make us damned mischievous
Englishmen.'
    We do not want to be, like the Greeks, powerful and
prosperous wherever we settle, but with a dead Greece behind
us. We do not want to be like the Jews of the Dispersion – a
potent force everywhere on the globe, but with no Jerusalem.

                              JOHN BUCHAN, *Hansard*. vol. 272, 24th
                                                   November 1932

At the same time, the greatest stirrer-up of energy of them all, Hugh
MacDiarmid, was already active in his life-long campaign for Scottish
independence, cultural revival, radicalism and the encouragement of Gaelic
and Scots. On many points, as he admitted himself, he embraced self-
contradictions, but on these he was always consistent. He stated them in
a letter of 1968:

(10.4)   An Independent Literary Tradition

I have devoted many years to seek to overcome the inability of
the academic authorities and literary circles in many countries
to recognise that Scotland is a separate and very different
country from England, that Scotland has an independent
literary tradition at odds in many vital respects with the
English tradition – and that it has always been, and remains,
the aim of the latter to eliminate the former and assimilate
Scottish Standards completely to English. Government agencies
like the Arts Council, the British Council, British consulates,
etc. have pursued this policy and been largely responsible for
the general identification abroad of what is merely English
as British, and these agencies have actively endeavoured to
frustrate my efforts to give foreign countries a true sense of
Scotland's difference, of the need for Scotland to build on

its own separate traditions without regard to England, and in particular to revive our native languages, Scots and Gaelic.

*   *   *

I think you will agree that I cannot lend my name and influence to a project which does not accept as of prime importance the encouragement of Scots and Gaelic, the necessity of Scottish Independence, and the recognition that in contradistinction to the situation in England a deep-seated Radicalism is the chief, and an irreversible, element of the Scottish political tradition and a prime requirement of Scottish conditions today and henceforth.

HUGH MACDIARMID, *Letters*. Ed. by Alan
Bold, London, 1984, pp. 872–3

Like Robert Burns, MacDiarmid scorned the advantages said to have been derived from the Union:

(10.5)   The Parrot Cry

Tell me the auld, auld story
O'hoo the Union brocht
Puir Scotland into being
As a country worth a thocht.
England, frae whom a' blessings flow
What could we dae withoot ye?
Then dinna threip it doon oor throats
As gin we e'er could doot ye!
    My feelings lang wi' gratitude
    Ha'e been sae sairly harrowed
    That dod! I think it's time
    The claith was owre the parrot!

Tell me o' Scottish enterprise
And canniness and thrift,
And hoo we're baith less Scots and mair
Than ever under George the Fifth,
And hoo to 'wider interests'
Oor ain we sacrifice
And yet tine naething by it
As aye the parrot cries.

Syne gie's a chance to think it oot
Aince we're a' weel awaur o't,
For, losh, I think it's time
The claith was owre the parrot!

Tell me o'love o' country
Content to see't decay,
And ony ither paradox
Ye think o' by the way.
I doot it needs a Hegel
Sic opposites to fuse;
Oor education's failin'
And canna gie's the views
    That were peculiar to us
    Afore oor vision narrowed
    And gar'd us think it time
    The claith was owre the parrot!

A parrot's weel eneuch at times
But whiles we'd liefer hear
A blackbird or a mavis
Singin' fu' blythe and clear.
Fetch ony native Scottish bird
Frae the eagle to the wren,
And faith! you'd hear a different sang
Frae this painted foreigner's then.
    The marine that brocht it owre
    Believed its every word
    —But we're a' deeved to daith
    Wi' his infernal bird.

HUGH MACDIARMID, *Complete Poems*.
Ed. by Michael Grieve and W.R. Aitken,
Harmondsworth, 1985, vol. I, pp. 192–3

MacDiarmid aimed not only to give new life to Scottish poetry and the use of Scots but to restore its relationship to contemporary literature in the rest of the world and extend its intellectual scope:

(10.6)   ## Scotland and the Infinite

Whatever Scotland is to me,
Be it aye pairt o' a' men see
O' Earth and o' Eternity

Wha winna hide their heids in't till
It seems the haill o' Space to fill,
As 'twere an unsurmounted hill.

He canna Scotland see wha yet
Canna see the Infinite,
And Scotland in true scale to it.

> HUGH MACDIARMID, *A Drunk Man Looks at*
> *the Thistle* (1926). Ed. by Kenneth Buthlay,
> Edinburgh, 1987, 11, pp. 2521–9

As in the 1880s, literary, political and institutional developments moved forward together. The National Library of Scotland was established in 1925 on the basis of the Advocates' Library founded in 1682, (like the National Portrait Gallery, this was financed by private generosity). In 1936 the Saltire Society was formed to work for 'the restoration of Scotland as a creative force in European civilisation'. The Scottish National Party was founded in 1934 by the fusion of two other parties. In 1939 the Government moved the Departments of the Scottish Office from London to Edinburgh.

From the time of MacDiarmid's early lyrics in the 1920s and 30s (although he too had his predecessors) the cultural revival of Scotland has grown in confidence and strength. This has been one of the great periods of Scottish literature in Gaelic, Scots and English, of painting and of music. Other aspects of Scottish life from folk song and dance to historical scholarship and the intelligent scrutiny of Scottish affairs have flourished. There have been notable discoveries in science. Political and cultural self-confidence are inter-related and each encourages the other.

For the whole of the century the aspiration for the restoration of the Scottish Parliament has been a major theme of Scottish politics, fluctuating in intensity, but never either satisfied or abandoned. All of the political parties have been committed to it, in one form or other at different times. The Liberals (now the Liberal Democrats) have never abandoned the policy which they first adopted in 1888 for a Scottish Parliament within a federal United Kingdom. The Scottish National Party has been equally consistent and has not deviated in aims from a statement which it adopted in 1946:

(10.7) Aims of the SNP

The People of Scotland, as members of one of the oldest nations in Europe, are the inheritors, bearers and transmitters of an historic tradition of liberty. They have in common with

the peoples of all other nations an inherent right to determine
their own destiny in accordance with the principles of justice
accepted by the social conscience of mankind. The aim of
the Scottish National Party is therefore 'Self-Government for
Scotland. The restoration of Scottish National sovereignty by
the establishment of a democratic Scottish Government whose
authority will be limited only by such agreements as will be
freely entered into with other nations in order to further
international co-operation and world peace.'

Scots Independent, January 1947

Labour and Conservative policies on the Scottish question have changed
frequently. like the Liberals, the Labour movement adopted the policy of
Home Rule towards the end of the last century. The annual report of the
Scottish Council of the Labour Party for 1918–19 recommended a Bill for
Home Rule which began:

(10.8)   ## Labour Policy on Home Rule, 1919

HOME RULE FOR SCOTLAND

Now that the War is ended and an era of reconstruction
begun, Scottish problems require the concentration of Scottish
brains and machinery upon their solution. Your Committee
is of [the] opinion that a determined effort should be made
to secure Home Rule for Scotland in the first Session of
Parliament, and that the question should be taken out of the
hands of place-hunting lawyers and vote-catching politicians
by the political and industrial efforts of the Labour Party in
Scotland which should co-ordinate all its forces to this end,
using any legitimate means, political and industrial, to secure
the establishment of a Scottish Parliament upon a completely
democratic basis, as briefly outlined below:-

WHEREAS,

Scotland, though temporarily deprived, without the
consent of her people, and by corrupt means, in 1707, of
the exercise of her right to self-determination, is presently,
as anciently, entitled to legislate for the governance of her
National affairs in a Parliament of her own, the full exercise of
that right is hereby restored.

H.J. HANHAM, *Scottish Nationalism*. London,
1970, p. 111

John Maclean, one of the great heroes of the Scottish left, said when he stood as a parliamentary candidate in the Gorbals in 1922:

(10.9)   John MacLean on the Scottish Republic

I ... stand out as a Scottish Republican candidate feeling sure that if Scotland had to elect a Parliament to sit in Glasgow it would vote for a working class Parliament ... the social revolution is possible sooner in Scotland than in England ... Scottish separation is part of the process of England's Imperial disintegration. ....This policy of a Workers' Republic in Scotland debars me from going to John Bull's London Parliament ... had the Labour men stayed in Glasgow and started a Scottish Parliament as did the genuine Irish in Dublin in 1918, England would have sat up and made concessions to Scotland just to keep her ramshackle Empire intact to bluff other countries.

P. BERRESFORD ELLIS and S. MAC
A'GOBHAINN, *The Scottish Insurrection of*
1820. London, 1970, pp. 298–9

But in spite of these aspirations and in spite of the almost annual Scottish Home Rule Bill presented to the House of Commons (several of which were carried on the 2nd reading), there was no real progress towards a Scottish Parliament. Many of those who had hoped to achieve it through the Liberal or Labour parties were disillusioned. Both parties favoured Home Rule when they were in opposition, but lost interest when they were in power. They were, after all, British parties with a large majority of English members who were not well-informed about Scottish matters and not particularly interested. Neither of these parties wanted to lose its Scottish MPs without whom they had much less chance of achieving power at Westminster. It was clear that there was a need for a Scottish party devoted to self-government as its principal aim. Several such parties and groups were founded in the 1920s and 30s and it was these which came together as the Scottish National Party in 1934.

At first the progress of the new party was painfully slow. This was not surprising. The British first-past-the-post electoral system is highly unfavourable to new parties. The Unionist view that the Union had been a voluntary agreement which had benefited Scotland had been asserted for so long that it had been accepted uncritically.

In 1949 John MacCormick decided to launch an all-party campaign to collect signatures to demonstrate Scottish opinion. This was the Covenant which called for a Parliament, but still within the framework of the United Kingdom. By the end of 1950 this had collected more than two million signatures. On Christmas morning Scottish opinion was further galvanised by the news that the Stone of Destiny had been removed from Westminster Abbey where it had rested since Edward I had seized it in 1296 as a symbol of the suppression of Scotland.

(10.10)   The Covenant of 1949–50

> We, the people of Scotland who subscribe this Engagement, declare our belief that reform in the constitution of our country is necessary to secure good government in accordance with our Scottish traditions and to promote the spiritual and economic welfare of our nation.
>
> We affirm that the desire for such reform is both deep and widespread through the whole community, transcending all political differences and sectional interests, and we undertake to continue united in purpose for its achievement.
>
> With that end in view we solemnly enter into this Covenant whereby we pledge ourselves, in all loyalty to the Crown and within the framework of the United Kingdom, to do everything in our power to secure for Scotland a Parliament with adequate legislative authority in Scottish affairs.

JOHN MACCORMICK, *The Flag in the Wind.*
London, 1955, p. 128

The reponse of both Labour and the Conservatives to the two million signatures was to say that the question must be settled by the normal parliamentary process.

George Elder Davie's important book, *The Democratic Intellect* was published in 1961. It brought a new dimension to the Scottish debate by revealing the way in which the values of the Scottish intellectual tradition had been largely lost in the course of the 19th Century by pressures for conformity with the English model. The following are a few short extracts from it:

(10.11)   The Democratic Intellect

> Throughout the nineteenth century, in spite of increasing assimilation of political and economic life, the Scots stuck to a policy of apartness in social ethics. However, amid the

recurrent tensions of the time, industrial and democratic, the old confident grip on the situation was noticeably slackening. Instead of the steady rhythm of independent institutional life, a new pattern emerged of alternation between catastrophe and renaissance, in which the distinctive national inheritance was more than once brought to the very brink of ruin only to be saved at the last minute by a sudden burst of reviving energy.

In the early years of the century, no doubt, the situation was much more promising than in England. Church, Law, and Education in the North had emerged from the eighteenth century in good shape and with growing international prestige. However, the peculiarly precarious situation of the Scottish system of government was forcibly and unexpectedly brought home when, with the repercussions of 1832 Parliamentary Reform, a desperate crisis of stress and strain shook to its foundations the interlocked network of institutions on whose co-operation depended whatever was distinctive in Scottish society. The Church and the Law suddenly found themselves irreconcilably involved in a deadlock over fundamentals which split the whole country for over two decades, embittering relations in all walks of life and bringing into doubt the continuing viability of the semi-autonomous status enjoyed since the Union. Already, amid the shock and passion of the original schism, indispensable props of the system had been surrendered – most notably, the prerogative of independent credit issue (1845), and it looked as if the central sectors of the Northern establishment were in no position to withstand much longer the pull of assimilation.

However, remarkably enough, this dangerous loss of ground seems not to have produced any feeling of ultimate defeat in the Scots, and, once the height of the crisis was over, they reacted with resilience and imagination to the chaos caused by the break-up of the balanced harmony of their institutions. The ruling idea was to re-establish the system on a new and perhaps sounder basis, by rallying the dissident factions round the educational system as that item above all others in the inheritance which divided the Scots least, and which thus might bridge the difference between Law and Church. In this way, it was hoped that the universities would assume responsibility for the nation's spiritual leadership in the room of the divided Church, and, in that capacity, achieve

the practical reaffirmation of the moral ideals of Scottish life in
a form appropriate to the nineteenth century.

Grudgingly endorsed in the Universities (Scotland)
Act of 1858 by a suspicious Parliament, this experiment in
national revival through education depended on a sagacious
combination of practicability and of principles which stood
in silent but emphatic contrast to the corresponding usages
in the South. In a reaffirmation of the genuinely democratic
character of the universities, every effort was made to develop
the traditional Scottish machinery designed to neutralise
the inequalities of scholastic and family backgrounds.
Junior classes, in which the Professor himself might teach
the elements, enabled the intellectually gifted to 'catch up',
and matriculation at sixteen and earlier was sometimes a
counteractive to the counter-democratic influence of the sixth
form. In this way, careers were opened to talents, scientific
as well as philological, in accordance with the spirit of the
nineteenth century, but, at the same time, lest this selection
and fostering of talents would produce a flood of one-sided
experts and bureaucratic specialists, general studies of a non-
utilitarian kind were given pride of place in the curriculum,
and, as in France, the path alike to science and to literature lay
through compulsory philosophy.

Statistics as well as legends bear out the relative success
of this programme of democratic intellectuality. But, from
the first, difficulties were created for the project by Scotland's
subordinate rôle in the United Kingdom, and in particular the
Union parliament, though sanctioning the experiment, gave little
financial or moral support to ideals so un-English as these. No
doubt, it was up to the Scots to press for fair treatment, but,
unfortunately, in a situation which called for concerted national
action, Scottish initiative was paralysed by a new intensification
of the nationwide sectarian strife, and in fact it was by this
time depressingly clear that this imaginative scheme of rallying
the country round its educational institutions and ideals was
having the effect not of resolving the stresses and strains of
Scottish society but merely of shifting them into the University
faculties, and above all into the philosophy classrooms, as into
the heart and centre of the nation's culture. No doubt, these
continuing dissensions impaired the academic routine less than
was sometimes alleged, but they made a bad impression over
the border, providing the Parliamentary parties unsympathetic

to Scotland with the opportunity they had long been waiting
for. In this way, recovery within less than twenty years
turned into ruin, and just as the crisis of a generation before
saw the loss to the Scots of their privileges in banking and
in finance, so too in this crisis of the 'seventies, they found
themselves suddenly deprived of their cherished autonomy in
education. Control of the system of state-schools passed into
the hands of the English board and an authoritative Royal
Commission decreed the reorganisation of the Universities
as specialist institutions on the model of London or of
Redbrick, and it began to look as if the end of the century
would see the effective abolition of the whole distinctive
Union system, especially as this educational onslaught was
contemporaneously seconded by a forceful Parliamentary
campaign in the religious sector, aimed at reducing the
Scottish establishment to a position comparable to southern
non-conformity.

*　　*　　*

In the Victorian Age Scottish intellectualism was eclipsed. The
deliberate break with the national cultural heritage occurred not
only in the spheres of Scottish philosophy and of pedagogical
method. On the contrary, it can easily be shown that in all the
chief departments of formal education – mathematical, classical
and scientific – there was an analogous abandonment of an
inheritance, and that, throughout most of the cultural field,
distinctively national ideals were played down in the interests of
uniformity, and the old traditions of democratic intellectualism
were discouraged in favour of social expediency.

*　　*　　*

It is our belief, however, that the conventions governing
Scottish teaching were at least as normal and reasonable as
the very different conventions governing teaching in England,
and at least as fruitful in promoting contributions to the
various branches of learning. Indeed, the primary object of
the following glimpses of mathematics, science and classics
is to restore life and meaning to the dimming legend of the
'Metaphysical Scotland' of 'the lads o' pairts'. At the same
time, however, we hope to give a credible and clear account
of the tortuous, dark revolution whereby a nation noted
educationally both for social mobility and for fixity of first

principle gradually reconciled itself to an alien system in
which principles traditionally did not matter and a rigid social
immobilism was the accepted thing.

        *   *   *

The democratic intellectualism which had distinguished
Scottish civilisation was being allowed to disappear and the
peculiar polymathic values it supported were, increasingly, at a
discount among the cultural leaders.

        *   *   *

There had been a failure of intellectual nerve among the Scots,
and the educated class of the new century, though still loyal
enough to inherited principles in a quiet way, had become
increasingly chary of public demonstrations of national
pretensions to intellectual independence.

GEORGE ELDER DAVIE, *The Democratic
Intellect*. Edinburgh, 1961, pp. xv–xviii,
105–6, 336–7

Dr Robert McIntyre won the SNP's first parliamentary seat at a by-election
in Motherwell in April 1945. From that time the party gathered momentum.
It won sixty-nine seats in the local government elections in 1967 and in
November of the same year Winnie Ewing overturned a large Labour majority
to win Hamilton with 46 per cent of the vote. The emphasis of her campaign
was on the need to return Scotland to normality like any other country:
'Stop the world, I want to get on.' The discovery of oil in Scottish waters
encouraged further support for the SNP which doubled its share of the vote
in each successive General Election between 1966 and 1974.

These events persuaded both the Conservatives and Labour that they
had to take the Scottish issue seriously. At the Conference of the Scottish
Conservative Party in Perth on 18th May 1968, Edward Heath, then Leader
of the Opposition, made the so-called Declaration of Perth. This pledged the
Conservatives to the establishment of an elected Scottish Assembly to sit in
Scotland as a single chamber and 'take part in legislation in conjunction with
Parliament'. Their policy changed three times in three years from an indirect
assembly, then no assembly and then to Heath's directly elected assembly.
The Conservatives won the election in 1970, but took no steps to implement
the Perth undertaking; but, in appearance at least, Heath's policy remained
in force for some years. Six months after Margaret Thatcher won the election
in October 1974 she said in a speech in Glasgow that 'an assembly must be a

top priority to ensure more decisions are taken in Scotland for Scotsmen'.
For a time all the major parties professed support for a Scottish Assembly
or Parliament.

Margaret Thatcher, the lady 'not for turning' did a U-turn on this. In
December 1976, during the debate on Labour's Scotland Act on devolution
she opposed the second reading. Two of her front-bench spokesmen, Alick
Buchanan-Smith and Malcolm Rifkind, resigned their appointments. Rifkind
explained why he supported a Scottish Assembly:

(10.12)   'A Legal System without a Legislation'

> Throughout the 270 years of Union, Scotland has required –
> and here it is very different from Wales – separate legislation
> throughout the whole sphere of domestic matters. This is
> a major anomaly, which the British Parliament has accepted
> because it has no alternative. It is an anomaly which has not
> always worked entirely to the advantage of Scotland because
> as a result of the requirements of a separate legal system,
> the British Parliament was unable to meet fully the need
> for modernising, reforming and improving the legal system.
> Scotland is the only territory on the face of the earth which has
> a legal system without a legislature to improve, modernise and
> amend it . . .
>
> There are other distinctive Scottish characteristics as
> well. Throughout the 18th and 19th centuries Scotland was
> governed in a different way from the rest of Britain, with
> different administrative powers, different local government
> and a different structure of education. In 1885 a Scottish
> Secretary was appointed, and in the 1920's he was elevated to
> Secretary of State. In the 1930's the Scottish Office was sent
> lock, stock and barrel to Edinburgh. All this administrative
> devolution was done by Conservative Governments, and it was
> not done out of a feeling of national sentiment, but because
> of the administrative requirements needed to achieve good
> government for the Scottish people.
>
> It may be asked why, if we had this enormous devolution
> and if Parliament, with a unitary system, is able to respond
> to the distinct needs of Scotland, this should not continue. It
> may be asked why, with a separate legal system and a separate
> Scottish Office, it is necessary to go any further and establish
> a directly elected assembly. The answer is that throughout the
> last 270 years a dynamic change has taken place. This is not

because the people have changed their minds but because of
the increasing complexity of government, requiring more and
more administrative devolution, and more powers to be given
to the Scottish Office.

We have now a Secretary of State for Scotland who is for
all practical purposes a Scottish Prime Minister. He covers a
Department the equivalent of which in Wales and England
is served by eight or nine Ministries. He has one Department,
and Scottish Members are expected to scrutinise his actions.
The Scottish Office has more civil servants than the European
Commission ... There has been a qualitative change in the
call for devolution. In the late 20th century the demand
for a separate Scottish legislature was the result of national
sentiment. That national sentiment still exists, but added to it
is the need for good government, good administration and a
better deal for Scottish people in the United Kingdom.

> Quoted by Sir David Steel in his 'Town and
> Gown' lecture. University of Strathclyde,
> November, 1991

The response of the Labour Party to the challenge of the SNP was equally
tormented. Shortly after Hugh Gaitskell became leader of the party he told
the Scottish Conference that devolution was an irrelevance. In September
1958, a special Scottish conference of the party in Scotland rejected Home
Rule, for the first time, and this remained their policy for the next sixteen
years. In 1968 the Government of Harold Wilson resorted to the familiar
tactic to delay awkward decisions by setting up a Royal Commission to
consider the constitutional question, first under Lord Crowther and then
under Lord Kilbrandon. They reported in October 1973. The following are
paragraphs from their summary of conclusions in a long detailed report:

(10.13)   The Kilbrandon Report

National feeling (Chapter 10)
(13) In Scotland and Wales dissatisfaction with government has
      an added dimension of national feeling. In Scotland the
      emphasis is largely placed on economic considerations; in
      Wales, while the economic factor is important, it is closely
      associated with a desire to preserve the Welsh language
      and culture (paragraphs 325–335).
(14) New political initiatives have been taken, but have not

succeeded in raising the prosperity of Scotland and
Wales to the desired level. In these circumstances
political nationalism has grown and put down stronger
roots (paragraphs 336–337).

(15) In neither Scotland nor Wales has the nationalist cause
attracted support anything like sufficient to constitute
a general vote for independence; but it has provided a
means for the people of Scotland and Wales to register
their feeling of national identity, and has focused
attention on the desire for changes in the system of
government which would acknowledge their separate
identities and special interests (paragraphs 339–356).

The background to our conclusions (Chapter 23)

(170) Devolution could do much to reduce discontent
with the system of government. It would counter
over-centralisation and, to a lesser extent, strengthen
democracy; in Scotland and Wales it would be a
response to national feeling (paragraph 1102).

Scotland and Wales (Chapter 24)

(173) Our preferred schemes all provide for the establishment
of Scottish and Welsh assemblies directly elected by the
single transferable vote system of proportional representation for a fixed term of four years (paragraphs 1116–1122).

The Kilbrandon Report, HMSO, 1973

The Labour Party leadership in Scotland was still reluctant to make any move
to return to a policy of Home Rule, or devolution, as it was now usually called.
In June 1974 a meeting of the Scottish Executive (which was poorly attended
because it coincided with a match between Scotland and Yugoslavia in the
football World Cup) rejected all five options in a Labour White Paper on
devolution. The London leadership regarded this as electoral suicide and
they secured a vote in favour of devolution at a special conference in August
1974. This has remained the official policy. At a General Election in October
1974 the SNP won 30 per cent of the vote and eleven seats and was in second
place in forty-two others.

Meanwhile, the Scottish situation continued to be analysed in books
and articles. One of the most notable of these was a book by H.J. Paton,
The Claim of Scotland, published in 1968. Paton had been a member of the
British delegation at the peace conference in 1919, Professor of Logic at
Glasgow and of Moral Philosophy at Oxford. He said that this book was

one that had to be written to protest against a centralising Government which, 'almost absent-mindedly, was destroying by stages everything which is distinctive of Scotland and has been the source of her greatness'. These are the concluding pages:

(10.14)   The Claim of Scotland

What Scotland wants and needs is genuine, and not bogus, autonomy. If hope of this is continually deferred, if interference from London becomes ever more extensive and more arbitrary, and if as a result Scotland appears to be going down hill and to be losing her national identity and her national pride, it is not surprising that some Scotsmen should begin to talk about independence. What is surprising is that this talk is so limited.

The high hopes raised by the signing of the Covenant in 1949 were smothered by well-tried methods of procrastination with the help of a Royal Commission. Since then London interference in Scottish affairs has steadily and insidiously increased: even the Scottish system of education is being knocked about to fit in with the latest innovations from the South. It is hardly surprising if the demand for independence has become stronger in Scotland, as also in Wales, and has won increasing support in Parliamentary elections.

This is the only kind of argument that English politicians cannot entirely ignore; but they try to sweep it aside as a 'protest' vote – generally against the Party to which they do not themselves belong. They are strangely reluctant to open their eyes to the truth and to see that it is a protest against both the main political Parties and against the London misgovernment which they practise and defend. The first reaction to the success of National Parties is to dismiss their policies, not merely as folly, but as 'criminal' folly. But abuse is not a substitute for argument. If there has been any criminal folly, it has been displayed by successive British Governments which have closed their ears to the most just and moderate claims.

The case argued throughout this book is that the ideal solution would be to have a complete federal system like that of the U.S.A., where the separate States have equality in the Senate as well as full representation in Congress. If this is impossible, as so many think, the next best solution would be to set up subordinate national parliaments with real, and not illusory, control over their own affairs. If this too is resolutely ruled out, what is left open to Scotsmen and Welshmen except to seek for independence? If reasonable Englishmen would only begin to try to understand the situation, it would be far better for everybody concerned.

There is a heavy burden of proof on those who assert that no matter what Scotland may desire, she is not entitled to the independence freely acknowledged as the common right of all other nations in the world. The burden is all the greater since Scotland entered freely into the Union with England and may reasonably claim that she has a further, and very special, right to leave it in equal freedom – a right certainly not weakened because the predominant partner has so often ignored the conditions of the Union. The Scots, like other reasonable men, may not insist on exercising all their acknowledged rights; but the brash denial of these rights might easily produce a different attitude. The topic of rights is one which reasonable Englishmen would do well to avoid. Their concern should rather be to remove the grievances from which Scotland suffers and to meet the demands which have been put forward with such moderation.

Again, it would be unconvincing to argue that whatever be the theoretical rights of Scotland, she is in practice incapable of independence. Scotsmen are not unacquainted with what happens in comparable sister countries in Europe, and especially in Scandinavia. They can see how well these countries manage their own affairs, how competent and progressive and trig they are, and how they grow richer rather than poorer even without the natural advantages which Scotland enjoys. They may even ask themselves how many Norwegians – whose standard of living has recently become higher than that of Britain – would wish to go back to their former dependence on Stockholm. It must carry little conviction to assert that Scotsmen alone could never manage their own country without some benevolent stranger breathing down their necks and supervising their every movement.

It is sometimes argued that an independent Scotland would have less influence on world affairs. This too is hardly plausible. At present she has no such influence – not even in matters that concern her deeply, such as the three-mile limit for territorial waters, where a tiny independent country like Iceland is able to defend her own interests. No one could

argue seriously that Eire has less influence in world affairs than
she had before she broke away.

It may seem more plausible to say that an independent
Scotland could not defend herself against external enemies.
This argument might have had some weight in the past, but
to-day it applies to Scotland no more than it does to all
independent European countries. We are all in the same boat,
and – if I may mix the metaphor – our safety depends on the
American nuclear umbrella. Furthermore there is no reason
whatever to suppose that an independent Scotland within
the Commonwealth would be unable or unwilling to enter
into the closest possible co-operation with England in all
matters concerned with defence. It might even be hoped that
the independence of Scotland could be a first step towards a
genuine British federation or confederation, or at least a close
defensive alliance, which Ireland too might be willing to join
on a footing of equality.

Perhaps the strongest argument for independence is that
without a change of heart in England modest measures of
self-government, even if they were permitted, could never cure
the ills from which Scotland suffers. The central government
would still be too strong, and English nationalism is so deeply
engrained that the interests of Scotland would always be
sacrificed to the real or imaginary interests of England. The sad
facts of history lend only too much support to this contention;
and even to-day the habit of deriding all Scottish claims
without any attempt to understand them is enough to make
some Scotsmen despair of any solution short of independence.
Is it too much to hope that our English brothers might at long
last develop a truly British patriotism which would regard
Britain as something more than an England possessed of a few
recalcitrant provinces not yet completely assimilated? England
has long enjoyed the most loyal partnership any nation has
ever had. If she still regards Scotland with suspicion and
distrust, is it not time that we should kiss and part?

Our discussion of Scotland's right to independence
is obviously incomplete, but it was necessary in order to
get the situation into perspective. It may help to show how
moderate and reasonable are the claims I have put forward
for a generous measure of self-government and to dispose of
the belief that they are manifestly crazy. It may also serve to
remind us that there can be many degrees of self-government

between a subordinate parliament on the Ulster model and the full-blown independence of Ireland.

A final plea

Throughout this chapter, and throughout this book, I have sought to present the claim of Scotland as essentially an appeal to right and reason. In so doing, I hope I have not seemed to set forth Scottish patriotism as if it were something remote and academic. Genuine patriotism is more like being in love: it has its roots deep in the hearts of men. Yet even a man in love is not precluded from giving rational answers to amiable or officious busybodies who seek to place obstacles in his way.

It is sometimes imagined that those who seek self-government for Scotland must hate the English as individuals. This is a profound mistake. Even if the greatest of modern Scottish poets has listed Anglophobia as his recreation, there may be in this an undercurrent of dry humour; and in any case there is no accounting for the ways of genius. If I have given any impression of sharing such a view I have failed in my object. From many long-standing personal friendships I know the best kind of Englishmen to be among the wisest and most just of men as well as the most charming. What I should like them to do is to direct their wisdom and justice to the plight of Scotland. She is in greater danger now than she was at Bannockburn because she has fewer means of defence.

If in the course of this plea for Scotland I have fallen into errors of details, I regret it; but in matters so complex and so changing some error is inevitable. I have tried to give a picture of the Scottish case as a whole, and this picture I believe to be substantially correct.

If I have shown bias and unfairness and occasional irritation, this too I regret; but it is hard not to feel some emotion as one examines the raw deal given to Scotland in the past and in the present; and for any one accustomed to civilised discussion it is difficult not to become irritated when her claim is dismissed off hand with a minimum of thought and an insufferable air of superiority. I could even forgive myself a little unfairness if it would help to sting some of our English brothers out of a complacent lack of interest which is the source of half our troubles. As to bias, it would require a very great deal of Scottish bias to counterbalance the amount of bias on the other side.

I have not attempted to put forward a detailed plan for a parliamentary and administrative system suited to modern conditions in Scotland, but for this I make no apology. Such plans have been drawn up, and readers may be referred for one example to the Memorandum of Evidence submitted by the Scottish Covenant Association to the Royal Commission on Scottish Affairs and published separately by the Hanover Press in March, 1953, under the title *The Case for Scottish Devolution*. My own aim has been only to describe, however roughly, the present problem and to outline the principles necessary for its solution. It is this problem that requires first of all to be understood. Once it is agreed that Scotland, if she so desires, should have a legislature for her own affairs, the time would come to discuss detailed proposals, and these would have to be made acceptable to a British government determined that English interests, real or supposed, would be given at least their just weight. Any kind of Scottish parliament, provided it had some real power, would to my mind be better than none; for in it the voice of Scotland could no longer be muffled and smothered, and it would be impossible to maintain that nobody knew what Scotland really wanted. This by itself would be an immense gain. No sensible man can suppose that all the ills of Scotland would immediately be cured, but at least she would have the possibility of taking an initiative denied to her at present, and the effects of this in every walk of life might be far-reaching indeed. What is so devastating is the feeling that she is at the mercy of events wholly beyond her control and is unable to develop naturally in her own distinctive way.

The claims of Scotland, so often dismissed as irrational, are fundamentally an appeal to reason and to common sense or common justice. Sometimes it may seem that this is why they receive so little attention. It almost looks as if British governments will yield only to violence, or at least to non-violent disobedience to the law: Ireland and Ulster and the suffragettes and Cyprus and India are cases in point. Amid all the Scottish discontents there have been extraordinarily few outbreaks of this kind – the defacing of some pillar boxes, the 'lifting' of a Scottish stone from Westminster Abbey, a couple of misguided Scottish students imprisoned, not because they did anything destructive, but because they were found in possession of explosives alleged to have been supplied by the

police. The bogey of a Scottish Republican Army comparable
to the I.R.A. never had any basis in fact. Intemperate language
may have been used by some agitators, but the Scots are a
law-abiding race and could not even under great provocation
take to the shooting which won Ireland her freedom. They
still retain a pathetic belief that the voice of reason may be
listened to even in the United Kingdom. Is it too much to ask
that our English brothers should be wise and generous enough
to understand?

Perhaps I may be allowed to end by adopting as my own
the words of a private letter sent to me by one of the wisest
men in Scotland – Sir Thomas Taylor, Principal of Aberdeen
University – shortly before his untimely death.

'Personally I am so sick of the mess that is being made of
my native country that I should be glad of anything that would
arouse contention and even passion, rather than that things
should be allowed to slide.'

H.J. PATON, *The Claim of Scotland*. London,
1968, pp. 267–72

John P. Mackintosh taught history at the Universities of Glasgow and
Edinburgh and was Professor of Politics at Strathclyde and Edinburgh.
In 1966 he was elected the Labour Member of Parliament for Berwick
and East Lothian. He was one of the most respected intellectuals in the
Scottish Labour Party and a leading advocate for devolution. His early
death in 1978, in the words of Chambers's *Scottish Biographical Dictionary*
'removed a major force in the Labour attempt to bridge the counterpulls
of unionism and nationalism'. Towards the end of his life he was moving
close to the position of the SNP, as he revealed in a long article, 'The New
Appeal of Nationalism', published in the *New Statesman* of 27th September
1974. This is his conclusion:

(10.15)   The Moment of Conversion

Starting from a low or almost negligible level, the SNP
proceeded to double its support at every general election.
And the bulk of this support came not for specific reasons,
not because voters wanted anything as precise as a Scottish
Parliament or the revenues from North Sea oil (though both of
these appeals have helped). The support came because a series
of events in the world and in the United Kingdom made the

British side of the dual nationality less and less attractive till
finally considerable numbers, for the first time for 200 years,
began to doubt whether it was worth preserving at all.

This decline in the self-esteem and self-confidence of
the British is something with which we are all familiar. There
was the evident slide from being a world power during the
war and even in the post-war years to the level of the major
European power. Britain had so many Commonwealth and
overseas interests that Anthony Eden could not see the
country relegated to the status of a mere European power in
1958 when the Common Market was formed. Soon after, we
were asking for permission to join, only to be rebuffed. Then
the question was whether Britain would be a liability to the
new Europe; we sank behind France and Germany as European
powers and now Chancellor Schmidt says he is too busy to
waste his time on 'the misery of England and Italy'.

And this process of decline has come home to people as
Britain has sought to achieve the same growth levels as the
EEC powers and has failed. One balance of payments crisis
has followed another, economic targets have been missed
and now the forecasts are that Britain in the 1980s will have
fallen behind till her standard of living is no higher than that of
Greece or Spain.

A once strong imperial power, Britain has not merely
abandoned almost all of its colonies but failed where the
Israelis later succeeded in an invasion of Suez in 1956. A
handful of white Rhodesians defied the Government in the late
1960s and it seemed as if all Britain could do was recapture the
island of Anguilla from some non-existent Mafia elements. In
general a gloom hangs over the country, a sense of failure. In
England, this has led to a lack of faith in both major political
parties and a massive swing in 1974 to the Liberals, and this
despite the nagging doubt that they have no answer to the
country's problems, that their chief merit is that they have not
yet had the opportunity to fail in office.

In Scotland, there is no such problem. With the dual
nationality, there is a simple alternative if the pride in being
British wanes; just be Scottish. It is an 'opt out' solution which
allows each person to imagine the kind of alternative to the
disappointment of being British which he or she wants. For
businessmen, such as Sir Hugh Fraser, an independent Scotland
would be less trade union dominated than the UK. For others,

self-government would mean no balance of payments problem and therefore more rapid growth and lower taxation. For internationalists, Scotland could at least take her place in the European Community after the English had insisted on burying their collective heads in the sand. For those who dislike EEC policies, Scotland could stand on its own like Norway proud and unsullied outside any such amorphous conglomerations. For the extreme Left, Scotland could achieve socialism easier than an England dominated by the multinationals and the City of London. In general, there is a sense of untapped energy and unused human resources; at least this is an available and cheering alternative which has not been tried and found wanting.

For all these reasons a point comes at different times with different individuals when they suddenly wonder if this nationalist idea which they have first ignored and then belittled does not make some sense after all. The precise moment and issue when this reaction occurs varies with the person concerned. For me, it came at an international conference when I had just heard a middle-ranking minister explain the present Government's position. He said that Britain must unilaterally rearrange the Treaty of Accession to the Common Market which had recently been ratified by Parliament. Britain was going to be much poorer than had been anticipated and could not afford her budgetary contributions. Other concessions were also needed. Till these were granted, Britain would continue to boycott the European Parliament and, if the concessions were not adequate, then the Treaty might have to be breached. My feeling of shame deepened with every word and when the chairman turned and asked me to speak, almost involuntarily, I found myself saying: 'I am from Scotland and I must dissociate myself from all that you have just heard.' As I left, the Parisian taxi driver said: 'From your accent, I gather you are not French – where do you come from?' Again, I found myself saying, 'Scotland.' 'Ah,' he replied, 'I hear it is a beautiful country with brave people; what a pity you have to cross England to get here.' I could not but agree.

So nationalism is making converts in many places for many reasons. It is the answer to so many of the present discontents. One must hand it to the SNP that their challenge is the central issue of this election in Scotland. They have

forced the other parties to fight on ground chosen by the SNP:
namely, what can these parties do for Scotland? And anything
that they suggest will always be inadequate, be it more
regional economic advantages or assemblies or a percentage
of oil revenues; it will all be inadequate so long as there is
no proper pride in being British. Only one thing will halt or
reverse the onward march of the SNP and that is a period of
government in London which is really successful so that it
ends with a satisfied electorate eager to vote positively for a
party that has once again restored the feeling that Britain is a
successful, worthwhile country to belong to for those who do
have other places where they can go and other traditions and
titles to which they can turn.

JOHN P. MACKINTOSH, 'The New Appeal
of Nationalism' in the *New Statesman* of
24th September 1974

Mackintosh's point about the decline of British power and relative prosperity
and the loss of Empire is, of course, one of the main reasons why the
relationship between Scotland and England has changed. In the 19th Century
the Union was acceptable to the Scots because it meant partnership with a
prosperous and powerful England in the Empire. Now that the Empire has
disappeared, so has the justification for the Union. As David Marquand has
said: 'Imperial Britain *was* Britain ... Empire was not an optional extra for
the British; it was their reason for being British as opposed to English or
Scots or Welsh. Deprived of Empire and plunged into Europe, "Britain" had
no meaning.'[1]

A book by an American sociologist, Michael Hechter, *Internal Colonialism*,
was published in 1975. This analysed the relationship from the 16th Century
to the present between England and the 'Celtic fringe', as he called Scotland,
Wales and Ireland. Hechter made specific what many people in Scotland had
long suspected, that there was a relationship between the denigration of the
'fringe' cultures and political domination and economic exploitation. Also,
that this process was carried out largely through the voluntary co-operation
of élites in the fringe countries for their own self-interest. This point in
particular hit home. Since the 18th Century we have been familiar with
Scots who do exactly this, either because they have been educated in
England, admire English wealth and power, or simply think English ways are
more fashionable and a requirement for social and economic advancement.
Hechter's conclusions were very similar to those of Franz Fanon about France
and the French colonies. They were subsequently explored in the Scottish

context by Craig Beveridge and Ronald Turnbull in their book, *The Eclipse of Scottish Culture* (1989):

(10.16)   The Denigration of Indigenous Culture

One of the defining characteristics of the colonial situation is that it must involve the interaction of at least two cultures – that of the conquering metropolitan élite (cosmopolitan culture) and of the indigenes (native culture) – and that the former is promulgated by the colonial authorities as being vastly superior for the realization of universal ends: salvation in one age; industrialization in another. One of the consequences of this denigration of indigenous culture is to undermine the native's will to resist the colonial régime. If he is defined as barbarian, perhaps he should try to reform himself by becoming more cosmopolitan. Failure to win high position within the colonial structure tends to be blamed on personal inadequacy, rather than any particular shortcomings of the system itself. The native's internalization of the colonist's view of him makes the realization of social control less problematic. Conversely, the renaissance of indigenous culture implies a serious threat to continued colonial domination.

It is evident that the mere fact of political incorporation substantially affected the course of development in the Celtic fringe by contributing to its economic, cultural, and political dependence. This can be seen with particular clarity in the economic sphere. Throughout the period, the English market was both relatively larger and wealthier than that of the Celtic regions, taken singly or in the aggregate. This initial difference became greatly magnified over time. Political incorporation also had a decisive effect on the progress of anglicization, which proceeded not only by government fiat, but through the voluntary assimilation of peripheral élites. Finally, by removing the locus of authority from the Celtic regions to London, incorporation stimulated apathy and corruption in the peripheral polities.

MICHAEL HECHTER, *Internal Colonialism*.
London, 1975, pp. 73, 80–1

Tom Nairn's influential book, *The Break-Up of Britain*, was published in 1977. From a different point of view, he reached a similar conclusion to Davie

and Hechter about Scotland in the 19th Century. Davie called it a failure
of intellectual nerve and Hechter a voluntary assimilation of an élite. Nairn
called it self-emasculation:

(10.17)   Self-Emasculation

It was not unusual for Empires to try and exploit the more
picturesque and *Völkisch* sides of their provinces, to pander
to petty local vanities and precious traditions (particularly
military ones). The Hapsburgs and Romanovs used the
technique for centuries, and Bismarck raised it to a new pitch
of perfection in Germany. What is remarkable in the Scottish
case is its success and solidity, and the degree to which
it was self-administered. Gramsci used a story, 'The Fable
of the Beaver', to illustrate the acquiescence of the Italian
bourgeoisie in fascism: 'The beaver, pursued by trappers who
want his testicles from which medicinal drugs can be extracted,
to save his life tears off his own testicles ... Why was there
no defence? Because the parties had little sense of human or
political dignity? But such factors are not natural phenomena,
deficiencies inherent in a people as permanent characteristics.
They are "historical facts", whose explanation is to be found in
past history and in the social conditions of the present ...'
      Adapting the fable to our argument one might say: in
the 19th century the Scottish bourgeoisie could hardly help
becoming conscious of its inherited *cojones* to some extent,
its capacity for nationalism; but this consciousness conflicted
with its real, economic interests in an unusual fashion, it was
forced to – at least – repress or 'sublimate' the impulse itself.
The emasculation was not enforced by gendarmes and Regius
Professors from London (this kind of treatment was reserved
for Gaels). It was a kind of self-imposed, very successful
Kulturkampf, one which naturally appears as 'neurosis' in
relation to standard models of development. Because of its
success the elements of 'pathology' inherent in it have become
embedded as modern 'national traits'; but these are not really
the natural phenomena, dating back to some Caledonian
Original Sin, which people feel them to be. As 'historical facts',
their *main* explanation is certainly to be located in the modern
era itself – that is, in the last century or so, up to the present.
      Let us consider some of the historical facts most relevant
to the phenomenon. During the age of nationalism it has

come to be taken for granted that the distinctively modern consciousness of nationality is 'natural': people are naturally, instinctively, national*ists* (and not merely aware of being different from other folk). But in reality nationalism was a historical construct, associated with certain social strata, at a certain characteristic period of their development. Amongst these, none was more important than the intelligentsia. The new commercial and industrial middle class was indisputably the dominant force in the process; yet the way this dominance was exerted – the form of their class hegemony – owed its character to new intellectuals. It was the latter who formulated the new ideologies that were needed, and manned the first new societies, parties and other organizations. It was they who, initially, enabled the bourgeoisie to 'enlarge its class sphere technically and ideologically', and so 'pose itself as an organism ... capable of absorbing the entire society', etc. By accomplishing this task, the intellectuals also won for themselves a new and greater social significance: no longer the servants of a closed aristocratic élite, they became vital elements in the cohesion of society as a whole.

Nationalism was the most important and effective of such new ideologies. Normally it developed through a recognizable number of phases, over several generations, in all those territories where new middle classes felt that tolerable 'development' for their people was impossible without rapid mobilization of their own resources and rejection of 'alien rule'. Normally, too, this process was a revolutionary one – whether or not it ever resulted in a successful *coup d'état* – in the sense that it meant trying to get rid of a non-adaptable landlord *ancien régime*, its 'reactionary' intellectual caste, corrupt and non-populist 'traditions', and so on. One may say that during this long period, over most of Europe, the standard function of an intellectual class was in this task. This is of course not to maintain that all intellectuals were xenophobes or flag-wavers. But the centre of gravity of their rôle *as* a class, their collective definition within modern social conditions, lay in the way they educated one folk or another.

In Scotland, the intelligentsia was deprived of this typical 'nationalist' rôle. Its new intellectual strata were to be, in a sense, unemployed on their home terrain. There was no call for the usual services. Here, the old régime and its intellectuals had crumbled away without firing a shot: they

were overwhelmed by the burgeoning growth of the Scottish
Industrial Revolution and the new entrepreneurial bourgeoisie
linked to it. No prolonged cultural subversion was required
to pull down its bastions. William Ferguson notes 'The decline
of the specifically Scottish intellectualism which throughout
the 18th century had without conscious effort sustained
the concept of a Scottish nation'. This decline was not to be
counterpointed by the rise of a new 'specifically Scottish'
culture, less intellectualist and more romantic, advancing the
new concept of nationality appropriate to the age.

Clearly, the country did not cease to produce individual
intellectuals from its own separate and quite advanced
educational system. The point is simply that they could not
constitute any longer a coherent, national 'class', in a sense
which it is quite hard to define but easy to recognize. The fact
was emphasized, rather than disproved, by the well-known
prominence of so many Victorian Scots in fields like medicine,
engineering, and the natural sciences. As Ferguson comments
again: 'The reputation won by Scotsmen in science ... did little
to enhance the culture of their country. This is far from being a
singular case, for science stands independent of national contexts
... For good or ill, therefore, science cannot nurture the irrational
bonds that make nations.' Irrational bonds: this overstates the
case, and concedes too much to German-romantic theories of
nationalism. The bonds are non-rational and non-intellectual,
rather than those of unreason. But the underlying point is valid:
a 'national culture', in that sense which had become newly
important, entailed an intellectual class able to express the
particular realities of a country, in a romantic manner accessible
to growing numbers of the reading public – a class operating
actively in the zone of general and literary culture (rather than
the specializations Scots became celebrated for).

The relationship between civil society and State in
Scotland precluded a fully national culture in this sense.
Instead, what it led to was a strange sort of sub-national
culture. An anomalous historical situation could not engender
a 'normal' culture: Scotland could not simply be adapted
to the new, basically nationalist, rules of cultural evolution.
But since the country could not help being affected by this
evolution, it produced something like a stunted, caricatural
version of it. The best title for this is perhaps 'cultural sub-
nationalism'. It was cultural, because of course it could not be

political; on the other hand this culture could not be straight-
forwardly nationalist either – a direct substitute for political
action, like (e.g.) so much Polish literature of the 19th century.
It could only be 'sub-nationalist', in the sense of venting its
national content in various crooked ways – neurotically, so to
speak, rather than directly.

Among the numerous strands in the neurosis, two are
especially prominent: cultural emigration, and the Kailyard
School. As we shall see, the two phenomena are in fact (and
contrary to appearances) closely connected. And they are
connected in a way which permits one to focus much more
clearly upon the significant popular-cultural reality underlying
both of them: vulgar tartanry.

In the most authoritative study of the Scottish 19th
century cultural scene, David Craig remarks: 'The historian is
left calling Victorian culture in Scotland "strangely rootless"
... We have to recognize that there did not emerge along with
modern Scotland a mature, "all-round" literature....' Later,
he ascribes this surprising 'void' in culture to intellectual
emigration: 'During the 19th century the country was emptied
of the *majority* of its notable literary talents – men who, if
they had stayed, might have thought to mediate their wisdom
through the rendering of specifically Scottish experience. Of
the leading British "sages" of the time an astonishingly high
proportion were of Scottish extraction – the Mills, Macaulay,
Carlyle, Ruskin, Gladstone.' Unemployable in their own
country, these and many later émigrés quite naturally found
themselves a function in the development of English culture.
For England was a milieu *par excellence* of just that 'mature,
allround' and literary thought-world Craig refers to. It was
an organic or 'rooted' national-romantic culture, in which
literature – from Coleridge and Carlyle up to F.R. Leavis and
E.P. Thompson – has consistently played a major role.

The rootless vacuum, the great 'absence', the 'cultural
schizophrenia' William Ferguson mentions in a similar context:
these are metaphors, which in turn invite decipherment. What
was the actual presence they denote, in Scotland – the books
they wrote and read, the thoughts they had, and so on? They
did not ponder mightily and movingly upon the reality of 19th
century Scotland – on the great Glasgow bourgeoisie of mid-
century and onwards, the new class conflicts, the continuing
tragedy of the Highlands. So what was there, instead of those

missing Zolas and George Eliots, those absent Thomas Manns
and Vergas? What there was increasingly from the 1820s
onwards, until it became a vast tide washing into the present
day, was the Scots 'Kailyard' tradition.

TOM NAIRN, *The Break-Up of Britain*.
London, 1977, pp. 152–7

The renaissance of the 1880s and 90s and its revival after the First World
War were a conscious reaction to the comparative decline in Scottish
self-confidence in the mid–19th Century. Culturally there has been an
unmistakable recovery of nerve and substantial achievement in many directions. This has been accompanied by a marked change in political attitudes
but, so far, aspirations towards self-determination have been frustrated.

Under the Labour Government of Jim Callaghan the Scotland Act was
finally adopted by the House of Commons in February 1978. This provided
for the establishment of a Scottish Assembly with powers only over certain
internal matters and financed by a block grant from the UK Treasury. To
satisfy opposition within the Labour Party this was to be subjected to a
referendum, requiring a 'Yes' vote by 40 per cent, not of those voting but of
all entitled to vote. This was a unique requirement in the whole of English,
Scottish and British parliamentary history. In every other decision a majority
of one of those voting had been sufficient. The 40 per cent of the electoral list
meant in effect that those who could not or did not vote, the dead, the ill,
the absent on business or holiday, as well as those hesitant or unsure were
effectively voting 'No'. If 40 per cent was not reached the Act required the
Government to lay before the House an order for its repeal.

The Referendum was held on 1st March 1979. 62.9 per cent of the
electorate voted, 51.6 per cent 'Yes' and 48.4 per cent 'No'. The 'Yes' vote
was 32.9 per cent of the electorate. Since every opinion poll on the subject
for decades had shown 75 per cent to 80 per cent in favour of a Scottish
Parliament this was a poor result. There were many reasons for this. It was a
Labour measure and, after the 'winter of discontent', Labour popularity was
at a low ebb. Their organisation in Scotland campaigned only half-heartedly
and three of their prominent members, Robin Cook, Tam Dalyell and Brian
Wilson led a vigorous 'No' campaign. The 'Yes' campaign was well funded
by the Conservative Party and commercial companies, but the 'No' side
had no such resources. The Conservatives confused the issue by saying
that they were not against devolution in principle but only against this
particular measure. They promised the immediate calling of a constitutional
conference, if the Referendum did not succeed. Perhaps the most damaging
factor of all was a television broadcast by Alec Douglas-Home, the former

Conservative Prime Minister who was widely respected in Scotland. He argued for a 'No' vote on the grounds that the Conservatives would introduce a better Act for an Assembly with greater powers, including the right to raise its own taxes.

Shortly after the Referendum, the Conservative Government of Margaret Thatcher came to power in the election of May 1979. The Scotland Act was repealed, but neither the Constitutional Conference nor the better Act ever appeared.

One of the reasons why the British parties tend to forget about Scotland or to misunderstand the issues is that the London press and media pay very little attention to them. George Orwell, who was of Scottish descent and spent more than two years in Jura towards the end of his life, commented on this in his column in *Tribune* on 14 February 1947:

(10.18)   The Scottish Case

> Up to date the Scottish Nationalist movement seems to have gone almost unnoticed in England. To take the nearest example to hand, I don't remember having seen it mentioned in *Tribune*, except occasionally in book reviews. It is true that it is a small movement, but it could grow, because there is a basis for it. In this country I don't think it is enough realised – I myself had no idea of it until a few years ago – that Scotland has a case against England. On economic grounds it may not be a very strong case. In the past, certainly, we have plundered Scotland shamefully, but whether it is *now* true that England as a whole exploits Scotland as a whole, and that Scotland would be better off if fully autonomous, is another question. The point is that many Scottish people, often quite moderate in outlook, are beginning to think about autonomy and to feel that they are pushed into an inferior position. They have a good deal of reason. In some areas, at any rate, Scotland is almost an occupied country. You have an English or anglicised upper class, and a Scottish working class which speaks with a markedly different accent, or even, part of the time, in a different language. This is a more dangerous kind of class division than any now existing in England. Given favourable circumstances it might develop in an ugly way, and the fact that there was a progressive Labour Government in London might not make much difference ...

> GEORGE ORWELL, *Collected Essays*. London,
> 1968, vol. 4, pp. 284–5

CHAPTER ELEVEN

The 20th Century after the Referendum of 1979

There is no doubt that the failure of the Scotland Act was a serious setback to the aspirations for Scottish self-government. It was a Labour measure, but the SNP took the blame. They had been the most energetic campaigners for a 'Yes' vote and were associated in the public mind with moves towards Scottish autonomy. In the election of May 1979, the SNP were reduced to 17.3 per cent of the vote and two seats. Since it has always been the pressure of support for the SNP which has spurred other parties to move in this direction, interest in the whole question of constitutional change in Scotland fell off the agenda. For some years the Conservative Government simply refused to regard it as an issue.

But there were others who refused to let it die. In particular a cross-party organisation, the Campaign for a Scottish Assembly (changed later for a Parliament) struggled to keep the aspiration alive. After many public meetings and conferences, and consultations with the political parties, they decided to work for a Constitutional Convention. They appointed a Steering Committee to study the whole question and make recommendations. Sir Robert Grieve was appointed Chairman and Jim Ross Secretary and there were fourteen other members. They reported in July 1988 in *A Claim of Right for Scotland*, a deliberate reference to the previous claims in 1689 and 1841 which were earlier responses to misgovernment (3.4 and 9.2).

Here I must declare an involvement. I was a member of this Committee and I was working on my book on Andrew Fletcher at the time. I had been writing about the Claim of Right of 1689 and I suggested that this would be an appropriate title for our report. It was largely drafted by Jim Ross, a retired civil servant of the Scottish Office who had worked on the Scotland Act. He was a long-standing member of the Labour Party and he had an exceptional ability to translate the discussion round the table into words acceptable to all of us.

The report was described by Neal Ascherson in the *Observer* of 31st July 1988 as 'the most penetrating constitutional critique of the United Kingdom I have read in this decade'. It makes detailed recommendations about how a Constitutional Convention could be set up and how it might work, but the opening section and the Epilogue deal with more general questions:

(11.1)

The 3rd Claim of Right, 1988

Part I
THE NEED FOR CHANGE IN SCOTTISH GOVERNMENT

1 Introduction

1.1 We were appointed because, in the opinion of Campaign for a Scottish Assembly, Parliamentary government under the present British constitution had failed Scotland and more than Parliamentary action was needed to redeem the failure. We share that view and in this report set out what we consider must be done if the health of Scottish government is to be restored.

1.2 Our direct concern is with Scotland only, but the failure to provide good government for Scotland is a product not merely of faulty British policy in relation to Scotland, but of fundamental flaws in the British constitution. We have identified these and pointed out their relevance to the problems of Scotland. They do not, however, afflict Scotland only. So far from giving Scotland an advantage over others, rectifying these defects would improve the government of the whole of the United Kingdom, more particularly those parts of it outside the London metropolitan belt.

1.3 In this report we frequently use the word 'English' where the word 'British' is conventionally used. We believe this clarifies many issues which the customary language of British government obscures. Although the government of the United Kingdom rests nominally with a 'British' Parliament, it is impossible to trace in the history or procedures of that Parliament any constitutional influence other than an English one. Scots are apt to bridle when 'Britain' is referred to as 'England'. But there is a fundamental truth in this nomenclature which Scots ought to recognise – and from which they ought to draw appropriate conclusions.

1.4   We do not wish to create ill-will between Scots and
        English. But our report must be based on a clear
        understanding of the motor forces of the 'British'
        State, the allocation of power within it, and the effects
        of these forces and that power on Scotland. That
        understanding can best begin with some essentials of
        Scottish history.

2 The Past: essential facts of Scottish History

2.1   Much ink is wasted on the question whether the Scots
        are a nation. Of course they are. They were both a
        nation and a state until 1707. The state was wound up
        by a Treaty which clearly recognised the nation and
        its right to distinctive government in a fundamental
        range of home affairs. The fact that institutional forms,
        however empty, reflecting these distinctions have been
        preserved to the present day demonstrates that no-one
        in British government has dared to suggest openly
        that the nation no longer exists or that the case for
        distinctiveness has now disappeared.

2.2   Scottish nationhood does not rest on constitutional
        history alone. It is supported by a culture reaching
        back over centuries and bearing European comparison
        in depth and quality, nourished from a relatively early
        stage by an education system once remarkable by
        European standards. Since the Union, the strength of
        that culture has fluctuated but there is no ground for
        any claim that, overall or even at any particular time,
        it has benefited from the Union. On the contrary the
        Union has always been, and remains, a threat to the
        survival of a distinctive culture in Scotland.

2.3   The international zenith reached by that culture in the
        late eighteenth century is sometimes facilely attributed
        to the Union, but that leaves for explanation the
        subsequent decline of the culture as the Union became
        more established. No doubt some benefit was derived
        from the relatively settled state of Scotland at the time.
        More, probably, stemmed from the minimal interference
        of London in Scottish affairs in those days. But the roots
        of that philosophical, literary and scientific flowering

lay in the social soil of Scotland itself and its long-established cross-fertilisation with mainland Europe.

2.4　That cross-fertilisation diminished as the pull of London increased and the effects of the removal of important stimuli to Scottish confidence and self respect were felt. In mid-nineteenth century Scottish culture eroded and became inward-looking in consequence. It has struggled with mixed success to revive as Scots realised what they were in danger of losing. The twentieth century, up to and including the present day, has been a period of extraordinary fertility in all fields of the Scottish arts; literature, visual and dramatic arts, music, traditional crafts, philosophic and historical studies. In particular the indigenous languages of Scotland, Gaelic and Scots, are being revived in education, the arts and social life. We think it no accident that this trend has accompanied an increasingly vigorous demand for a Scottish say in Scotland's government.

2.5　The nation was not conquered but it did not freely agree to the Union of the Parliaments in 1707. We need not go into the details of the negotiations about the Union. What is beyond dispute is that the main impetus for Union came from the English and it was brought about for English reasons of state. Likewise, the form of Union was not what the Scots would have chosen but what the English were prepared to concede. However, the considerable guarantees which Scots won in the Treaty of Union reflected the fact that, until the Treaty was implemented, they had a Parliament of their own to speak for them.

2.6　The matters on which the Treaty guaranteed the Scots their own institutions and policies represented the bulk of civil life and government at the time; the Church, the Law and Education. However, there was never any mechanism for enforcing respect for the terms of the Treaty of Union. Many of its major provisions have been violated, and its spirit has never affected the huge areas of government which have evolved since. The say of Scotland in its own government has diminished, is diminishing and ought to be increased.

2.7   The forms of Scottish autonomy which, until recently,
        had multiplied for almost a century are misleading. The
        Scottish Office can be distinguished from a Whitehall
        Department only in the sense that it is not physically
        located in Whitehall (and much of its most important
        work is done in Whitehall). The Secretary of State
        may be either Scotland's man in the Cabinet or the
        Cabinet's man in Scotland, but in the last resort he is
        invariably the latter. Today, he can be little else, since
        he must impose on Scotland policies against which an
        overwhelming majority of Scots have voted.

2.8   The apparent strengthening of Scottish institutions
        of government since 1885; the creation of a Secretary
        of State, the enlargement of the functions of the
        Scottish Office, the extension of Scottish Parliamentary
        Committees; has been accompanied by an increasing
        centralisation and standardisation of British government
        practice which has more than offset any decentrali-
        sation of administrative units.

3 The Present, and the Future being forced upon us

3.1   Scotland has a team of Ministers and an administration
        who are supposed to exist in order to provide Scotland
        with distinctive government according to Scottish
        wishes in those fields of British government which affect
        Scotland only. They cannot possibly do so.

3.2   The creation of these offices and procedures was a sop
        to Scottish discontent, not a response to Scottish needs.
        The team of Ministers is chosen from whichever political
        party has won a British general election. That election
        must be fought on British, not Scottish, issues. The Scots
        cannot concentrate on Scottish issues when casting their
        votes, but must simultaneously reflect their opinions
        on such matters as foreign policy, defence, the EEC, and
        Northern Ireland. So far as the Scots vote for United
        Kingdom parties, these parties will themselves regard
        Scottish issues as subsidiary to the winning of British
        votes. At present, the Scots cannot vote for other than
        a UK party without implying a vote for independence.
        And the political arithmetic of the United Kingdom

means that the Scots are constantly exposed to the risk of having matters of concern only to them prescribed by a government against which they have voted not narrowly but overwhelmingly. Yet Scottish Ministers and the Scottish administration must implement these policies, even where their implementation affects only Scotland.

3.3   Scottish Ministers and the Scottish Office are not the only parts of the special machinery of current Scottish government. But the other parts are no more effective.

3.4   There is a Scottish Grand Committee for general debate of Scottish issues in Parliament; there are Scottish Standing Committees for detailed consideration of Scottish legislation; and there used to be a Select Committee on Scottish Affairs to scrutinise the working of Government policy in Scotland.

3.5   The Scottish Grand Committee rarely votes. Its debates have no effect except so far as the Government chooses to pay attention to them and its agenda is subject to Government manipulation. The Scottish Standing Committees operate only when the Government chooses to handle Scottish legislation separately. If it prefers to combine Scottish legislation with English, it can usually find an excuse for doing so. And if need be, Scottish Standing Committees can be filled out with English members. The Select Committee on Scottish Affairs must have a Government majority, no matter how slight a minority the Government may be in Scotland.

3.6   Even this unsuitable and inadequate 'government' of Scotland is no longer working. There is a constitutional flaw in the present machinery of Scottish government: it can work only within a limited range of election results. Providing a Scottish Ministerial team, Scottish Whips and Government representation on Standing and Select Committees, requires a certain minimum number of Government party MPs from Scottish constituencies. There is no guarantee of such a number being elected.

3.7   At present the governing party is below the minimum

and there is no certainty that this situation will be short-lived. As a result, we have no Select Committee on Scottish Affairs, so Government policy in Scotland is not subject to the scrutiny thought necessary elsewhere. And the use of the other elements of Scottish Parliamentary procedures is being minimised.

3.8   We are not aware of any other instance, at least in what is regarded as the democratic world, of a territory which has a distinctive corpus of law and an acknowledged right to distinctive policies but yet has no body expressly elected to safeguard and supervise these. The existing machinery of Scottish government is an attempt either to create an illusion or to achieve the impossible.

3.9   In that attempt it was bound to fail eventually and the failure can no longer be hidden. The choice of adhering to present Scottish government is not available. Either we advance to an Assembly, or we retreat to the point at which Scottish institutions are an empty shell and Scottish government is, in practice, indistinguishable from that of any English region. The latter process has already begun.

3.10   So far as Scottish Ministers and the Scottish Office have a real, as distinct from an illusory, purpose it is merely to solicit for Scotland a larger share of what the British Government of the day thinks Scotland ought to want. Even when this soliciting succeeds, it regularly fails to produce what Scotland wants and there can be little confidence that it produces what Scotland needs. It is also invidious within the United Kingdom. It arouses the jealousy of English regions and it concentrates Scottish attention on lobbying in London rather than initiating in Scotland. It creates the very dependency culture of which the present Government professes to disapprove.

3.11   Because of the constitutional flaws long latent in Scottish government, also because it is now imagined elsewhere that Scotland has an unfair advantage, Scottish government as developed over the last century is being rapidly eroded. It cannot be preserved. It must be rejuvenated or it will fade away.

4 The English Constitution – an Illusion of Democracy

4.1   The English constitution provides for only one source
        of power; the Crown-in-Parliament. That one source is
        now mainly embodied in the Prime Minister, who has
        appropriated almost all the royal prerogatives. She/he
        appoints Ministers who, with rare exceptions, can be
        dismissed at will, and has further formidable powers of
        patronage. Because of Party discipline and the personal
        ambition of members the consequence is that, so far
        from Parliament controlling the Executive (which is the
        constitutional theory), it is the Prime Minister as head
        of the Executive who controls Parliament.

4.2   Historically, the power of Parliament evolved as a
        means of curbing the arbitrary power of Monarchs. We
        have now reached the point where the Prime Minister
        has in practice a degree of arbitrary power few, if
        any, English and no Scottish Monarchs have rivalled.
        Yet he or she still hides behind the fiction of royal
        sanction and the pretence of deference to Parliament
        to give legitimacy to a concentration of power without
        parallel in western society. The American constitution
        was framed largely with a view to making such a
        development impossible. Even the centralised and
        Executive-biassed French constitution distributes power,
        demonstrated by the recent balance between the
        President and Prime Minister there.

4.3   Every feature of the English constitution, every right
        the citizen has, can be changed by a simple majority
        of this subordinated Parliament. That applies even to
        the requirement to hold Parliamentary elections every
        five years – or at all. It applies to the very existence
        of Parliament, with no more than minor delaying
        qualifications.

4.4   As a product of these constitutional facts, Parliamentary
        procedures are subject to heavy pressure to conform
        with Government convenience and rest on the tacit
        assumption that the primary purpose of Parliament is to
        facilitate Government business. The power of dissolving
        Parliament has largely passed to the Prime Minister who,
        with rare exceptions, can manipulate it both to benefit

and to control her/his party. In fact, if not in theory,
the Prime Minister is Head of State, Chief Executive and
Chief Legislator, and while in office is not circumscribed
by any clear or binding constitutional limitations.
Against all this there is in the United Kingdom not a
single alternative source of secure constitutional power
at any level.

4.5   This unique concentration of power is reinforced by
a voting system which has always been commended
as yielding strong government. In the English case,
a system which already gives government excessive
power adds to that power through the voting system.
Specifically, a large majority of the electorate may have
voted against the Prime Minister wielding the enormous
powers described above, supported by a crushing
Parliamentary majority.

4.6   The effects on Scotland now can be statistically measured.
In the last election, political parties expressing the
intention of creating a Scottish Assembly won 57% of
the United Kingdom votes cast and 76% of the Scottish
votes cast. In spite of which there is currently a Prime
Minister dedicated to preventing the creation of a
Scottish Assembly and equipped, within the terms of
the English constitution, with overwhelming powers to
frustrate opposition to her aims.

4.7   It is sometimes said that Scotland cannot complain
when it is governed by a Party which is in a minority
in Scotland, since the same can happen to England. In
marginal cases, where voters in England are almost
equally divided between Parties, there may be something
in this point. But there is no possibility of England
ever being governed by a Party which had won only a
seventh of the seats and a quarter of the votes there.

4.8   It would be wrong to isolate any one of the above
features. Any one of them might be tolerable without
the others. Taken together they represent an indulgence
to Party dogma and a hazard to human rights, in
particular to the rights of minorities. Within the United
Kingdom the Scots are a minority which cannot ever
feel secure under a constitution which, in effect, renders

the Treaty of Union a contradiction in terms, because it makes no provision for the safeguarding of any rights or guarantees and does not even require a majority of the electorate to override such rights and guarantees as may once have been offered.

4.9   Some may argue that all the above is irrelevant because the Scots had a referendum on the Assembly issue in 1979 and failed to vote for it. That is a misrepresentation on three counts. First, by the criteria of British general elections, which are regarded by British Governments as justifying policy and constitutional changes of every kind and magnitude, the Scots did vote for an Assembly in 1979 but were refused it. Secondly, during the referendum campaign, the Conservative Party promised that, in the event of a 'No' vote, it would propose a constitutional conference to consider the improvement of the government of Scotland. The implications of the negative votes, let alone the abstentions, are therefore suspect. Thirdly, no referendum is forever. All current evidence suggests that the demand for an Assembly is now much stronger.

Epilogue

Scotland faces a crisis of identity and survival. It is now being governed without consent and subject to the declared intention of having imposed upon it a radical change of outlook and behaviour pattern which it shows no sign of wanting. All questions as to whether consent should be a part of Government are brushed aside. The comments of Adam Smith are put to uses which would have astonished him, Scottish history is selectively distorted and the Scots are told that their votes are lying; that they secretly love what they constantly vote against.

Scotland is not alone in suffering from the absence of consent in Government. The problem afflicts the United Kingdom as a whole. We have a Government which openly boasts its contempt for consensus and a constitution which allows it to demonstrate that contempt in practice. But Scotland is unique both in its title to complain and in its awareness of what is being done to it.

None of this has anything to do with the merits or demerits of particular policies at particular times, or with the degree of conviction with which people believe in these policies. Many a conviction politician, contemptuous of democracy, has done some marginal good in passing. Mussolini allegedly made the Italian trains run on time. The crucial questions are power and consent; making power accountable and setting limits to what can be done without general consent.

These questions will not be adequately answered in the United Kingdom until the concentration of power that masquerades as 'the Crown-in-Parliament' has been broken up. Government can be carried on with consent only through a system of checks and balances capable of restraining those who lack a sense of restraint. Stripping away the power of politicians outside Whitehall (and incidentally increasing the powers of Ministers inside Whitehall) restores power not to the people but to the powerful. The choice we are promised in consequence will in practice be the choice the powerful choose to offer us. Through effectively answerable representative institutions we can edit the choices for ourselves.

Whether Government interferes unnecessarily or fails to interfere where it should, political institutions answerable alike to consumers and producers, rich and poor, provide the means of correcting it. If these institutions are removed, restricted or censored, Governments do not get accurate messages – or can ignore any messages they do not like. If past conduct of politics has given cause for complaint, the answer is to open up and improve politics to give more accurate messages sooner, not to close politics down so that the few remaining politicians can invent the messages for themselves.

It is a sign of both the fraudulence and the fragility of the English constitution that representative bodies and their activities, the lifeblood of government by consent, can be systematically closed down by a minority Westminster Government without there being any constitutional means of even giving them pause for thought. It is the ultimate condemnation of that constitution that so many people, in Scotland and beyond, have recently been searching in the House of Lords for the last remnants of British democracy.

Scotland, if it is to remain Scotland, can no longer live with such a constitution and has nothing to hope for from it. Scots have shown it more tolerance than it deserves. They must now show enterprise by starting the reform of their own Government. They have the opportunity, in the process, to start the reform of the English constitution; to serve as the grit in the oyster which produces the pearl.

It is a mistake to suppose, as some who realise the defects of our present form of Government do, that the route to reform must lie through simultaneous reorganisation of the Government of all parts of the United Kingdom. That will lead merely to many further years of talk and an uncertain prospect of action. Tidiness of system is a minor consideration. The United Kingdom has been an anomaly from its inception and is a glaring anomaly now.

It is unrealistic to argue that the improvement of government must be prevented if it cannot be fitted within some preconceived symmetry. New anomalies that force people to think are far more likely to be constructive than impossible ambitions to eliminate anomaly.

Even if Scots had greater hopes than they have of voting into office a Party more sympathetic to the needs of Scotland, it would be against the long-term interests of Scotland to offer credibility to the existing constitution. There is no need for Scots to feel selfish in undermining it. They can confidently challenge others to defend it.

We are under no illusions about the seriousness of what we recommend. Contesting the authority of established government is not a light matter. We would not recommend it if we did not feel that British Government has so decayed that there is little hope of its being reformed within the framework of its traditional procedures. Setting up a Scottish Constitutional Convention and subsequently establishing a Scottish Assembly cannot by themselves achieve the essential reforms of British Government, but they are essential if any remnant of distinctive Scottish Government is to be saved, and they could create the groundswell necessary to set the British reform process on its way.

The Constitutional Convention proposed in this report was duly established by the Members of Parliament and Councillors of the Labour and Liberal Democrat Parties, the Trade Unions, Churches and other bodies. At their first meeting on 30th March 1989 they signed the following document, confusingly also called A Claim of Right for Scotland:

(11.2)   # The 4th Claim of Right, 1989

We, gathered as the Scottish Constitutional Convention, do hereby acknowledge the sovereign right of the Scottish people to determine the form of Government best suited to their needs, and do hereby declare and pledge that in all our actions and deliberations their interests shall be paramount.

We further declare and pledge that our actions and deliberations shall be directed to the following ends:

To agree a scheme for an Assembly or Parliament for Scotland;

To mobilise Scottish opinion and ensure the approval of the Scottish people for that scheme; and

To assert the right of the Scottish people to secure the implementation of that scheme.

A Claim of Right for Scotland, Edinburgh,
1989

That declaration is a rejection of the English doctrine that sovereignty rests at Westminster. It is also in contradiction to Tony Blair's statement that Labour's devolution proposals would leave the sovereignty of Westminster intact.

In August 1988 Jim Sillars published a pamphlet, *No Turning Back: The Case for Scottish Independence within the European Community*. The policy of 'Independence in Europe' was approved by the Conference of the SNP in September:

(11.3)   Member State Status a Priority Objective

For Scots the question is whether we shall participate in the new debate about Europe's future? I argue that we must, because whatever future is created for Europe is our future too. Do we as a small northern nation, speaking as a nation and not as a region in London's domain, have anything positive to contribute? I believe we do. We may indeed have been part of the British Empire, but we have avoided the hangover from that period which has so deeply affected, and flawed, English policy towards Europe and the international community.

The Scots are far from a perfect people. But our national life has exhibited certain traits which do supply the basis upon which we can contribute effectively to a debate about how we and our partners live and work in harmony. If the European Community is to progress and face some of its pressing difficulties, then there must be a spirit of give and take. There must be an ability to put aside self-interest for the sake of others. There has to be a capacity to care about other peoples. There has to be the sense of being part of a wider humanity. There has to be a strong impulse towards an internationalist view of the world.

I believe those positive qualities required to advance the European Community along a road of co-operation and a growing sense of co-responsibility, are to be found among the Scottish people. Whereas Mrs Thatcher and Neil Kinnock bask in the glory of looking after the narrow British interest, the Scots shrink in shame if accused of such an outlook when setting out their own causes for complaint within the common market of Britain.

Tell someone from the South-East that he or she is talking like a British nationalist and the reply will be 'So, what's wrong with that?' Tell a Scot that he or she is narrowly nationalistic and we feel guilty, because there is a strong internationalist element in our make-up. I noticed that when Mrs Thatcher addressed the General Assembly of the Church of Scotland, and gave them a distorted history lesson on the great figures of the Scottish Enlightenment, that she avoided (or was ignorant of) the role of Burns in that period, and the profound mark his cry for internationalism has left upon the Scottish character.

The Scots nation has the qualities to help build the new Europe, but it cannot do so from the position of a region whose views do not register with the larger unit to which we are currently yoked. Scottish internationalism is blocked by England's narrow mentality, which stereotypes and then derides our partners in Europe. In our present lowly status we can contribute little to the development of the Community. Our wider vision and international outlook has no stage upon which to bring its influence.

This pamphlet argues that the European Community matters now to Scotland, and will matter more in future because its power will surely increase at the expense of Westminster and all other nation state parliaments.

It argues that it is the height of irresponsibility for the Scots to sit back and let others make decisions which will affect us, and that it is immoral to stand back from a political process where men and women of goodwill are trying to mend the fractures which weaken Europe and weld together a strong but civilised economic and political entity able to increase the prosperity of its peoples, and act constructively in world affairs.

This pamphlet argues that only by seeking independence within the European Community – internal independence – can Scotland play a full role and thus fulfil our obligations, not only to the people who will inherit this nation after the present generation has gone, but to our fellow European citizens with whom we share the Community.

As later parts will demonstrate, it is in Scotland's self-interest to demand the internal independence here advocated. But it would be a betrayal of the internationalist outlook about which we have always been so proud, if self-interest alone was the motivation for changing our constitutional and political status for the better. Scotland can gain more from Europe through internal independence. But Scotland can also contribute more. For too long, the Scots have been cast

in a fringe or, at best, provincial role, which we have played
to perfection. Our political life reflects that reality. Scottish
Questions in the House of Commons concentrates solely on
domestic issues which, important as they are, are only part of
the world in which we live. The Scottish Grand Committee is
a more eloquent version of the parochial Scottish Question
Time, and in no debate about Scotland on the floor of the
Commons have our representatives lifted their eyes above the
level of Carter Bar.

This obsession with local matters retards Scottish political
development. We are spectators and not players when the
international community grapples with the problems and big
issues that shape and mould the world in which we live. We
are cut off from and play no part in the events and institutions
through which the world fashions its international legal order.
Great issues of principle which come to determine the conduct
of states pass us by, for we have no part in their determination.
We are a lesser people because of this self-imposed isolation.

Because we cast ourselves in a lesser role, we think and
act at a lower level than we ought to. Not for us the great
initiatives taken by other small countries to facilitate the
tension-relaxing meetings of the great and potentially world-
destructive powers; or the important initiatives by such as the
Scandinavians in stimulating and then focusing world attention
and action upon threat to the global environment.

✽   ✽   ✽

A SHARP REMINDER ABOUT SEPARATISM

Some words in the political vocabulary carry a permanent
pejorative quality which, if attached to an idea or a party,
can prove a permanent handicap. 'Separatism' is one of those
words. It conjures up images of breaking something up, of
isolation, of turning away from others, of narrow-mindedness,
of unreasonable self-interest. It is the label which unionist
parties stuck upon the SNP as it rose to prominence in the
1960s and 1970s.

The SNP was never able to overcome the problem. It
was forced into ever more sophisticated rebuttals of the
separatist charge, but in a sense the more it explained the
more convincing the label appeared. After 1979 not much was

heard about separatism, but that was because the SNP faded. When next the party bursts through to a prominence which threatens London's hegemony, the separatist chorus will be heard again from both Labour and Tory.

Next time the charge will be that we are 'double separatists', seeking to break away from not only our large English market, but from the 323 million European market offered by the Community. No matter how well argued is our explanation of how Scotland should be able to negotiate a special deal for access of Scottish goods and services, we shall not escape the fatal gibe.

Those who say the withdrawal group want a double-take on separatism, and thus a double jeopardy for the Scottish economy, will have a powerful argument to buttress their claim. It is against the interests of the Community for it to break at the edges, and the economic and political power represented by its market of 323 million people would be deployed to the full in driving home to the Scots that leaving carries a penalty.

Against that reality, those arguing for withdrawal could only offer the speculation (some would say naive hope) that in the actual negotiations it would not be as bad as forecast, and that the Community would give us similar access benefits to those obtaining to full members. As industry after industry assessed its position, realising that the stability of current certainty was to give way to uncertainty which could end in being effectively locked out from their present European customers, the clamour against the double separatists would grow and grow.

It would be utter folly for the SNP to take a lead from those of our members who seek to maintain the option of withdrawal. We would be handing to the unionist parties a separatist stick with which they could beat to death the idea of Scottish independence.

EUROPE IN THE NEW WORLD ORDER: WHITHER SCOTLAND?

There is now under way one of the great shifts in world economic power and influence. Most were unaware of it in the 1960s and 1970s, but it is unmistakable in the 1980s. We are heading for the century of the Pacific, and this is underlined by the fact that consistently over these past few years, the United

States has done more trade with Pacific countries than with
Europe. That did not happen before. On the Pacific rim of S.E.
Asia the economic growth in some countries is of the order of
8–11 per cent per year.

We have entered the technological era in which people
with intellectual power, energy and drive are the vital resource
that fuels growth. Whereas Europe has an ageing population,
whose energy is waning, the countries on the Pacific rim
have a high proportion of young people able to seize the
opportunities offered by the new technologies.

That does not mean that all is lost for Europe. Our relative
position will change, but we still have built-in advantages of
technical traditions and political stability, with benefits still
to be had from the creation of a single market. Europe is not
heading for an economic abyss, but it does face new world
challenges to its industry, its economic strength relative to
others, and, as a consequence, its political influence in world
affairs.

The great sea change in economic power distribution
to which I refer cannot be reversed. Indeed it should be
welcomed by internationalists, because a world more evenly
balanced in terms of economic power is likely to be a more
stable one politically. We should also be happy to see peoples
who have been traditionally poor and exploited creating an
indigenous strength, reaching new levels of independence, and
growing in prosperity.

Scotland cannot avoid the consequences of these changes.
The issue for us is a three part one, whether we shall face the
new world as a debilitated EC region devoid of influence,
whether we shall be an integral and influential part of its
substantial whole through member state status, or whether
we shall try to swim alone, nominally independent of all
major trade/economic groupings while in reality being heavily
dependent upon their attitude to us.

WE CANNOT LEAVE SCOTLAND DANGEROUSLY EXPOSED

Strangely, both the British unionists and the Scottish withdrawal
group, while advancing different views, would leave us in the
same dangerously exposed position.

The British unionists would keep Scotland as she is, or at
best with an Assembly for domestic affairs which would have

no direct say in the development of Community policy. They would keep us firmly on the fringe, away from the power and decision centres. Others would decide for us, and we would do their bidding.

If it were to be successful, the withdrawal option would see our industry, which sells 80 per cent of its products into the Community, deprived of access as of right to that large market; the benefits of and access to the vast technological research and development which European industry and governments are capable of launching and sustaining would not be available in anything like its present form; our financial institutions would be permanently locked out of Europe when they are so excellently placed to expand within it.

Scotland's future is now inextricably bound up with the European Community, and the Community's future will be decided by how its peoples, governments, and institutions respond to the new world economic developments. Scots are part of its peoples, but we have no government that represents our unique viewpoint on collective policy, and our institutions reflect our provincial status, pleaders who have no governmental power base within the Council or Commission on which to operate. That weak condition is what we have to alter.

The policy of internal independence, that is member state status, should become a priority objective of the whole Scottish nation, and the centrepiece of SNP policy.

Independence within Europe destroys, at a stroke, the separatist gibe about breaking away, disrupting relations, going off into isolation. But it has far more attraction than simply supplying a negative answer to a negative set of concepts.

Internal independence has positive benefits. The translation of Scotland from province to member state will cause no problems for our industry, service sector, or trade union movement. For them there will be no dislocation: the free flow that is developing with their markets or, in the case of the trade unions, the increasing co-operation with fellow European trade unionists, will not be adversely affected. Indeed, their position would be enhanced.

Internal independence means elevating Scotland to a new political level of direct influence. It will place us in the centres of decision-making as of right. Our trade union movement, our industrialists, our financial community, the local authorities,

our farmers, and fishermen will have a government speaking
and acting for them directly.

To underline the difference that would make, one need
only refer to Ravenscraig and other plants that used to be the
Scottish steel industry. With Scotland only a region of the
United Kingdom, the Community has regarded Ravenscraig
as a peripheral part of the British steel industry, and in that
British context no special account could be taken of its vital
role in the Scottish economy. But were Scotland a member
state, our steel industry would no longer be an adjunct of
British steel. It would be recognised in Europe for what it is: a
national steel industry. No Community Commission or Council
of Ministers would dream of asking a member state to drive a
knife into the heart of its industrial base.

> JIM SILLARS, *No Turning Back: The Case*
> *for Scottish Independence within the European*
> *Community*. 1988, pp. 2–3, 6–9

Two months later Sillars overturned a Labour majority of 19,000 to win a
by-election for the SNP in Govan. As with Winnie Ewing's win at Hamilton
twenty-one years earlier, the effect was to give a revived urgency to
the constitutional issue. It was probably the reason why Labour, usually
suspicious of co-operation with other parties, decided to participate in the
Constitutional Convention. Together with the Liberal Democrats and the
other organisations they gradually evolved a joint policy for a devolved
Scottish Parliament elected by proportional representation. The SNP did
not participate. They had unhappy memories of the consequences of
campaigning for a Labour policy in the Referendum of 1979. In any case,
they could hardly support an organisation which said that its object was
not to annul the Union, but to strengthen it.

William McIlvanney is a distinguished novelist and also a penetrating
critic of the Scottish situation. In 1991 he published a collection of essays,
Surviving the Shipwreck. This is from the essay, 'The Shallowing of Scotland':

(11.4)   The Great Divide

For Scotland is one of the most intense talking-shops I have
ever been in. Here the Ancient Mariner haunts many pubs and
Socrates sometimes wears a bunnet, and women at bus-stops
say serious things about the world. The talk may touch on
anything from the essential Scottish sporting hero to politics.

But, in my experience, two common factors will tend to recur regardless of the subject under debate: the talk will at some point connect with non-material values and it will, frequently at the same time, challenge current social orthodoxies. There are reasons why this should be so.

Scotland was born poor. There are two main ways to react to poverty. One is to fall in love with money, since that is what you do not have. The other is to generate values beyond the economic, since otherwise you acknowledge your own inferiority unless you can acquire wealth. Scotland grew up with the potential to do both.

The country contained that implicit division within itself, like the internal striations in an apparently solid rock that only needed some natural calamity in order to become a fissure. Scotland's calamity came in 1707. The Act of Union made a separation in the nation that created a unique and confused historical legacy. The people were separated from their legislature. This meant that insofar as democratic government is the fulfilment of the people's will, Scots would be denied the means of self-government. Yet they retained the characteristics of a nation without the political identity of one.

This situation had one major side-effect. The Act of Union had not been brought about by the will of the people. It had been brought about by the will of a few entrepreneurial spirits. They traded in the sovereignty of Scotland for two gains: money in hand and the opportunity of advancement. That opportunity lay primarily in London. It was the rationalisation and consolidation of a trend that had begun with the removal of King James's court to England in 1603. The division in Scotland had become explicit. There was on the one side an Anglicised minority, a controlling establishment whose motivation was accepting the materialistic values that made sense of the English connection. There was, on the other side, a more radically Scottish majority whose motivation was the maintenance of a distinctly Scottish identity and for whom the cost of realising that motivation was adopting the deeper, non-materialistic values that were needed to make sense of their determined Scottishness.

The division has never been a clean one. Each side has infiltrated the other. The self-interest of the minority has often been tempered by the weight of community values ranged against it. The community values of the majority have often been compromised by the secession of greater or lesser numbers of Scots to the pursuit of materialism. That is why the Scots have been simultaneously both the furtherers of English materialism and imperialism and potentially its greatest subverters.

The results of this dichotomy, which had been fore-shadowed by the intensity of the Reformation in Scotland, were cultural as well as political. This ambiguity in the nation's sense of itself helps to explain why two major Scottish writers, who have achieved international reputations, have a status so dramatically different in their own country. Sir Walter Scott conquered Europe but he remains marginal to most Scots' sense of themselves. Robert Burns still represents Scottishness so effectively that he retains for many, even today, the authority of a talking icon.

But the greatest single effect of 1707, the year of the Great Divide in the Scottish psyche, has been felt continuously for nearly 300 years. You can take the people out of the parliament but you can't take the parliament out of the people. In that imaginary Scottish Parliament without powers that has been sitting in uninterrupted session for so long in some dark corner of Scotland's dream of itself, one brute fact has been re-enacted again and again: it is the majority who form the opposition, the minority the government.

That is a trauma-inducing state of affairs in a democracy. No wonder the Scottish psyche is a strange place. No wonder Scots are called argumentative. No wonder a union representative in Vancouver, an expatriate Scot, told me his union wouldn't allow him to speak on television because the sound of a Scottish accent in a political context sent householders off on a quick search for the Reds under their beds. If Scots have a long history of being agin the government, it isn't surprising. The government was never theirs. That was the shattering result of 1707: the majority of Scottish people were disenfranchised from their potential rights. They have not yet won them back. The Act of Union effectively put Scotland politically in a timelock, moved it aside out of the mainstream so that by the time universal suffrage arrived it couldn't mean as much as it might have. For Scots it was circumscribed by the events of 1707.

The growth of the British Labour Movement seemed to offer a way out of the impasse. Much of the movement's energy and most of its radicalism came from Scotland. The majority in permanent opposition had found a vehicle for their discontent. That vehicle has certainly carried the aspirations of the Scottish people forward, no matter how often it has stalled, but now it may have broken down completely.

WILLIAM MCILVANNEY, *Surviving the Shipwreck*. Edinburgh, 1991, pp. 138–9

In November 1991, David Steel gave the 'Town and Gown' lecture in the University of Strathclyde and took the need for constitutional reform as his theme:

(11.5)   The Undeniable Right of the Scots

It is clear that the whole panoply of Scottish democratic procedure through Westminster is not working. The lack of democratic accountability is beyond a joke. It has become a scandal.

When people talk about possible anomalies arising from the restoration of a Scottish parliament within the UK I acknowledge that there may be some, but they are as nothing compared with the unacceptable collapse of democratic accountability over the government of Scotland.

I mention all of this because the case for Scottish self-government is normally argued from a Scottish standpoint ignoring the equally forceful Westminster case for reform. The Scottish Constitutional Convention was correct to limit its remit to the Scottish case and the Scottish solution. To delve into the consequences for Westminster would have been beyond its remit, but speaking for myself I have no qualms about accepting both a reduction in Scottish MP numbers and in our voting powers on English legislation. We have had a Scottish Grand Committee for years, so what is wrong with an English Grand Committee performing a similar function? Nor can I shed tears at the possible disappearance of the post of Secretary of State for Scotland.

These are small sacrifices compared with the great gain of restoring control over our own government in Scotland. The English should be relieved at seeing the end of Scottish legislation in Westminster, freeing up the parliamentary timetable for other matters.

You would think that agreement on securing a Scottish parliament within the Union would not be too difficult to achieve. Successive opinion polls tell us that is what the great majority of Scots want to see.

In 1968 the leader of the Conservative Party in the so-called 'Declaration of Perth' committed the party to 'give the people of Scotland genuine participation in the making of decisions .. and we propose the creation of a Scottish elected Assembly'.

In a critical intervention in the 1979 referendum Lord Home said, 'I should hesitate to vote no if I did not think that the parties will keep the devolution issue at the top of their priorities.' Far from doing so, under Mrs Thatcher the Conservatives reneged on all promises, and they now tell us there is no option between accepting what we have now, or busting up the UK and going for total independence. Thus they avoid the inevitable pain of thought along with the Nationalists who are equally happy to accept such a one-dimensional confrontation.

Fortunately there are some sane voices among Conservatives and Nationalists who do not like this futile stance. Individuals have helped us consistently in the Convention, and the door remains open to their parties. It is not beyond the wit of man to devise an acceptable form of Scottish self-government. We have advocated a parliament with taxation powers. Our enemies interpret this as tax-increasing powers but they could just as well be tax-reducing powers. If Shetland Council could obtain a barrelage throughput levy on oil landed there a Scottish parliament would certainly have been able to achieve the same.

I want to encourage those Conservatives who support a rethink. Forget about a Royal Commission – we had one in the seventies which incidentally argued for a reduction in the number of Scottish MP's – and forget about some kind of senatorial talking shop. They should join us to refine and promote the Convention's scheme.

To Nationalists I would say: You can stick to your principles of total independence which only a minority of Scots support and still unite behind our scheme as what you would regard as a halfway house.

The curse of Scotland has been its internal divisions. But for these we would have seen a revision of the 1707 Act of

Union and the restoration of a Scottish parliament years ago. Now is a time for unity. I feel certain that we can secure this during the next parliament.

The Claim of Right pointed out that the matters on which Treaty of Union 'guaranteed the Scots their own institutions and policies represented the bulk of life and government at the time; the Church, the Law and Education. However there was never any mechanism for enforcing respect for the terms of the Treaty of Union. Many of its major provisions have been violated, and its spirit has never affected the huge areas of government which have evolved since.

'The say of Scotland in its own government has diminished, is diminishing and ought to be increased.'

That is the critical point round which we could all unite. In the words Sir Walter Scott wrote in *The Heart of Midlothian*: 'When we had a king and a chancellor and a parliament – men o' our ain – we could aye peeble them wi' stones when they werena guid bairns. But naebody's nails can reach the length o' Lunnon.'

It is difficult to understand on what logic the *right* of the Scottish people to determine their own future is denied by the present government. After all they extend that right to the people of Northern Ireland, not only in Border polls but most recently Article 10 of the Anglo/Irish Agreement refers to achieving 'devolution on a basis which secures widespread acceptance in Northern Ireland'. Moreover in 1982 the then Prime Minister enunciated a policy of doubtful constitutional validity when she declared that the wishes of the Falkland Islanders were 'paramount' – not that their interests had to be safeguarded, not that their view had to be consulted, but that the wishes of these 2000 people would in any discussion with the Argentine be paramount. That doctrine has led to expenditure since the end of the Falklands war of over £3000 million on various aspects of the 'Fortress Falklands' policy, far in excess of the wildest estimates of the cost of establishing self-determination for five million Scots.

Yet the constitutional claim of the right of the Scots to demand renegotiation of the terms and mechanisms of the 1707 Act of Union is undeniable. Even the English constitutional theorist Professor Dicey conceded that while legislative sovereignty was vested in parliament political

sovereignty lay with the people. The Lord President of the
Court of Session, the late Lord Cooper, in his celebrated 1953
judgement was quite specific about this:

'The principle of the unlimited sovereignty of Parliament
is a distinctively English principle which has no counterpart
in Scottish constitutional law ... Considering that the Union
legislation extinguished the Parliaments of Scotland and
England and replaced them by a new Parliament, I have
difficulty in seeing why it should have been supposed that the
new Parliament of Great Britain must inherit all the peculiar
characteristics of the English Parliament but none of the
Scottish Parliament, as if all that happened in 1707 was that
Scottish representatives were admitted to the Parliament of
England. This is not what was done.'

SIR DAVID STEEL, 'Town and Gown'
Lecture. University of Strathclyde,
November 1991

The General Election in April 1992 was another disappointment for the
supporters of Scottish self-government. It had been widely expected that
Labour would win in the United Kingdom as a whole and would therefore
be able to carry out its promise to legislate for a Scottish Parliament in its
first year of office; also that the SNP vote would rise to reflect the demand
for independence, which a poll in the *Scotsman* in January 1992 had put at
50 per cent; and that the Conservatives would probably lose all but one or
two of their seats in Scotland. The result was different. The Conservatives
retained control over the United Kingdom. In Scotland the Labour share
of the vote went down slightly, from 42.4 per cent to 39.0 per cent, but
they held forty-nine of the seventy-two seats. The SNP share of the vote
went up from 14 per cent to 21.5 per cent, but such are the vagaries
of the electoral system that this gave them only three seats. The Liberal
Democrats went down from 19.2 per cent to 13.1. per cent, but this gave
them nine seats. The Conservative vote actually rose slightly, from 24 per
cent to 25.7 per cent and this gave them eleven seats. During the campaign
John Major had made the defence of the Union a major issue. Since then
Conservatives have suggested that this was the reason why they did better
than anyone expected in Scotland. Probably the real reason is that Margaret
Thatcher had been so unpopular in Scotland that any successor was bound
to do better.

One of the most striking reactions to this result was a demonstration
of more than 25,000 people during the European Summit in Edinburgh

in December 1992. The following 'Democracy Declaration of Scotland', addressed to the heads of the European Governments, was adopted by acclamation and signed by the Labour Party, the Liberal Democrats and the Scottish National Party:

(11.6) The Right to National Self-Determination

A warm welcome to Scotland, one of Europe's oldest nations. The Edinburgh Summit is the latest event in a long history binding Scotland to its European neighbours.

Today we share with you a commitment to Europe's democratic future. Scotland's ancient Parliament was adjourned in 1707, before the birth of modern European democracy. Since that time Scotland has remained a nation with its own separate legal system and national institutions. Today the majority in Scotland demand the recall of our own Parliament as a modern and democratic body empowering all our citizens.

And yet you have come to a nation denied democracy by the present British government. At the April 1992 General Election in Britain, 75% of Scottish voters supported parties calling for a Scottish Parliament. A government that won only 25% of the Scottish vote, with only 11 out of 72 Scottish Members of Parliament, ignores this clear majority for constitutional change in Scotland.

This government now imposes its minority policies on Scotland through an executive Scottish Office with more civil servants than Brussels, yet with no Scottish legislature to examine or pass such policies. The people of Scotland face problems and opportunities which can best be dealt with by our own Scottish Parliament. We know of no other nation placed in such a predicament and you can surely understand why we are calling for a constitutional referendum to enable democratic renewal within our country.

We recognise that on the Summit Agenda is the issue of the definition and implementation of the principle of subsidiarity. Let it be brought to your attention that subsidiarity – decision-making at the level closest to the people concerned – is being denied to the people of Scotland by the British state. It limits subsidiarity to relations between London and Brussels and seeks to remain the most centralised state in the European Community.

For us, however, the claim to our Parliament is not a

matter to be left to interpretation but is ours of right – the
right of national self-determination. The central issue at stake
is that of sovereignty. The unwritten British constitution,
founded on the notion of the absolute sovereignty of the
Westminster Parliament, gives Scotland no constitutional right
of democratic control over its own affairs, let alone provides
the right of national self-determination or fundamental
individual rights for its citizens. This concept of sovereignty has
always been unacceptable to the Scots constitutional tradition
of limited government or popular sovereignty. Today, in the
modern world, it is no longer acceptable in practice to us.

Therefore we call upon the people of Europe and the
Government leaders at the Summit to recognise Scotland's
right to national self-determination – the right to our own
Parliament. We have voted for this right, we have asked for a
referendum – now we appeal to you to raise our claim with the
British Government as a matter of principle. We have now an
historic opportunity of a peaceful and democratic assertion of
our national right. There is no issue of violence or of ethnicity.
For us rights are a means as well as an end in itself. The
recognition of our right causes no harm to any other nation or
people. We invite the President of the European Parliament to
consider our case by meeting a representative delegation from
Scotland.

At the heart of our nation's history, at the centre of
Europe's future, lies rule by consent of the people. The call
of our times is that of democratic renewal. When the eyes of
the world are upon our capital, Edinburgh, we are confident
that the peoples and governments of Europe will recognise
the appeal of its host nation. We therefore raise our demand
without fear or favour – Scotland demands democracy.

Democracy Declaration of Scotland, December 1992

During the election campaign in 1992 the Conservative Prime Minister, John
Major, and Secretary of State for Scotland, Ian Lang, promised that they
would 'take stock' of the Scottish situation. The result of this approach is a
White Paper, *Scotland in the Union*, published in March 1993. This still refused
to move towards a Scottish Parliament. It did say that the Government
was committed to devolve decision-making power in Scotland, but the
Government meant this in their own ideological sense of decisions over
such personal matters as the purchase of a council house or the choice of

a school. It repeatedly emphasised that Scotland must be recognised as a nation. Very little practical change followed, but there is a distinct change in the tone of the language. Since Michael Forsyth became Secretary of State, he has gone further in this direction. He has deliberately invoked the symbols of Scottish nationality, even arranging for return of the Stone of Destiny, on St Andrew's Day, 1996. As Lindsay Paterson said in the Autumn 1996 issue of *Scottish Affairs*, 'we are all nationalists now', in a certain sense at least.

(11.7)　　　　　　　　　　# Taking Stock

9.1　The Government are deeply committed in principle to
the diffusion of power. In their drive to devolve more
decision-making power to Scotland and within Scotland,
the Government will continually seek ways of extending
choice and opportunity in such a way as to enable
the people of Scotland to have more say over their
own lives. Enabling Scots to have more real decision-
making power in their own hands is at the heart of the
Government's strategy for the future. The Government
wish to confer more real rights on ordinary Scots.

*　　*　　*

10.3　And if the Union is to flourish in the future a more
concerted recognition of Scotland's status as a nation
will be necessary. It should be a mark of Scotland's
self-confidence in her own status as a nation that she
shares her sovereignty with the other parts of the United
Kingdom. But the willingness to share that sovereignty
must never be taken for granted.

10.4　This White Paper indicates some of the ways in which
such recognition can be given. But there are others. For
example, there should be more acknowledgement from
all parts of the United Kingdom of the significance of the
major institutions of Scottish life – the legal system, the
professions, the Churches, the Universities, the learned
societies and the financial institutions – and of Scottish
cultural excellence and the arts. Scottish pride in these
should be shared by the rest of the United Kingdom and
their distinctive features should be promoted abroad.

10.5 Parliament in Westminster is the Parliament of the whole of the United Kingdom. It is at the heart of our democracy and its Members enjoy equal rights, regardless of which part of the United Kingdom they represent. The Government remains committed to ensuring that it is seen as fully a United Kingdom Parliament, reflecting in its composition, institutions and ceremonial, the diversity of the Kingdom's constituent parts.

10.6 We should not hesitate to create, when appropriate, new bodies to take account of the distinctive Scottish identity. Sometimes such organisations will be in the public sector, such as Scottish Natural Heritage. On other occasions they will belong to the private sector, such as Scottish Power. In either instance the case for establishing new Scottish institutions will be closely examined.

*   *   *

10.11 The people of Scotland rightly aspire to a special place for their country within the United Kingdom and throughout the wider world. At the same time they want their Scottishness to be recognised, understood and respected. The Union must be flexible enough to take account of this and to ensure that Scottish aspirations are met and distinctive Scottish qualities recognised. It is the Government's task to ensure this, and through the proposals in this White Paper the Government intend to achieve it.

Scotland in the Union: A Partnership for Good.
Edinburgh, HMSO, Cm2225, March 1993,
pp. 35, 38–9

Since the 1992 Election, Labour and the SNP have been so far ahead in the opinion polls and in European and local elections that Scottish politics seemed to be resolving into a straight fight between them, which means between devolution and independence. Presumably for this reason, the *Scotsman* and the BBC arranged the 'Great Debate' on 13th February 1995 between the two party leaders, George Robertson and Alex Salmond in the old Royal High School in Edinburgh, now known in anticipation, as New Parliament House. The opening statements in the debate follow:

(11.8)   The Great Debate, 13th February 1995

LESLEY RIDDOCH

Good evening and welcome to the 'Scotsman Great Debate' in the historic old Royal High School here in Edinburgh.

If there is a change of Government at the next election, this building could house the first Scottish Parliament since 1707. The Conservatives' position on that couldn't be clearer: they want no constitutional change, the Union must remain sacrosanct. But over recent months there has been a great debate. Opposition parties demand a Parliament – Labour's would be devolved from Westminster, the Nationalists would govern an independent Scotland. Last year the challenge was laid down for a public debate between the two men whose parties cast the lion's share of votes in Scotland – Shadow Scottish Secretary, George Robertson and the Leader of the Scottish National Party, Alex Salmond.

Tonight, that fiercely anticipated debate becomes a reality. In a few moments the Leaders will be questioned by a panel of three eminent Scottish journalists, and later the audience of three hundred who've packed this chamber will have their say. But now the question: devolution or independence? Each Party Leader has the chance to make his case. First, after the toss of a coin, is Alex Salmond.

ALEX SALMOND MP

Thank you, Lesley. Well, ladies and gentlemen, our debate this evening in this Parliament building is about Scotland's future. I want to outline the case for a future that can be achieved both speedily and safely – that future is independence in Europe. Scotland is an ancient nation state, it still has the trappings of statehood: a legal system, education system, established churches, sporting teams, yet without the democratic heart-beat of nationhood – an independent Parliament. This is a vacuum which stifles our voice in Europe and leads to economic and social decline at home. Now as we approach the Millennium there is an opportunity to overcome the eighteenth-century trap of the present union with England. Membership of the new European Union, membership that would be guaranteed to Scotland as to England by the process of independence, would allow Scotland a direct voice at the political nerve-centre of a market of three hundred and seventy million people.

The advantages of such membership for small nations are not in dispute. Sweden, Austria, Finland have all been convinced of the benefits. The economic prospects of Ireland have been transformed by independent membership, and the Netherlands, Denmark and Belgium are all major players in the European scene. Even tiny Luxembourg with a population smaller than this capital city of Edinburgh, has status in Europe. How could it be argued then that Scots and Scots alone are not talented enough or skilled enough or wise enough to run our own affairs alongside all of these other nations?

For years unionists, and I include in that description not just the 'do nothing unionists' like John Major, but also the 'do as little as possible unionists' like George Robertson – unionists have argued that independence would lead to the closure of industry, the sundering of families. Tonight I expect you will hear more of these fears and smears, not just about Scotland but about borders and barriers and bogeymen everywhere. The reality of Scotland's experience is that industries have closed, jobs have been exported from Rosyth to Rolls-Royce, families have been sundered by emigration. But these things have happened not because of independence but because of dependence – dependence on an outdated political arrangement.

The present-day reality is of a borderless continent with free trade, free movement and freedom of employment. There is a stark contrast between the SNP's open vision of the new Europe and Labour's narrow view of regional Scotland cowering behind the walls of fortress Britain. Scotland has the right to regain our sovereignty – indeed, this is the only choice we can make for ourselves. Devolution would require the votes of England to bring it about, but independence requires only the votes of Scotland. Even our most bitter unionist opponent, the Prime Minister himself, has admitted that there is no English veto on Scottish independence. For far too long we've accepted a situation in which Scotland cannot get the Government we choose without the same choice being made by England.

Devolution would not solve that question, the real question, the Westminster question, it would leave the commanding heights not just of the Scottish economy, but of Scottish democracy itself, they still would be left in London.

Achieving devolution is difficult, as we know from bitter experience. For over a hundred years Labour has promised home rule for Scotland. During this century they've been in Government for twenty years and yet the promise has never been delivered. Now we see a Labour Party which has let down those who passionately believe that Labour would abandon nuclear weapons, let down those who desperately want justice from the Social Security system, the restoration of benefits for sixteen- and seventeen-year-olds. If Labour is prepared to renege ... if Labour is prepared to renege on its commitments to young people, on its commitment to nuclear disarmament, to tear up its own constitution, then how on earth can we trust their commitment to Scotland?

Labour supports Scotland when Scotland supports the SNP. That is a fact in Scottish politics demonstrated time after time. Now, a few weeks ago, in debate with me, my opponent this evening said that his mission in politics was to save the union. That's exactly the same mission as Ian Lang, the Secretary of State for Scotland. Well, my mission in politics is to save Scotland, to reach the best constitutional settlement for the Scottish people. Independence offers the power to change Scotland for good, to build a new Scotland in the new Europe. Thank you very much.

LESLEY RIDDOCH

Thank you to Alex Salmond. Now we hear the case for devolution from George Robertson. George.

GEORGE ROBERTSON MP

Thanks Lesley. The Scottish people want a Scottish Parliament but they don't want to break up their country. They say it peacefully and they say it reasonably and they're right. A strong and powerful Scottish Parliament is Labour's promise, taking the power out of Whitehall and returning it to the people, strengthening and renewing our national democracy. And this Scottish Parliament will make a difference. No more poll taxes and the scandal of unelected quangos, sweeping away the hospital trusts and opt-out schools and returning water to democratic control – that's the difference our Parliament could make. And it will entirely avoid the chaos of fragmenting Britain and ripping Scotland out of the country which the Scots have helped to build. Do we really want to make foreigners of our family and friends down south? Do we really want a separate Scottish currency, changing money for a

weekend trip to Blackpool or to shop at the Gateshead Metro
Centre? Because that's what it means. Never mind the trouble
for companies and industries as the Scottish pound fluctuates.
Are we seriously entranced with the idea of a separate Scottish
armed forces with Alex Salmond here as the Commander-in-
Chief? And do we really need to face the costs and the agonies
of unpicking the tax and benefit systems and arguing over our
share of the national debt? Separatism offers only chaos and
confusion and the Scottish people don't want it.

Labour will empower the Scottish people, not smash up
the country that we know and live in. And Labour didn't just
build the Scottish Parliament plan alone, we had the guts to
join others in this historic project. Other parties joined the
convention, even if the Tories and the Nationalists stayed
away, and together with the churches and the unions, small
businesses and local Councils and a huge range of civic groups,
we built the plan, a plan forged in detail, forged together
and built to last. A real law-making Parliament, elected on
a proportional system impossible for any faction or any
area to dominate, with equality of representation between
men and women, financing which is fair and flexible and a
direct voice in Europe which retains the clout of being part
of the British delegation. And it'll have powers which matter
over housing, health and education, water and transport,
the arts and the universities, the criminal justice system and
economic development and much more. Real power and real
power where it matters in daily life. Power to make new laws
and to improve others, power to innovate and to change,
to experiment and to develop. Making a Scottish Health
Service that the people deserve, making Scotland's education
system as good as it once was, fitting skills and training to the
demands of today's economy and getting our youngsters, our
youngsters especially, back to work.

But only Labour can enhance Scotland's role in Britain – a
new and a different Britain, a new Labour Britain. Signing the
Social Chapter on day one, introducing a national minimum
wage as a safety net for all, investing in skills, cracking down
on crime and committed to the goal of full employment. The
Nationalists used to tell the Scottish people don't vote Labour
because they can't win in England, now they tell the Scottish
people don't vote Labour because Labour is winning in
England. But we're winning in Scotland too and we're winning

everywhere. The late John Smith, one of Scotland's greatest sons, lived and worked for the day when he would stand here in this very building in Edinburgh at the opening of the first Scottish Parliament in three hundred years. Well, we will finish his unfinished business and Scotland will have its Parliament, make no mistake about it, but only Labour can deliver that Parliament because only Labour can and will get rid of the Tories.

LESLEY RIDDOCH, ALEX SALMOND,
GEORGE ROBERTSON, The Great Debate,
13th February 1995

Of course, it cannot be taken for granted that one of the two options, devolution or independence, will now be easily achieved. The supporters of the *status quo*, even if they are a small minority, will no doubt fight vigorously as they did in 1979. A new uncertainty was introduced by the announcement by Tony Blair in June 1996, without consultation with the partners in the Constitutional Convention, that a referendum with two questions would be held by a Labour Government before they legislated for devolution. The old certainty had gone that had been associated with John Smith, who died on 12th May 1994. As the previous leader of the Party he had spoken of unfinished business and the 'settled will of the Scottish people', and the Labour Party had repeatedly argued that no referendum was necessary. Now unpredictable hazards, reminiscent of 1979, had again been introduced.

This book began in the period when Edward I of England seized the Stone of Destiny as a symbol of his intention to destroy the independence of Scotland. It ends at the time, 700 years later, when it has been returned. Is this only a gesture to Scottish opinion, beads for the natives? Or might it eventually be seen as symbolic of the return of real power and freedom to Scotland? On the night before the installation of the Stone in Edinburgh Castle on 30th November 1996, the Scottish Centre for Economic and Social Research held a meeting in the old Royal High School, or New Parliament House, which overflowed into the yard outside. It adopted the following Declaration:

(11.9)   Build on the Stone

We the undersigned, drawn from all parts of this ancient nation of Scotland, have assembled here in Edinburgh tonight to welcome home the Stone of Destiny, the historic symbol of our nationhood that for 700 years has been held at Westminster against both treaty and law.

We are from all backgrounds and from many traditions. Some of us were born in countries furth of Scotland. We have different pasts but we seek a common future – a future as citizens of a prosperous, just and independent Scotland.

We now pledge ourselves and exhort our fellow Scots to build on the Stone – to work together to restore the substance of nationhood to our country and to establish a free and independent Parliament that is founded firmly on the sovereignty of the Scottish people.

We commit our untiring efforts and energies to the establishment of such a Parliament and to the re-birth of Scotland as an independent nation once again, a full partner in the counsels of Europe and the World.

Declaration adopted at meeting in New
Parliament House, 29th November 1996

Creachadh

'Tìr nam beann, nan gleann 's nan gaisgeach':
tha na glinn 's na beanntan againn fhathast
is còmhnardan tarbhach nan tuathanach,
gun luaidh air tràighean is eisirean,
eathraichean-iasgaich air chiallaidh
is mòintichean falamh de dhaoine,
Cluaidh air chluainidh,
eileanan ga reic ri eilthirich
is tobraichean ola gan spùinneadh,
is sinn fhathast a' bruidhinn mu shaorsa.
Ach tha cus de ar coimhearsnaich
glaiste an daorsa:
fo chuing nan tabloid 's nam video,
deooh is drogaichean
gan togail á dòrainn
's gan tilleadh
gu staid nas miosa.
Rinn sinn prìosanan dhuinn fhìn,
's tha thìd aig na gaisgich
tilleadh
's am Bastille seo a chreachadh.

Storming

'Land of mountains, glens and heroes':
we have the glens and mountains still
and the farmers' productive plains,
not to mention beaches and oysters,
laid-up fishing-boats
and unfrequented moors,
Clyde retired,
islands sold to foreigners,
oil wells plundered
while we still talk about freedom.
Too many of our neighbours
also locked in thralldom:
yoked to tabloids and videos,
with drink and drugs
lifting them from despair
and returning them
to worse conditions.
We have made prisons for ourselves
and it is high time the heroes
returned
to storm this Bastille.

DERICK S. THOMSON

APPENDIX

The Treaty of Union

1   **The Articles of Union agreed in London on 22nd July 1706 by the Commissioners of Scotland and England.** (*Acts of the Parliament of Scotland*, vol. XI, pp. 201–5)

I.   THAT the two Kingdoms of Scotland and England shall upon the first day of May next ensuing the date hereof, and for ever after be United into one Kingdom by the name of GREAT BRITTAIN and that the Ensigns Armorial of the said United Kingdom be such as Her Majesty shall appoint And the Crosses of St Andrew and St George be conjoyn'd in such manner as Her Majesty shall think fit, and us'd in all Flags, Banners, Standards and Ensigns both at Sea and Land.

II.   THAT the Succession to the Monarchy of the United Kingdom of Great Brittain, and of the Dominions thereunto belonging after Her most Sacred Majesty and in default of Issue of Her Majesty, be remain and continue to the most Excellent Princess SOPHIA Electoress and Dutchess Dowager of HANNOVER, and the Heires of Her body being Protestants, upon whom the Crown of England is Setled by an Act of Parliament made in England in the Twelfth year of the Reign of his late Majesty King William the Third Entituled an Act for the further Limitation of the Crown and better securing the Rights and Libertys of the Subject, and that all Papists, and persons marrying Papists shall be Excluded from, and for ever incapable to Inherit, Possess or Enjoy the Imperial Crown of Great Brittain and the Dominions thereunto belonging, or any part thereof, and in every such Case the Crown and Government shall from time to time Descend to, and be Enjoyed by such person being a Protestant, as should have Inherited and Enjoyed the same, in case such Papist, or Person marrying a Papist was naturally Dead, according to the Provision for the descent of the Crown of England made by one other Act of Parliament in England in the first year of the Reign of their late Majestys King William and Queen Mary Entituled an Act Declaring the Rights and Libertys of the Subject, and Settling the Succession of the Crown.

III.   THAT the United Kingdom of Great Brittain be Represented by one and the same Parliament to be Stil'd the Parliament of Great Brittain.

IV.   THAT all the Subjects of the United Kingdom of Great Brittain shall from and after the Union have full freedom and Intercours of Trade and Navigation to, and from any Port, or Place within the said United Kingdom, and the Dominions and Plantations thereunto belonging. And that there be a Communication of all other Rights Privileges and Advantages which do, or may belong to the Subjects of either Kingdom, Except, where it is otherwise Expressly agreed in these Articles.

V.   THAT all Ships belonging to Her Majestys Subjects of Scotland at the time of Signing this Treaty for the Union of the two Kingdoms (tho' Forreign Built) shall be deem'd and pass as Ships of the Built of Great Brittain, The Owner, or where there are more Owners, one or more of the Owners, within Twelve Months after the Union, making Oath that at the time of Signing the said Treaty the same did[1] belong to him, or them, or to some other Subject, or Subjects of Scotland to be particularly nam'd, with the places of their respective abodes, and that the same doth then belong to him, or them, and that no Forreigner directly or indirectly hath any share, part, or interest therein Which Oath shall be made before the Chief Officer, or Officers of the Customs in the Port next to the abode of the said Owner, or Owners, And the said Officer, or Officers shall be Impowered to Administer the said Oath, And the Oath being so Administred shall be attested by the Officer, or Officers who Administred the same, And being Registred by the said Officer, or Officers shall be delivered to the Master of the Ship for security of her Navigation, and a Duplicat thereof shall be transmitted by the said Officer, or Officers, to the Chief Officer, or Officers of the Customs in the Port of Edinburgh to be there Entered in a Register, and from thence to be sent to the Port of London, to be there Entered in the General Register of all Trading Ships belonging to Great Brittain.

VI.   THAT all parts of the United Kingdom, for ever, from and after the Union shall have the same Allowances and Encouragements, and be under the same Prohibitions Restrictions and Regulations of Trade, and lyable to the same Customs and Dutys on Import and Export, and that the Allowances, Encouragements, Prohibitions, Restrictions, and Regulations, and Regulations of Trade, and the Customs and Dutys on Import and Export, Settled in England when the Union Commences shall from, and after the Union, take place throughout the whole United Kingdom.[2]

VII.   THAT all parts of the United Kingdom be for ever, from and after the Union lyable to the same Excises upon all Excisable Liquors,[3] and that the Excise settled in England on such Liquors when the Union Commences take place, throughout the whole United Kingdom.

VIII.   THAT from and after the Union all Forreign Salt which shall be Imported into Scotland shall be Charg'd at the Importation there with the same Dutys as the like Salt is now Charged with being Imported into England and to be Levied and Secur'd in the same manner,[4] But Scotland shall for the space of Seven Years from the said Union, be Exempted from the paying in Scotland for Salt made there, the Duty, or Excise, now payable for Salt made in England, but from the Expiration of the said Seven Years shall be Subject and Lyable to the same Dutys for Salt made in Scotland, as shall be then payable for Salt made in England to be Levied and Secur'd in the same manner, and with the like Drawbacks and Allowances as in England,[5] And during the said Seven years, there shall be paid in England for all Salt made in Scotland, and Imported from thence into England, the same Dutys upon the Importation as shall be payable, for Salt made in England to be Levied, and Secur'd in the same manner as the Dutys on Forreign Salt are to be Levied and Secur'd in England, And that during the said Seven years, no Salt whatsoever be brought from Scotland to England by Land in any manner, under the penalty of forfeiting the Salt and the Cattle and Carriages made use of in bringing the same and paying Twenty Shillings for every Bushel of such Salt, and proportionably for a greater or lesser quantity for which the Carrier, as well as the Owner shall be lyable joyntly and severally and the person bringing or carrying the same, to be Imprison'd by any one Justice of the Peace by the space of Six Months without Bail; and untill the penalty be paid, And that during the said Seven years, all Salted Flesh, or Fish, Exported from Scotland to England, or made use of for Victwalling of Ships in Scotland, and all Flesh put on board in Scotland to be Exported to parts beyond the Seas which shall be

Salted with Scotch Salt or any mixture therewith, shall be forfeited and may be Seiz'd, And that from and after the Union the Laws and Acts of Parliament in Scotland for Pineing, Curing and Packing of Herrings White Fish and Salmon for Exportation, with Forreign Salt only, and for preventing of Frauds in Cureing and Packing of Fish be Continued in Force in Scotland subject to such alterations, as shall be made by the Parliament of Great Brittain, and that all Fish Exported from Scotland to parts beyond the Seas which shall be Cur'd with Foreign Salt only, shall have the same Eases Praemiums and Drawbacks as are, or shall be allowed to such persons as Export the like Fish from England, and if any matters or fraud relating to the said Duty's on Salt shall hereafter appear which are not sufficiently provided against by this Article, the same shall be subject to such further Provisions as shall be thought fit by the Parliament of Great Brittain.

IX.   THAT whenever the Summe of One Million Nine Hundred Ninty Seven Thousand Seven Hundred and Sixty three pounds Eight Shillings and Four pence half penny, shall be Enacted by the Parliament of Great Brittain, to be raised in that part of the United Kingdom now call'd England on Land and other things usually Charg'd in Acts of Parliament there for granting an Aid to the Crown by a Land Tax, That part of the United Kingdom now called Scotland, shall be Charged by the same Act, with a further Summe of Forty Eight Thousand pounds, free of all Charges, as the Quota of Scotland to such Tax, and so proportionably for any greater, or lesser Summe raised in England by any Tax, on Land, and other things usually Charg'd together with the Land And that such Quota for Scotland, in the Cases aforesaid be rais'd and collected in the same manner as the Cess now is in Scotland, But subject to such Regulations in the manner of Collecting as shall be made by the Parliament of Great Brittain.

X.   THAT during the Continuance of the respective Dutys on Stampt Paper, Vellome and Parchment by the several Acts now in force in England, Scotland shall not be Charg'd with the same respective Dutys.

XI.   THAT during the Continuance of the Dutys payable in England on Windows and Lights which Determins on the first day of August One Thousand Seven Hundred and Ten, Scotland shall not be Charged with the same Dutys.

XII.   THAT during the Continuance of the Dutys payable in England on
         Coales Culm, and Cynders which determins the Thirtieth day of
         September One Thousand Seven Hundred and Ten, Scotland shall
         not be Charg'd therewith for Coales Culm and Cynders consum'd
         there, But shall be charg'd with the same Dutys as in England, for
         all Coal, Culm, and Cynders not consum'd in Scotland.

XIII.   THAT during the Continuance of the Duty payable in England
         on Mault which determins the Twenty fourth day of June one
         Thousand Seven Hundred and Seven, Scotland shall not be Charg'd
         with that Duty.

XIV.   THAT the Kingdom of Scotland be not Charg'd, with any other
         Dutys laid on by the Parliament of England before the Union
         Except those Consented to in this Treaty, in regard it is agreed
         that all necessary Provision shall be made by the Parliament of
         Scotland for the Publick Charge and Service of that Kingdom
         for the year One Thousand Seven Hundred and Seven Provided
         nevertheless that if the Parliament of England shall think fit to lay
         any further Impositions by way of Customs, or such Excises with
         which by virtue of this Treaty Scotland is to be Charg'd Equally
         with England In such Case Scotland shall be Lyable to the same
         Customs and Excises and have an Equivalent to be Settled by the
         Parliament of Great Britain[6] and seing it cannot be supposed that
         the Parliament of Great Brittain will ever lay any sorts of Burthens
         upon the United Kingdom, but what they shall find of necessity
         at that time for the preservation and good of the whole and with
         due regard to the Circumstances and Abilitys of every part of the
         United Kingdom, Therefore it is agreed that there be no further
         Exemption insisted on for any part of the United Kingdom, But
         that the Consideration of any Exemptions beyond what are already
         agreed on in this Treaty shall be left to the Determination of the
         Parliament of Great Brittain.

XV.   WHEREAS by the Terms of this Treaty the Subjects of Scotland for
         preserving an equality of Trade throughout the United Kingdom,
         will be lyable to several Customs and Excises now payable in
         England which will be applicable towards payment of the Debts
         of England Contracted before the Union, It is agreed that Scotland
         shall have an Equivalent for what the Subjects thereof shall be
         so Charg'd towards Payment of the said Debts of England in
         all particulars whatsoever in manner following vizt That before

the Union of the said Kingdoms the summe of Three Hundred Ninty Eight Thousand and Eightie Five pound Ten shillings be Granted to her Majesty by the Parliament of England for the uses aftermentioned being the Equivalent to be answer'd to Scotland for such parts of the said Customs and Excises, upon all Excisable Liquors, with which that Kingdom is to be Charg'd upon the Union, as will be applicable to the payment of the said debts of England according to the proportions which the present Customs in Scotland being Thirty Thousand pounds p^r Anñ do bear to the Customs in England Computed at One Million Three Hundred Forty one Thousand Five Hundred and Fifty nine pounds p^r Anñ and which the present Excises on Excisable Liquors in Scotland being Thirty Three Thousand and Five Hundred pounds p^r Anñ do bear to the Excises on Excisable Liquors in England Computed at Nine Hundred Forty Seven Thousand Six Hundred and Two Pound p Anñ Which summe of Three Hundred Ninty Eight Thousand Eighty five pounds Ten shillings shall be due and payable from the time of the Union, And in regard that after the Union Scotland becoming lyable to the same Customs and Dutys payable on Import and Export, and to the same Excises on all Excisable Liquors as in England, as well upon that account, as upon the account of the Encrease of Trade and People (which will be the happy consequence of the Union) the said Revenues will much Improve beyond the before mentioned annual Values thereof, of which no present Estimate can be made, Yet nevertheless for the reasons aforesaid there ought to be a proportionable Equivalent answered to Scotland, It is agreed That after the Union there shall be an Account kept of the said Dutys arising in Scotland, to the End it may appear what ought to be answer'd to Scotland as an Equivalent for such proportion of the said Encrease as shall be applicable to the payment of the Debts of England, And for the further, and more Effectual answering the several ends hereafter mentioned It is agreed That from and after the Union the whole Encrease of the Revenues of Customs and Dutys on Import and Export and Excise upon Excisable Liquors in Scotland, over and above the annual produce of the said respective Dutys as above stated shall go, and be apply'd for the Term of seven years to the uses hereafter mentioned And that upon the said account there shall be answered to Scotland annually from the end of Seven years after the Union, an Equivalent in Proportion to such part of the said Encrease as shall be applicable to the Debts of England,[7] And whereas from the Expiration of Seven years after the Union, Scotland is to be lyable to the same Dutys for Salt made

in Scotland as shall be then payable for Salt made in England It
is agreed that when such Dutys take place there an Equivalent
shall be answered to Scotland for such part thereof as shall be
apply'd towards payment of the Debts of England of which Dutys
an Account shall be kept to the end it may appear what is to be
answered to Scotland as the said Equivalent, And generally that
an Equivalent shall be answered to Scotland for such parts of the
English Debts as Scotland may hereafter become lyable to pay by
reason of the Union other then such for which Appropriations
have been made by Parliament in England, of the Customs, or
other Dutys on Export, or Import Excises on all Excisable Liquors,[8]
or Salt, In respect of which Debts, Equivalents are herein before
provided And as for the Uses to which the said Summe of Three
Hundred Ninty Eight Thousand Eighty five pounds Ten Shillings to
be granted as aforesaid, and all other moneys which are to be
answered or allowed to Scotland as aforesaid It is agreed[9] That
out of the said Sume of Three Hundred Ninty Eight Thousand Eighty
five pound Tenn Shillings all the publick Debts of the Kingdom of
Scotland, And also the Capital Stock, or Fund of the Affrican and
Indian Company of Scotland advanc'd, together with the Interest
for the said Capital Stock after the Rate of Five pounds p Cent.
P Anñ from the respective times of the Payment thereof shall be
paid, upon payment of which Capital Stock and Interest, It is agreed
the said Company be disolv'd and cease, and also That from the
time of passing the Act of Parliament in England for raising the
said Summe of Three Hundred Ninty Eight Thousand Eighty five
pounds Tenn Shillings the said Company shall neither Trade, nor
Grant Licence to Trade,[10] And as to the Overplus of the said Sume
of Three Hundred Ninty Eight Thousand Eighty five pound Ten
Shillings, after the payment of[11] the said Debts of the Kingdom
of Scotland, and the said Capital Stock and Interest, and also the
whole Encrease of the said Revenues of Customs Dutys and Excises,
above the present Value which shall arise in Scotland during the
said Term of Seven Years Together with the Equivalent which shall
become due upon Account of the Improvement thereof in Scotland
after the said Term, And also as to all other sums, which according
to the agreements aforsaid may become payable to Scotland by
way of Equivalent for what that Kingdom shall hereafter become
lyable towards payment of the Debts of England, It is agreed That
the same be apply'd in manner following viz[t] That[12] out of the
same, what Consideration shall be found necessary to be had for
any losses which privat persons may sustain by reducing the Coyn

of Scotland to the Standard and Value of the Coyn of England may be made good, And afterwards the same shall be wholly applyed towards Encourageing and Promoting the Fisheries and such other Manufacturys and Improvements in Scotland as may most Conduce to the General Good of the United Kingdom, And It is agreed that Her Majesty be Impowred to appoint Commissioners who shall be accountable to the Parliament of Great Britain for disposing the said Summe of Three Hundred, Nynty Eight Thousand Eighty five pounds Ten Shillings and all other moneys which shall arise to Scotland upon the agreements aforsaid, to the purposes before mentioned Which Commissioners shall be Impowred to Call for, Receive and Dispose of the said moneys in manner aforesaid, And to Inspect the Books of the several Collectors of the said Revenues, and of all other Dutys, from whence an Equivalent may arise, And that the Collectors and Mannagers of the said Revenues and Dutys be Obliged to give to the said Commissioners Subscribed Authentick Abbreviats of the Produce of such Revenues and Dutys arising in their respective Districts, And that the said Commissioners shall have their Office within the Limits of Scotland, and shall in such Office Keep Books containing Accounts of the Amount of the Equivalents, and how the same shall have been disposed of from time to time which may be Inspected by any of the Subjects who shall desire the same.

XVI.   THAT from and after the Union the Coyn shall be of the same Standard and Value throughout the United Kingdom as now in England, And a Mint shall be Continued in Scotland under the same Rules as the Mint in England[13] Subject to such Regulations as Her Majesty, Her Heires, or Successors, or the Parliament of Great Brittain shall think fit.

XVII.   THAT from and after the Union the same Weights and Measures shall be used throughout the United Kingdom, as are now Established in England, and Standards of Weights and Measures shall be Kept by those Burroughs in Scotland to whom the keeping the Standards of Weights and Measures now in use there do's of Special Right belong. All which Standards shall be sent down to such respective Burroughs from the Standards kept in the Exchequer at Westminster Subject nevertheless to such Regulations as the Parliament of Great Brittain shall think fit.

XVIII. THAT the Laws Concerning Regulation of Trade, Customs and such

Excises to which Scotland is, by virtue of this Treaty to be lyable, be the same in Scotland, from and after the Union as in England And That all other Laws in use within the Kingdom of Scotland doe after the Union and notwithstanding thereof remain in the same force as before (Except such as are Contrary to, or Inconsistent with the Terms of this Treaty) but alterable, by the Parliament of Great Britain, with this difference betwixt the Laws concerning Publick Right, Pollicy and Civil Government, and those which concern privat Right, That the Laws which concern Publick Right, Policy and Civil Government may be made the same throughout the whole United Kingdom, But that no alteration be made in Laws which Concern Privat Right Except for evident utility of the Subjects within Scotland.

XIX.   THAT the Court of Session, or College of Justice do, after the Union and notwithstanding thereof Remain, in all time coming within Scotland, as it is now Constituted by the Laws of that Kingdom, and with the same Authority and Priviledges as before the Union, Subject nevertheless to such Regulations for the better Adminis-tration of Justice, as shall be made by the Parliament of Great Brittain[14] And That the Court of Justiciary do also after the Union, and notwithstanding thereof, remain in all time coming within Scotland as it is now Constituted by the Laws of that Kingdom And with the same Authority and Priviledges as before the Union, Subject nevertheless to such Regulations as shall be made by the Parliament of Great Brittain And without prejudice of other Rights of Justiciary, And That all Admiralty Jurisdictions, be under the Lord High Admiral, or Commissioners for the Admiralty of Great Brittain for the time being And that the Court of Admiralty now Established in Scotland Be Continued, And that all Reviews, Reductions, or Suspensions of the Sentences in Maritim Cases Competent to the Jurisdiction of that Court remain in the same manner after the Union, as now in Scotland, until the Parliament of Great Brittain shall make such Regulations and Alterations as shall be judg'd Expedient for the whole United Kingdom so as there be always Continued in Scotland a Court of Admiralty such as is in England, for determination of all Maritim Cases, relating to Private Rights in Scotland, Competent to the Jurisdiction of the Admiralty Court Subject nevertheless to such Regulations, and Alterations as shall be thought proper to be made by the Parliament of Great Brittain, and that the Heretable Rights of Admiralty and Vice Admiraltys in Scotland be reserved to the respective proprietors, as Rights of property Subject nevertheless as to the manner of Exercising such Heretable Rights, to such Regulations and Alterations as shall be thought proper to be made by the Parliament of Great Brittain And That all other Courts now in being within the Kingdom of Scotland do remain, But subject to Alterations by the Parliament of Great Brittain And That, all Inferior Courts within the said Limits doe Remain subordinat as they are now to the Supreme Courts of Justice within the same in all time coming And that no Causes in Scotland be Cognoscable, by the Courts of Chancery, Queens Bench, Common Pleas, or any other Court in Westminster Hall, And that the said Courts, or any other, of the like nature after the Union shall have no Power to Cognosce, Review, or Alter the Acts, or Sentences of the Judicatures within Scotland, or Stop the Execution of the same, And That there be a Court of Exchequer in Scotland after the Union, for deciding Questions Concerning the Revenues of Customs and Excises there, having the same Power and Authority in such Cases as the Court of Exchequer has in England And That the said Court of Exchequer in Scotland have power of passing Signatures, Gifts, Tutories, and in other things as the Court of Exchequer at present in Scotland hath, And that the Court of Exchequer that now is in Scotland do Remain until a New Court of Exchequer be settled by the Parliament of Great Brittain in Scotland after the Union, And That after the Union The Queens Majesty and Her Royal Successors, may Continue a Privy Council in Scotland for preserving of Publick Peace and Order, until the Parliament of Great Brittain shall think fit to alter it, or Establish any other Effectual Methode for that end.

XX.   THAT all Heretable Offices[15], Heretable Jurisdictions, Offices for Life, and Jurisdictions for Life be reserved, to the Owners thereof as Rights of Property in the same manner as they are now enjoy'd by the Laws of Scotland notwithstanding of this Treaty.

XXI.   THAT the Rights and Priviledges of the Royal Burrowghs in Scotland as they now are doe Remain entire after the Union and notwithstanding thereof.

XXII.   THAT by virtue of this Treaty of the Peers of Scotland at the time of the Union Sixteen shall be the Number to Sit and Vote in the House of Lords, and Forty Five the Number of the Representatives of Scotland in the House of Commons of the Parliament of Great Brittain And that when Her Majesty, Her Heires, or Successors

shall Declare Her, or their pleasure for holding the first, or any
subsequent Parliament of Great Brittain until the Parliament of
Great Brittain shall make further Provision therein A Writ do issue
under the Great Seal of the United Kingdom Directed to the Privy
Council of Scotland Commanding them to Cause Sixteen Peers who
are to Sit in the House of Lords to be summon'd to Parliament and
Forty Five Members to be Elected to Sit in the House of Commons
of the Parliament of Great Brittain according to the Agreement in
this Treaty in such manner as by[16] the Parliament of Scotland shall
be Settled before the Union, And that the Names of the Persons
so summon'd and Elected shall be Returned by the Privy Council
of Scotland into the Court from whence the said Writ did issue,
And That if Her Majesty on, or before the first day of May next,
on which day the Union is to take place, shall Declare under
the Great Seal of England That it is Expedient that the Lords of
Parliament of England, and Commons of the present Parliament of
England should be the Members of the respective Houses of the
First Parliament of Great Brittain, for, and on the part of England,
Then the said Lords of Parliament of England, and Commons of
the present Parliament of England shall be the Members of the
respective Houses of the first Parliament of Great Brittain, for,
and on the part of England And Her Majesty may by Her Royal
Proclamation under the Great Seal of Great Brittain, appoint the
said first Parliament of Great Brittain to meet, at such time and Place
as Her Majesty shall think fit, which time shall not be less than Fifty
days after the date of such Proclamation, and the time and place of
the meeting of such Parliament being so appointed, a Writ shall be
immediatly issued under the Great Seal of Great Brittain Directed
to the Privy Council of Scotland for the Summoning the Sixteen
Peers and for Electing Forty Five Members by whom Scotland is to
be represented in the Parliament of Great Brittain And the Lords
of Parliament of England and the Sixteen Peers of Scotland, such
Sixteen Peers being summoned and return'd in the manner agreed
in this Treaty, And the Members of the House of Commons of
the said Parliament of England and the Forty five Members for
Scotland, such Forty five Members being Elected and Return'd
in the manner agreed in this Treaty, shall assemble and meet
respectively in their respective Houses of the Parliament of Great
Brittain at such time and place as shall be so appointed by Her
Majesty, and shall be the two Houses of the First Parliament of Great
Brittain And that Parliament may Continue for such time only as the
present Parliament of England might have Continued if the Union

of the two Kingdoms had not been made unless sooner disolved by Her Majesty, And That every one of the Lords of Parliament, of Great Brittain, and every member of the House of Commons of the Parliament of Great Brittain, in the first & all succeeding Parliaments of Great Brittain, until the Parliament of Great Brittain shall otherwise direct, shall take the respective Oaths appointed to be taken, Instead of the Oaths of Allegiance and Supremacy by an Act of Parliament made in England in the first year of the Reign of the late King William and Queen Mary Intituled an Act for the Abrogating of the Oaths, of Supremacy and Allegiance and appointing other Oaths and make, subscribe and audibly Repeat the Declaration mention'd in an Act of Parliament made in England in the Thirtieth year of the Reign of King Charles the Second Entituled an Act for the more effectwall preserving the King's person and Government by disabling Papists from sitting in either House of Parliament and shall Take & Subscribe the Oath mention'd in an Act of Parliament made in England in the first year of Her Majestys Reign Intituled An Act to Declare the Alterations in the Oath appointed to be taken by the Act Intituled An Act for the further Security of His Majestys Person & the Succession of the Crown in the Protestant Line, and for Extinguishing the hopes of the pretended Prince of Wales and all other Pretenders and their open and secret abbettors and for Declaring the Association to be determin'd, at such time and in such manner as the Members of both Houses of Parliament of England are by the said respective Acts directed to take, make and Subscribe the same upon the Penaltys & Disabilitys in the said respective Acts contain'd And it is declar'd and agreed that these Words, This Realm, The Crown of this Realm, and the Queen of this Realm mentioned in the Oaths and Declaration contained in the aforesaid Acts, which were Intended to Signify the Crown and Realm of England shall be understood of the Crown & Realm of GREAT BRITTAIN, and that in that Sence the said Oaths, and Declaration be taken & subscrib'd by the Members of both Houses of the Parliament of Great Brittain.

XXIII. THAT the forsaid Sixteen Peers of Scotland mentioned in the last preceeding Article to sit in the House of Lords of the Parliament of Great Brittain shall have all privileges of Parliament which the Peers of England now have, and which they, or any Peers of Great Brittain shall have after the Union, and particularly the Right of Siting upon the Tryalls of Peers, And in Case of the Tryal of any Peer in time of Adjournment, or Prorogation of Parliament the said Sixteen Peers

shall be summon'd in the same manner and have the same Powers
and Privileges at such Tryal as any other Peers of Great Brittain And
that in Case any Tryalls of Peers, shall hereafter happen when there
is no Parliament in being, The Sixteen Peers of Scotland who sate
in the last preceeding Parliament shall be summon'd in the same
manner, and have the same Powers and Privileges at such Tryals as
any other Peers of Great Brittain, And That all Peers of Scotland and
their Successors to their Honours and Dignitys shall from and after
the Union be Peers of Great Britain, and have Rank and Precedency
next and Immediatly after the Peers of the like Orders and Degrees
in England at the time of the Union, And before all Peers of Great
Brittain of the like Orders and Degrees who may be Created after
the Union, and shall be Tryed as Peers of Great Brittain, and shall
Enjoy all priviledges of Peers as fully as the Peers of England do
now, or as they, or any other Peers of Great Britain may hereafter
Enjoy the same, Except the Right & Privilege of Sitting in the House
of Lords, and the Privileges depending thereon and particularly the
Right of Sitting upon the Tryalls of Peers.

XXIV.   THAT from and after the Union there be One Great Seal for the
        United Kingdom of Great Brittain, which shall be different from the
        Great Seal now us'd in either Kingdom, And that the quartering the
        Arms[17] as may best suit the Union be left to Her Majesty, And that in
        the mean time the Great Seal of England be us'd as the Great Seal of
        the United Kingdom, And that the Great Seal of the United Kingdom
        be us'd for Sealing Writs to Elect and Summon the Parliament of
        Great Brittain, and for Sealing all Treatys with Forreign Princes
        and States, and all Publick Acts, Instruments and Orders of State
        which Concern the whole United Kingdom, And in all other matters
        Relating to England, as the Great Seal of England is now us'd, And
        that a Seal in Scotland after the Union be always kept and made use
        of in all things relating to Privat Rights, or Grants, which have usually
        passed the Great Seal of Scotland, and which only concern Offices,
        Grants Commissions and Privat Rights within that Kingdom, And
        that until such Seal shall be appointed by Her Majesty the present
        Great Seal of Scotland shall be us'd for such purposes, and that the
        Privy Seal, Signet, Casset, Signet of the Justiciary Court, Quarter Seal
        and Seals of Courts now used in Scotland be Continued, but that
        the said Seals be Altered and Adapted to the State of the Union
        as Her Majesty shall think fit, And the said Seals and all of them
        and the Keepers of them shall be subject to such Regulations as the
        Parliament of Great Brittain shall hereafter make.[18]

XXV.   THAT all Laws and Statutes in either Kingdom, so far as they are Contrary to, or Inconsistent with the Terms of these Articles, or any of them, shall from and after the Union Cease and become void and shall be so Declared to be by the respective Parliaments of the said Kingdoms.

The Treaty of Union

2   **Amendments (apart from minor adjustments of spelling and punctuation) agreed by the Scottish Parliament between 3rd October 1706 and 16th January 1707.** (*Acts of the Parliament of Scotland*, vol. XI, pp. 406–14)

Art. V
For 'signing' in line 2, read 'ratifying'.
At (1) insert:
'in haill or in part'.

Art. VI
After 'Encouragements' in lines 2 and 4 insert 'and drawbacks'.
At (2) insert:
'excepting and reserving the Duties upon Export and Import of such particular Commodities from which any persons the Subjects of either Kingdom are specially Liberated and Exempted by their private Rights which after the Union are to remain safe and entire to them in all respects as before the same And that from and after the Union no Scots Cattle carried into England shall be lyable to any other Duties either on the publick or private Accounts than these Duties to which the Cattle of England are or shall be lyable within the said Kingdom. And seeing by the Laws of England there are Rewards granted upon the Exportation of certain kinds of Grain wherein Oats grinded or ungrinded are not expressed, that from and after the Union when Oats shall be sold at fifteen shillings Sterling per quarter or under there shall be payed two shillings and six pence Sterling for every quarter of the Oat-meal exported in the terms of the Law whereby and so long as Rewards are granted for Exportation of other Grains And that the Bear of Scotland have the same Rewards as Barley. And in respect the Importation of Victual into Scotland from any place beyond Sea would prove a Discouragement to Tillage, Therefore that the Prohibition as now in force by the Law of Scotland against Importation of Victual from Ireland or any other place beyond Sea into Scotland, do

after the Union remain in the same force as now it is until more proper and effectwall ways be provided by the Parliament of Great Britain for discouraging the Importation of the said Victual from beyond Sea.'

Art. VII
At (3) insert:

'excepting only that the thirty four Gallons English Barrel of Beer or Ale amounting to twelve Gallons Scots present measure sold in Scotland by the Brewer at nine shillings six pence Sterling excluding all Duties and Retailed including Duties and the Retailers profit at two pence the Scots pint or eight part of the Scots Gallon, be not after the Union lyable on account of the present Excise upon Exciseable Liquors in England, to any higher Imposition than two shilling Sterling upon the forsaid thirty four Gallons English barrel, being twelve gallons the present Scots measure'.

Art. VIII
At (4) insert:

'But in regard the Duties of great quantities of foreign Salt Imported may be very heavie on the Merchants Importers; That therefore all forreign Salt imported into Scotland shall be Cellared and Locked up under the custody of the Merchant Importer and the Officers imployed for levying the Duties upon Salt And that the Merchant may have what quantities thereof his occasion may require not under a Weigh or fourtie bushells at a time; Giving security for the duty of what quantity he receives payable in six Months'.

At (5) delete from 'And that during the said seven years' to end of Article and insert:

'with this exception that Scotland shall after the said seven years remain exempted from the Duty of two shillings and four pence a Bushell on home Salt Imposed by ane Act made in England in the Ninth and Tenth of King William the Third of England And if the Parliament of Great Britain shall at or before the expiring of the said seven years substitute any other fund in place of the said two shillings and four pence of Excise on the bushel of Home Salt, Scotland shall after the said seven years, bear a proportion of the said Fund, and have an Equivalent in the Terms of this Treaty, And that during the said seven years there shall be payed in England for all Salt made in Scotland and imported from thence into England the same duties upon the Importation as shall be payable for Salt made in England to be levied and secured in the same manner as the Duties on forreign Salt are to be levied and secured in England. And that after the said seven years how long the said Duty of two shillings four pence a Bushel upon Salt is continued in England the said two shillings four pence a Bushel shall be payable for all Salt made in Scotland and imported into England, to be levied and secured in the same manner And that during the continuance of the Duty of two shillings four pence a Bushel upon Salt made in England no Salt whatsoever be brought from Scotland to England by Land in any manner under the penalty of forfeiting the Salt and the Cattle and Carriages made use of in bringing the same and paying twenty shillings for every Bushel of such Salt, and proportionably for a grater or lesser quantity, for which the Carrier as well as the Owner shall be lyable jointly and severally, And the persons bringing or carrying the same, to be imprisoned by any one Justice of the Peace, by the space of six months without Bail, and until the penalty be payed: And for Establishing an equality in Trade That all Fleshes exported from Scotland to England and put on Board in Scotland to be Exported to parts beyond the Seas and provisions for ships in Scotland and for forreign voyages may be salted with Scots Salt paying the same Dutie for what Salt is so employed as the like quantity of such Salt pays in England and under the same penalties forfeitures and provisions for preventing of frauds as are mentioned in the Laws of England And that from and after the Union the Laws and Acts of Parliament in Scotland for Pineing Curing and Packing of Herrings White Fish and Salmond for Exportation with Forreign Salt only without any mixture of British or Irish Salt and for preventing of frauds in Curing and Packing of Fish be continued in force in Scotland subject to such alterations as shall be made by the Parliament of Great Britain And that all Fish exported from Scotland to parts beyond the Seas which shall be Cured with Forreign Salt only and without mixture of British or Irish Salt, shall have the same Eases Praemiums and Drawbacks as are or shall be allowed to such persons as Export the like Fish from England: And that for Encouragement of the Herring Fishing there shall be allowed and payed to the Subjects Inhabitants of Great Britain during the present allowances for other Fishes ten shillings five pence Sterling for every Barrel of White Herrings which shall be exported from Scotland; And that there shall be allowed five shillings Sterling for every Barrel of Beef or Pork salted with Foreign Salt without mixture of British or Irish Salt and Exported for sale from Scotland to parts beyond Sea alterable by the Parliament of Great Britain. And if any matters of fraud relating to the said Duties on Salt shall hereafter appear which are not sufficiently provided against by this Article the same shall be subject to such further provisions as shall be thought fit by the Parliament of Great Britain.'

Art. XIV

At (6) insert:

'With this further provision That any Malt to be made and consumed in that part of the United Kingdom now called Scotland shall not be charged with any Imposition upon Malt during this present War.'

Art. XV

At (7) delete from 'And whereas from the Expiration' to 'as the said Equivalent' (6 lines)

At (8) delete 'or salt'

At (9) delete from 'That out of the said Sume' to 'Kingdom of Scotland' (3 lines) and add:

'That in the first place out of the forsaid Sum what consideration shall be found necessary to be had for any Losses which privat persons may sustain by reducing the Coin of Scotland to the Standard and Value of the Coin of England may be made good. In the next place'.

At (10) add:

'Providing that if the said Stock and Interest shall not be paid in twelve months after the Commencement of the Union That then the said Company may from thence forward Trade or give Licence to Trade until the said hail Capital Stock and Interest shall be payed'.

At (11) after 'payment of' delete: 'the said debts of the Kingdom of Scotland'; insert: 'what consideration shall be had for loses in repairing the Coin and paying'.

At (12) delete from 'out of the Same' to 'and afterwards' (3 lines); insert: 'That all the publick Debts of the Kingdom of Scotland as shall be adjusted by this present Parliament shall be payed and that two thousand pounds per annum for the space of seven years shall be applied towards Encouraging and Promoting the Manufacture of coarse Wool within these shires which produce the Wool And that the first two thousand pounds sterling be payed at Martinmas next, and so yearly at Martinmas during the space forsaid'.

Art. XVI

At (13) insert: 'And the present Officers of the Mint continued'.
Insert 'and Alterations' after 'such Regulations'.

Art. XIX

At (14) insert:
'And that hereafter none shall be named by Her Majesty or Her Royal Successors to be Ordinary Lords of Session but such who have served in the Colledge of Justice as Advocats or Principal Clerks of Session for the space of five years, or as Writers to the Signet for the space of ten years With this provision That no Writer to the Signet be capable to be admitted a Lord of the Session unless he undergo a private and publick Tryal on the Civil Law before the Faculty of Advocats and be found by then qualified for the said Office two years before he be named to be a Lord of the Session, yet so as the Qualifications made or to be made for capacitating persons to be named Ordinary Lords of Session may be altered by the Parliament of Great Brittain'.

Art. XX

At (15) insert 'Superiorities'.

Art. XXII

At (16) delete: from 'the Parliament of Scotland' to 'the Union' (2 lines)
Insert: 'a subsequent Act of this present Session of the Parliament of Scotland shall be settled; Which Act is hereby Declared to be as valid as if it were a part and ingrossed in this Treaty'.

Art. XXIV

At (17) insert: 'and the Rank and Precedency of the Lyon King of Arms of the Kingdom of Scotland'
At (18) add:
'And that the Crown, Scepter and Sword of State, the Records of Parliament, and all other Records, Rolls and Registers whatsoever, both publick and private generall and particular, and Warrands

thereof Continue to be keeped as they are within that part of the United Kingdom now called Scotland, and that they shall so remain in all time coming notwithstanding of the Union.'

PAUL H. SCOTT, *Andrew Fletcher and the Treaty of Union*. Edinburgh, Saltire Society, 1994

BOOKS FOR FURTHER READING

THE PAST

The most recent, and the best, one-volume history is *Scotland: A New History* by Michael Lynch (Pimlico). There are two very good histories in several volumes – *The Edinburgh History of Scotland* in four volumes, edited by Gordon Donaldson, was originally published in the late 60s and 70s and has recently been re-issued in paperback by the Mercat Press. The eight smaller volumes of *The New History of Scotland*, first published in the 80s with Jenny Wormold as the General Editor, has been re-issued by Edinburgh University Press.

On the Wars of Independence, the standard work is G.W.S. Barrow's *Robert Bruce and the Community of the Realm of Scotland* (EUP), and Andrew Fisher's *William Wallace* and R.C. Paterson's *For the Lion* (both John Donald) are also useful. On the events leading to the Union, both William Ferguson's *Scotland's Relations with England: A Survey to 1707* and Paul H. Scott's *Andrew Fletcher and the Treaty of Union* have been re-issued by the Saltire Society. There is a recent collection of essays about the Disruption, *Scotland in the Age of the Disruption*, edited by Stewart J. Brown and Michael Fry (EUP). Lindsay Paterson in *The Autonomy of Modern Scotland* (EUP) demonstrates that even after the Union Scotland had more autonomy than many nominally independent countries, with the important exception that it had no power to legislate.

Scotland: A Concise Cultural History, edited by Paul H. Scott (Mainstream), has essays by leading authorities on all aspects of Scottish culture. *The Scottish Enlightenment: A Hotbed of Genius*, edited by David Daiches, Peter Jones and Jean Jones (Saltire Society) is an admirable account of the Scottish Enlightenment. Roderick Watson's *The Literature of Scotland* (Macmillan), Duncan Macmillan's *Scottish Art* and John Purser's *Scotland's Music* (both Mainstream) are indispensable.

THE PRESENT

Two collections of essays give a general view of contemporary Scotland: *Anatomy of Scotland*, edited by Magnus Linklater and Robin Denniston (Chambers), and *Scotland in the 20th Century*, edited by T.M. Devine and

R.J. Finlay, (EUP). *A Claim of Right for Scotland*, edited by Owen Dudley Edwards (Polygon), reprints the 1988 document with comments on it from several points of view. The history of the Home Rule movement is examined in Andrew Marr's *The Battle for Scotland* (Penguin), Richard J. Finlay's *Independent and Free* (John Donald), James Mitchell's *Strategies for Self-Government* (Polygon) and *Restless Nation* by Alan Clements, Kenny Farquharson and Kirsty Wark (Mainstream). There are analyses of the Scottish situation, politically and culturally, in William McIlvanney's *Surviving the Shipwreck* (Mainstream), Angus Calder's *Revolving Culture* (I.B. Tauris) and in Paul H. Scott's *Scotland in Europe* (Canongate), *Towards Independence* (Polygon) and *Defoe in Edinburgh* (Tuckwell).

REFERENCES TO COMMENTARY

CHAPTER ONE

1 David Daiches in a Radio Scotland broadcast on 30 November 1996.
2 James Boswell, *Boswell on the Grand Tour Germany and Switzerland* (London 1953), pp. 125–6.

CHAPTER TWO

1 A.M. Stewart, Introduction to *The Complaynt of Scotland* (c 1550) (Edinburgh Scottish Text Society, 1979) p. XXXIV.
2 John Mair, *The Complaynt of Scotland* Translated by Archibald Constable, (Edinburgh, Scottish History Society, 1892), p. 214.
3 C.F. Arrowood, Introduction to his translation of George Buchanan's *The Power of the Crown in Scotland* (Austin 1949), pp. 11–12.

CHAPTER THREE

1 P. Hume Brown, *History of Scotland* (Cambridge, 1912), vol. II, p. 73.
2 Sir Walter Scott, *Rob Roy*, chapter 20.
3 P. Hume Brown, op. cit., pp. 74–5.
4 Polyodore Vergil, *Historia Anglica*, vol. II, pp. 1539–40. Quoted in R.L. Mackie, *King James IV of Scotland* (Edinburgh, 1958), p. 93.
5 P. Hume Brown, op. cit., pp. 240–1.

CHAPTER FIVE

1 Daniel Defoe, *Tour Thro the Whole Island of Great Britain* (edition of 1763, London) pp. 52–3.
2 George Ridpath, *An Account of the Proceedings of the Parliament of Scotland which met at Edinburgh May 6 1703*, pp. A 4–5.
3 Duke of Hamilton, Historical Manuscripts Commission 10th Report. App. Pt. IV, (1885), p. 370. On Hamilton generally see my *Andrew Fletcher and the Treaty of Union*, especially pp. 138–44.

4 Earl of Mar, *State Papers and Letters addressed to William Carstares* (Edinburgh, 1774), pp. 743–4.
5 George Lockhart of Carnwath, *Memoirs* (1714). An edition with the title, *Scotland's Ruine* has been published by the Association for Scottish Literary Studies (Aberdeen, 1995).
6 Sir John Clerk of Penicuik, *History of Scotland and England*, translated by Douglas Duncan (Edinburgh, Scottish History Society, 1993).

CHAPTER SIX

1 John Hill Burton in A.V. Dicey and R.S. Rait, *Thoughts on the Union* (London, 1920), pp. 2–3.
2 Daniel Defoe, op. cit., vol. III, p. 33.
3 Sir John Clerk of Penicuik, in Scottish History Society, *Miscellany X* (Edinburgh, 1965), p. 182.
4 Adam Smith, *Correspondence*. Ed. by E.C. Mossner and I.S. Ross (Oxford, 1977), p. 68.
5 Sir John Clerk of Penicuik, *History of Scotland*, op. cit., pp. 173 and 186.

CHAPTER SEVEN

1 John Sibbald Gibson, *Edinburgh in the '45* (Edinburgh, Saltire Society, 1995), pp. 51–2.
2 Robert Wodrow, *Early Letters (1698–1709)*, (Edinburgh, Scottish History Society, 1937), p. 291.
3 John MacQueen, *Progress and Poetry* (Edinburgh, 1982), p. 5.
4 For example in his letter of 26 April 1764 to Hugh Blair, *Letters of David Hume*. Ed. by J.Y.T. Greig (Oxford, 1932), vol. I, p. 436.
5 Nicholas Phillipson, *Hume* (London, 1989), p. 12.
6 David Hume, *Selected Essays*. Ed. by Stephen Copley and Andrew Edgar (Oxford, 1993), p. 311.
7 Adam Smith, *The Wealth of Nations* (1776), (London, Everyman's Library Edition, 1971), vol. I, pp. 204 and 216.
8 P. Berresford Ellis and S. MacA'Gobhainn, *The Scottish Insurrection of 1820* (London, 1970), pp. 298–9.
9 Robert Burns, 'Deserted Village', l. 425, from Robert Burns, *Letters*. Ed. by J. De Lancey Ferguson (Oxford, 1931), vol. II, p. 18.

CHAPTER NINE

1 Sydney and Olive Checkland, *The New History of Scotland 1832–1914: Industry and Ethos* (London, 1984), p. 117.
2 Sir Walter Scott, *Heart of Midlothian*, chapter XXVIII.

3 Bruce Lenman, *The New History of Scotland: 1746–1832 Integration, Enlightenment and Industrialisation* (London, 1981), pp. 58 and 148.

4 J.G. Lockhart, *Memoirs of Sir Walter Scott* (1837–8). Edition of 1900, London, vol. V, p. 445.

5 Quoted in Sir Reginald Coupland, *Welsh and Scottish Nationalism* (London, 1954), pp. 284–5.

6 Roderick Watson, 'Scottish Literature in the Twentieth Century', in *Scotland in the 20th Century*. Ed. by T.M. Devine and R.J. Finlay (Edinburgh, 1996), p. 287.

CHAPTER TEN

1 Quoted by Murray Ritchie, *The Herald*, 16th December 1996.

INDEX OF DOCUMENTS AND AUTHORS